SCHOOL DIDACTICS AND LEARNING

A school didactic model framing an analysis of pedagogical implications of learning theory

Michael Uljens

*Department of Education
Åbo Akademi University
Vasa, Finland*

Psychology Press
a member of the Taylor & Francis group

To Ritva, Mette and Reidar

Copyright © 1997 by Psychology Press Ltd,
a member of the Taylor & Francis Group
　All rights reserved. No part of this book may be reproduced in any form,
　by photostat, microform, retrieval system, or any other means without the
　prior written permission of the publisher.

Psychology Press Ltd
27 Church Road
Hove
East Sussex, BN3 2FA
UK

British Library Cataloguing in Publication Data
A catalogue record for this book is available from the British Library

　ISBN 0-86377-700-7 (Hbk)

Typeset by Acorn Bookwork, Salisbury, Wilts
Printed and bound in the United Kingdom by TJ International Ltd, Padstow, Cornwall

Contents

Acknowledgements v

PART I: Towards a Model of School Didactics 1

1. **Introduction** 3
   Background and Aim 3
   The Problems 5
   The Approach 7

2. **Didactics and the Teaching–Studying–Learning Process** 13
   Introduction 13
   On Teaching 13
   Educational Theory and Pedagogical Practice 18
   Questions to be Posed within a Theory of Didactics 21
   On Learning 27
   The Process and Result of Learning 27
   Maturation, Experience and Learning 29
   Conclusion 34
   On Teaching, Studying and Learning 34
   The Relation between Studying and Learning 36
   The Relation between Teaching and Studying 39
   The Socio-cultural Situation 41
   Conclusion 42
   Didactics as the Science of the Teaching–Studying–Learning Process 43
   The Concept of Didactics 44
   Didactics as Theory and Doctrine 48
   Didactics, Instruction and Education 49
   Didactics and Learning Theory 52
   Conclusion 55

3. **A Model of School Didactics** 59
   Forms, Levels and Contexts of Pedagogical Activity 59
   A School Didactic Model 64
   Planning—A Network of Intentions 67
   Conclusion 74
   The Interactive Teaching–Studying–Learning Process 75
   Evaluation 81
   Contexts 83
   Why School Didactics? 87
   A Model or a Theory of School Didactics? 93
   Comparison of the School Didactic Model and Some German Approaches 95
   Erudition-centred Theory of Didactics 95
   The Berlin Model 106
   A Descriptive Model, a Normative Model, or Both? 112
   Two Ways of Understanding Value-relatedness in Didactics 113

PART II: School Didactics and Pedagogical Implications of Learning Theory 123

4. **Analyzing Learning Theory—Its Aim and Design** 125
   Introduction 125
   The School Didactic Model and Theory of Learning 125
   Epistemological and Ontological Inquiries as the Instruments of Analysis 130

5. **The Object of Analysis—Cognitivist Learning Theory** 139
   Introduction 139
   The Cognitivist Approach 140
   Cognitivism and the Theory of Learning 151

6. **Cognitivism—Causal Theory of Perception, Representational Epistemology and Ontological Dualism** 167
   The Epistemological Mind–World Problem 167
   The Process of Learning 168
   The Result of Learning 170
   Cognitivism and Representational Epistemology 176
   The Ontological Mind–Brain Problem 181
   The Process of Learning 182
   The Result of Learning 186
   The Ontological Position of Cognitivism—Property Dualism and Functionalism 188
   Summary 192

7. **Pedagogical Implications of Cognitivist Learning Theory** 197
   Introduction 197
   Teaching and the Epistemological Mind–World Problem 203
   Teaching and the Learning Process 203
   Teaching and the Learning Result 212
   Teaching and the Ontological Mind–Brain Problem 218
   Teaching and the Learning Process 218
   Teaching and the Learning Result 229

PART III: Discussion 235

8. **Closing Thoughts and Perspectives** 237
   Introduction 237
   The School Didactic Model and the Pedagogical Implications Arrived At 237
   Teaching as Intentional Activity and Teaching as Success 240
   Teachers' Intentions, the Curriculum and Students' Interests 241
   Reflective Pedagogical Practice and Theory of Didactics 247
   A Model of Teachers' Pedagogical Reflection and Didactic Theory 249
   Conclusion 253

References 255
Author index 274
Subject index 278

Acknowledgements

In this book a theory of school didactics is proposed. As the term "didactics" is not in frequent use in the Anglo-American world it should be noted that this study is mainly carried out within the framework of Nordic and German research traditions on the theory of education and instruction, i.e. *Didaktik*. Although there are many similarities between the German, Nordic and Anglo-American traditions many differences also exist. Therefore some emphasis is laid on a clear explication of the school didactic theory and its features. It is hoped that the reader will be able to approach the use of the concept of didactics (didaktik) open mindedly when reading this book.

One of the main ideas of the book is to approach the so called intentional and interactive teaching–studying–learning process as it occurs in historically developed institutionalized education framed by a collective curriculum and other contextual factors. Thus the point of departure is not taken in traditional curriculum theory or in the needs of academic teacher education. It is, however, possible to use the theory developed both as a research model and a thought model for teachers.

The theory is not a *normative* theory, i.e. it does not say towards what goals education should aim at. Neither is the present theory a *descriptive* one, i.e. it does not mirror the reality as such on an ontological level. Rather the theory presented is a *reflective theory of didactics*. The theory is an explication of how instructional processes in the institutionalized school may be experienced. Second, as the theory may be used as a thought model and a research model its reflective nature is emphasized. As the theory is not a copy of the outer reality as such, it is not a rationalist model: it does not reach the essence of reality. Finally, the theory is a culturally regional theory, not a universal one.

The book also defends the thesis that in order to conceptually capture the complexity of pedagogical reality it is necessary to adopt a relatively broad perspective. Therefore, limiting one's pedagogical interest to developing principles of education and teaching based on learning theory is not enough if we want to understand the pedagogical process. Even if it would be possible to develop such instructional principles guiding practice by starting from learning theory, it is certainly not possible to develop instructional theory on the basis of learning theory. Similarly it is not possible to create theories of learning starting from instructional theory. However, whereas it may be that it is possible to develop learning theory without relating it to instructional theory it seems more difficult to develop instructional theory without saying anything about learning. The aim in the second part of this book is therefore to investigate pedagogical implications of learning theory. In doing this I would like to draw the reader's attention to two things. First, when the analysis of pedagogical implications of learning theory is carried out this is done within the frames of the instructional or didactic theory outlined in the first part of the study. Second, cognitive learning theory is, for different reasons, chosen as the object of analysis in the second part of the book. This should not be taken to mean that I am a one-eyed defender of cognitivism. On the contrary I am critical of most of the assumptions lying behind cognitive learning theory. The reason for still choosing cognitive learning theory as the object of analysis in the second part of the book was simply that I thought it better to choose a widely known approach to learning, in order not to confuse the reader too much, since the book deals with the theory of didactics, which is not well known in the English speaking world. In addition the epistemological and ontological analysis of cognitive learning theory that precedes the chapter on pedagogical implications also offers a considerable challenge for many readers. The approach and structure of the book would remain the same whether activity theory or cultural-historical theory of learning had been chosen as the object of analysis.

It is always pleasant to reflect on the path that led to a finished book. Combined with the rewarding experiences of insight I very much appreciate having had the time and opportunity to bring this work to an end. Naturally many discussions with my colleagues and scholars in the field come to my mind. I especially want to express my deepest thanks to the following three colleagues and friends.

First of all I want to thank my friend licentiate Åke Holmström. Without the numerous challenging and rewarding discussions we had through the years, many of the thoughts presented in this book would never have emerged.

Professor Pertti Kansanen of Helsinki University is one of the European didacticians and one of the few Nordic scholars who moves smoothly within and between German *Didaktik* and Anglo-American instructional research. What Professor Kansanen has meant to me in writing this book, will be obvious to the reader.

Ference Marton, professor in education at the University of Gothenburg, inspired me to formulate and approach fundamental problems. I deeply appreciate his interest in my thinking. Traces of the phenomenographic approach are visible in this volume.

In addition to these three colleagues and friends I also want to mention the following scholars who significantly and in different ways have been important in working on the book.

I very much appreciate Professor Stefan Hopmann for his kindness in helping me to move into the German tradition of *Didaktik*. I also appreciate that he and PhD Kurt Riquarts made it possible for me to follow the comparative project *Didaktik meets Curriculum*. My discussions with Professor Emeritus Wolfgang Klafki at Marburg University led me to many insights concerning fundamental questions to be posed in didactics as well as about how to answer them, especially with respect to normative problems. Professor Peter Menck at Siegen University has commented upon various strengths and problems with the thoughts that are presented here. All his points have been relevant and significant for the development of the present study. I also had rewarding discussions with Professor Hilbert Meyer from Oldenburg University on the theory of didactics and how it may be related to teachers' pedagogical practice. Last, but not least, I thank Professor Ewald Terhart at Ruhr-Universität Bochum, for his detailed evaluation of the study in December 1995.

From among my Nordic colleagues and friends I especially want to thank the following: Professor Biörg. B. Gundem's views of the curriculum development have been helpful. PhD Sigrun Gudmundsdottir's empirical studies have taught me many things. Professor Roger Säljö has taught me to better understand school practice as culturally embedded activity. Professor Tomas Englund has presented valuable comments on the role of content as it is constructed in the classroom framed by a complex cultural and political web. I remember discussions with docent Tomas Kroksmark on some of the issues touched upon here. I also want to thank Professor Per-Johan Ödman for interesting discussions on hermeneutics.

Of my colleagues at Åbo Akademi University in Vasa I would like to thank my friend and colleague licentiate Jan Sjöberg, for his interest in educational theory and Professor Håkan Andersson at the Department of Education in Vasa, who has for many years been a colleague with whom I have had valuable discussions on matters discussed in this study. I also thank associate Professor Anna-Lena Østern and Professor Ulla

Lahtinen for their support of many of the conclusions developed in the study and highly appreciate their collegial support. Among the many other colleagues at the Department of Teacher Education, where I worked as a researcher in didactics, (1987–1991) I especially thank Professor Claes-Goran Wenestam for reading the manuscript, and associate Professor Kaj Sjoholm for many inspiring discussions. I am also grateful for the critical evaluation, especially of the psychological part of this book, made by Professor Pekka Niemi at the Department of Psychology. Finally I want to mention Rector for Åbo Akademi University Bengt Stenlund whose support, in its own way, came to be important to me.

It has not been easy to write this book in English for two reasons. First Swedish, not English, is my mother tongue. The other reason is that many of the concepts used in the German, Finnish and Swedish literature are not easy to translate into English. I therefore appreciate that Stiftelsens för Åbo Akademi Forskningsintitut financed the proofreading of the manuscript by Rolf Lindholm at the Department of English, University of Vasa. He also translated the German quotes into English.

I am grateful to have had the opportunity to write parts of this book while working as researcher at the Department of Teacher Education and the Department of Education at Åbo Akademi University in Vasa. Research grants from Academy of Finland, Nordiska Forskarakademin, Stiftelsens för Åbo Akademi Forskningsinstitut and Deutscher Akademischer Austauschdienst have enabled me to work on this book both in Finland, Sweden and Germany.

Finally, I appreciate that Psychology Press accepted this book for publication.

Michael Uljens

TOWARDS A MODEL OF SCHOOL DIDACTICS

1 Introduction

BACKGROUND AND AIM

Institutional education is an intentional and interactive process through which individuals become encultured into the complex web of human competence and social networks constituting societies. Becoming encultured requires the student's intentional development of competence and personal identity.

The human ability to learn is a fundamental prerequisite for this process to occur. Without accepting this, practical educational activity is rather meaningless. However, we know well that intentional teaching does not always lead to learning. Nor does an individual's intentional study activity necessarily lead to what was striven for. Therefore, as teaching intends to support the student's activities aiming at learning, it may be asked how teaching and learning are related more precisely.

If pedagogical practice aims at supporting learning, then it is also relevant to ask how educational theory is related to learning. One reason why this question is important is that insights into teaching and learning are considered to constitute aspects of a teacher's professional competence (Francis, 1985).

Individual teachers' understanding of teaching and learning varies considerably (Pratt, 1992; Prawat, 1992; Prosser, Trigwell, & Taylor, 1994). Also, educational theories relate differently to learning theory. Yet educational or instructional theory should be quite explicit with respect to how learning is dealt with (Diederich, 1988, p.34).

4 SCHOOL DIDACTICS AND LEARNING

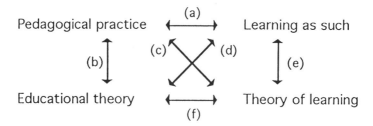

FIG. 1.1 Four interrelated factors of importance in specifying the relation between educational theory and learning.

In order to explain how educational theory is related to learning, it is useful to discriminate between the theory of learning and learning as an empirical phenomenon. Similarly we may discriminate between educational theory and pedagogical practice. We thus have four interrelated factors—learning, theory of learning, pedagogical practice and educational theory (see Fig. 1.1).

The following comments may be made in relation to the figure presented above:

(a) Pedagogical practice aims at facilitating learning;
(b) Educational theory aims at providing conceptual structures by which pedagogical practice may be described, analysed, understood and, sometimes, guided;
(c) Pedagogical principles are often developed on the basis of learning theory. In a narrower sense, teachers' understanding (or personal theories) of learning may affect their way of teaching. These principles should not be equated with the concept of "educational theory";
(d) Educational theory is indirectly related to learning as an empirical phenomenon since pedagogical practice aims at facilitating the individual's learning process;
(e) The theory of learning aims at providing a conceptual framework by means of which learning may be described and understood;
(f) Learning theory is related to educational theory as the pedagogical process aims at facilitating learning, and as it is possible to develop prescriptive pedagogical principles guiding practice on the basis of learning theory.

Of the relations described above, that between learning theory and pedagogical practice (c) is the most extensively developed. A traditional position concerning this relation is that knowledge of human learning may be useful in decision-making in pedagogical practice or in order to develop instructional materials or methods (e.g. Rein, 1912).

The object of this study is not, however, limited to the relation between pedagogical practice and learning theory. The aim is also to try to determine the relation between educational theory and learning theory (f). The reason is that both educational theory and theory of learning are important to pedagogical practice, but in different ways. While learning theory can be prescriptively related to pedagogical practice in that principles for teaching may be developed starting from learning theory, this is not necessarily the case with educational theory. Educational theory may also be related to pedagogical practice in a descriptive or analytic way, and does not necessarily state how teaching should be carried out. It can be delimited to pointing out fundamental constituents of pedagogical practice and it may actualize questions requiring prescriptive or normative decisions.

As educational theory may be related to pedagogical practice in different ways, we can see that the specification of the relation between theory of learning and educational theory is dependent on the nature of educational theory. Therefore the primary aim of this study is to outline a didactic model valid for the pedagogical reality in schools, which in turn gives us the possibility of specifying how learning is dealt with.

THE PROBLEMS

Granted that prescriptive pedagogical assumptions, developed on the basis of learning theory, are too narrow to enable us to fully understand the complexity of pedagogical reality, we must try to define the relation between learning theory and educational theory in some other way.

A fundamental starting-point is that learning must be of interest to educational theory (Hollo, 1927, p.119). The primary argument for this is that the aim of educational practice is to support the individual's attainment of competence. As an increase or change of competence is often thought to be reached through learning, it is argued that teachers may use knowledge of the process of human learning when organizing situations facilitating the attainment of competence. If this position which should not be regarded as self-evident, is accepted (cf. Bannister, 1982; Desforges, 1985), then a theory that purports to be valid for pedagogical practice must acknowledge the fact. The question then is how educational theory or theory of didactics acknowledges learning theory in offering a conceptual system supposed to be valid for pedagogical practice.

The First Problem

The first problem in this study is to reflect on what questions educational theory should answer in order to be suitable for pedagogical purposes, i.e. relevant in terms of offering instruments by which we can handle the complexity of pedagogical reality in a satisfying way. Part one of this study is devoted to that problem.

As a result of this part of the study, a didactic model is outlined. The model developed is identified as a model of "school didactics". School didactics is defined as a field of research within general education. This field is limited to research and theory aiming at understanding the pedagogical practice (*Erziehung* and *Bildung*) which takes place in institutionalized educational settings guided by a curriculum collectively agreed upon. A conceptual structure within the school didactic field of research is thus not to be understood as a general theory of education or teaching.

The aim of presenting this descriptive model is twofold. First, it may be viewed as an effort to contribute to the development of didactic theory. Second, the model also offers a framework for the following investigation into pedagogical implications emanating from learning theory. It is considered valuable that the solution offered concerning the first problem, i.e. the didactic model presented, offers the framework for analysing learning theory in the second part of this study.

The Second Problem

The second problem in this study is to investigate the pedagogical implications of the cognitivist theory of learning. This part of the study is to be conceived as a clarification of the pedagogical model presented; if pedagogical practice aims at affecting an individual's possibilities of reaching competence through the process of learning, then it is reasonable to expect that the theory of didactics recognizes learning theory. The answer to this problem offered by the model presented here is that learning theory is accepted as having a prescriptive function in two different but related ways.

Firstly, learning theory is assumed to play a role in pedagogical practice since a teacher may reflect analytically on theories of learning, i.e. what it means to attain a certain degree of competence and further that the teacher, on the basis of such reflection, makes decisions on how to organize and carry out the teaching–studying–learning process. (The expression "teaching–studying–learning process" is shortened to the acronym TSL process in this study.) In doing this the teacher reflects analytically and acts in a normative or prescriptive fashion; if acquiring competence "X" means "Y" then one should do "Z".

Secondly, precisely because of this it is important to investigate what kind of pedagogical implications different theories of learning have. Therefore the second part of this study is devoted to an analysis of cognitivist learning theory. Prescriptive propositions may thus be handled within the framework of an otherwise descriptive didactic model. Yet, even though we may use descriptive didactic theory as a general frame of reference in this study, it does not offer us the instruments to analyse theories of learning themselves. Rather, the didactic frame of reference shows us why and how learning as a phenomenon is important in the theory of didactics and in pedagogical practice.

The chosen level of analysis, when the cognitivist theory of learning is investigated, is the philosophy of mind. This was considered a reasonable level since it contained problems that every learning theory deals with in one way or another. Two problems were chosen. Firstly, the relation between an individual's conceptual knowledge and external reality, and, secondly, the problem of how to describe this conceptual knowledge.

The first problem deals with what it is to have knowledge of the world. Since teaching and education often aim at increasing, developing or changing an individual's knowledge, the question of what it means to possess knowledge is naturally a fundamental one from a pedagogical perspective. This is identified as the epistemological mind–world problem.

The second question deals with the problem of how to describe an individual's understanding of the world, his knowledge, mental representation, conceptual structure, etc. In order to be able to change this understanding or conceptual knowledge structure, i.e. to facilitate learning, we must decide how we want to describe what it is to be aware of something. In particular, we must know how we want to describe and discuss a change in this awareness of something. This question is identified as the ontological mind–brain problem.

Having investigated how the cognitivist theory of learning appears in the light of these two problems, we are ready to return to a didactic level of reasoning. Instructional implications of cognitivist learning theory are organized on the basis of the analysis carried out on the level of the philosophy of mind.

THE APPROACH

A Phenomenological–hermeneutical Approach. In its concern with how the reality of institutionalized education is constituted and what is required in order to describe it conceptually, the approach of this study is phenomenological. If such description is taken to mean that an aspect of educational reality is described as it appears to a subject who tries to reach some kind of essence (*Wesenserfassung*), then parts of this study may be seen as a phenomenological investigation. In fact, this is precisely the way the school didactic model was originally developed; it was an explication of how one part of educational reality was experienced.

Phenomenologically, theoretical knowledge of the educational field was bracketed through the "epoché". In phenomenological terms, being in the "natural attitude", a kind of eidetic reduction was carried out; questions that had to be answered in order to reach a description of the TSL process in schools were reflected on. However, in this view of phenomenological pedagogy there was no need for a "transcendental subject" in reduction (Danner, 1989, pp.155–156; Karlsson, 1993; Uljens, 1992a, pp.31–37). The bracketing refers only to the developmental process through which a first version of the model was constructed (see e.g. Uljens, 1993a). This phase did not consciously have its point of departure in any specific theoretical school of thought. My personal experience in the field of education formed the basis for this first phase of reflection. However, this was considered only as a first step to be followed by a hermeneutical phase. Having reached a first delimitation and structure it was possible to investigate this model in relation to previous theory in the field. This phase was crucial since a new model gets its cultural meaning and role only in relation to previous and contemporary scientific discourse. Only by such a comparative discussion can the features of the present model be communicated.

Methodologically, this second phase does not fall within a phenomenological description. The phase of hermeneutic interpretation in the research process was reached (Dilthey, 1958). To explicitly relate the pedagogical model developed to other contemporary approaches may be characterized as a kind of historical, social and cultural reflection; the historicity of the thoughts developed was accepted. Therefore, claims and perspectives put forth are seen as regional, not universal, truths. In this matter Schleiermacher (1957, p.20) asks about the generality of educational theory: "To what extent can our theories be regarded as generally valid? Will it be possible to devise a universal theory of education, that is, one that is valid for all times and places?".[1] In conformity with Schleiermacher the position of this study is that a universal theory of education is not possible. This view of scientific knowledge also sees the discipline of education as a cultural science; educational theory makes sense only in a cultural and historical perspective. Analytical propositions developed should not therefore be disconnected from the culture within which they have been produced.

The hermeneutic process of relating an early version of the model (Uljens, 1993a) to previous theory led to further development of the model. As a result, some parts were emphasized more and others less. This phase of the analysis may be described by the "hermeneutic circle";

the interpreted object was the phenomenologically described model. The "hermeneutical difference" between the model and previous theory was dealt with in terms of the hermeneutic circle, and reached the position presented in this study. In Gadamer's terms the different "horizons" were brought closer to each other, the horizons being the original model and the research tradition of didactics. The model was thus partly developed through a "discussion with the tradition" (Gadamer, 1960).

In this study Ricoeur's (1989, pp.114ff.) view of the relation between phenomenology and hermeneutics is also supported, i.e. a hermeneutic phenomenology is accepted. This position accepts the problem of meaning as the fundamental one both in interpretation theory and phenomenology. As Ricoeur (1989, p.114) notes, in order for meaning to become a hermeneutic problem "the central question of phenomenology must be recognized as a question of meaning". The problem of meaning in phenomenology refers to the nature of an experience, which again has a lingual aspect as discussed in Ricoeur (1989, p.115):

> Experience can be said, it demands to be said. To bring it to language is not to change it to something else, but, in articulating and developing it, to make it become itself.

A second perspective on the relation between phenomenology and hermeneutics advocated by Ricoeur and conceived of as relevant here, is the distanciation from the "experience of belonging" (ibid., p.116). That is, there is a connection between the hermeneutic concept of distanciation and the phenomenological epoché (bracketing), as long as the epoché is conceived of as "the intentional movement of consciousness towards meaning". In other words, to distance us from lived experience means to "interrupt lived experience in order to signify it" (ibid., p.116). Ricoeur concludes (p.117):

> [H]ermeneutical distanciation is to belonging as, in phenomenology, the *epoché* is to lived experience. Hermeneutics similarly begin when . . . we interrupt the relation of belongingness in order to signify it.

The relevance of this position to the present study is the following. Sometimes it is claimed that pedagogical practice is primary in relation to educational theory, i.e. that practice is not dependent on theory. Schleiermacher's widely referred position from 1826 may exemplify this:

> Still, it is nevertheless a fact that in every domain that goes under the name of Art, in a narrower sense, practice is much older than theory, so that it can simply not be said that practice gets its own definite character only with

theory. The dignity of practice is independent of theory; practice only becomes more conscious with theory.[2]

The view expressed requires some comments. Naturally the educational practice (*Bildungswirklichkeit*) is much older compared with a contemporary understanding of theory. Educational practice also continues to exist regardless of our description of it in the naive sense that it does not cease to exist if we stop talking about it. At least it would continue to exist as past "lived experience" (Van Manen, 1991). However, in such past lived experience the meaning of the experience is not always evident. Therefore, precisely as Schleiermacher argues, a fundamental feature of theory is that it helps us to deepen our understanding of pedagogical reality. Hollo (1927, p.12) expresses this by saying that we may become educationally "seeing" by the help of theory.

However, a deepening of our understanding must not be compared with a more detailed description of practice. To deepen our understanding is more; every description always has a constitutive function as well. Thus some kind of reflection is connected with every practice. Even identifying something as pedagogical is a result of some kind of reflection.

Taken for granted that some kind of reflection is always connected with practice in a constitutive fashion, i.e. that practice gets its meaning only by virtue of this reflection, then practice is not, as Schleiermacher claims, independent of theory. In this respect educational theory would be primary in relation to practice; theory defines the essence or the meaning of educational reality.

Thus, the conclusion is that instead of claiming that theory is secondary to practice or that practice is secondary to theory, we should ask: "What kind of reflection is present in practice?" This position should not be connected with solipsism but rather with critical realism (or "epistemic" realism, Putnam, 1988). In this view the world itself does not contain the limits for how it may be described. Only the describers themselves may decide upon which rules are to be followed, since the description is made in relation to previous knowledge and with certain interests in a given cultural and historical context. This means that scientific models can be tested empirically, provided that the assumptions behind them are accepted. This view also allows us to compare scientific models with the models teachers have. Against this background the methodology of the first part of the present study may be characterized as a continuous shifting between conceptual analysis and theory-generating activity.

The main role of the model, with respect to empirical research, is that it offers a framework for an empirical research programme as well as a thought model for teachers. Yet a view according to which theory would be a picture of an outer reality is not accepted. Therefore a difference between the notions model and theory is not important on an ontological level. Both theories and models reflect ways in which we experience reality.

On a conceptual level the difference between a model and a theory could be defined as follows: a theory is a model of the world that is explicit with respect to the tradition of educational science. The next question would naturally be: What is counted as being scientific? The answers to that question vary depending on more fundamental assumptions, of which one, the relation between theory and reality, was indicated above. However, the actual conceptual structure is not a theory in the sense that it would offer explanations of our observations of the pedagogical reality; it is not a predictive theory. Rather, it is a constitutive theory defining what institutionalized education is about in the first place. Differently expressed, the analysis carried out is an ontological one as it asks about the fundamental nature of the institutionalized teaching–studying–learning process.

The Structure of the Study

In order to make the reading of this study easier, I will briefly present the main components of it here and show how they are related to each other. The study is divided into two parts. The aim of the first part is to put forth a model of school didactics. The development of this model is to be seen as one of the main results of the present study.

The structure of the first part is as follows. The second chapter discusses teaching, studying and learning and how the relations between these concepts may be defined. It is also shown how didactics may be seen as the science of what is called the TSL process.

After this a school didactic model is presented in the third chapter. The model is related to two influential German approaches, Wolfgang Klafki's position within the erudition-centred theory of didactics (*bildungstheoretischer Didaktik*) and the so called Berlin model of didactics (P. Heimann, W. Schulz). As the problems of normativity and prescriptivity are fundamental to every educational theory, a separate section is devoted to this problem. It is shown in what sense and respects the theory presented is on the one hand analytical-descriptive and on the other normative-prescriptive.

In the second part of this study the model developed is used to frame an analysis of the pedagogical implications of learning theory. In Chapter 4 it is shown how the school didactic model is related to learning. Then the instruments of analysis are presented, i.e. the epistemological and ontological problems used to approach the cognitivist school on learning theory. Special attention is devoted to the process and result of learning as these aspects of learning are naturally related to many different types of decisions made in teaching.

Having shown how the cognitivist approach to learning may be characterized with respect to the epistemological and ontological problems in Chapter 6, the pedagogical implications of cognitivism discussed in the light of this analysis are presented in Chapter 7. In the final chapter teachers' professional competence is discussed with regard to the use of didactics in reflection on practice.

In sum the study shows how the descriptive model of school didactics presented may be used both as a research model in educational research and as an instrument in teachers' pedagogical reflection.

NOTES

1. *[W]elchen Grad von Allgemeingültigheit kann wohl unsere Theorien haben?* Wird es möglich sein, eine allgemeingültige Pädagogik aufzustellen, d.h. für alle Zeiten und Räume?".
2. Ist doch überhaupt auf jedem Gebiete, das Kunst heißt im engeren Sinne, die Praxis viel älter als die Theorie, so daß man nicht einmal sagen kann, die Praxis bekomme ihren bestimmten Charakter erst mit der Theorie. Die Dignität der Praxis ist unabhängig von der Theorie; die Praxis wird nur mit der Theorie eine bewusstere. (Schleiermacher, 1957, p.11)

2 Didactics and the Teaching–Studying–Learning Process

INTRODUCTION

The general aim of this chapter is to actualize and discuss questions about didactics. This second chapter paints a landscape of problems, fields and questions that are systematically approached in Chapter 3 by presenting a didactic model.

The chapter begins by reflecting on what a theory or model of didactics is needed for. We will see that the way of answering this question decisively determines how didactics is approached and conclusively developed.

Having delimited the object of the theory of teaching our attention is turned to the process of learning. After delimiting teaching and learning, the relation between the two is specified. Also, the relation between studying and teaching, as well as between studying and learning, is developed. Special attention is paid to the learner's intentionality and the socio-cultural situation as a constituent in the TSL process. In the final section the concept of didactics is introduced. It is suggested that didactics generally should be conceived of as the science of the TSL process. Finally, it is suggested how didactics may be related to instruction and education as well as what it means to view didactics from a normative-prescriptive and analytic-descriptive perspective.

ON TEACHING

In trying to define teaching[1] we may begin with the etymological roots of the concept.

It is not surprising, from a Nordic perspective, that the Middle English term *lernen* can mean both to learn and to teach. In Swedish the same term can be used both for teaching and learning; but the derivation of teaching from Old English pointed out by Smith (1987, p.11) is interesting. He writes:

> It [teaching] comes from the Old English *taecan* which is in turn derived from the Old Teutonic *taikjan*, the root of which is *teik*, meaning to show, and is traceable to Sanskrit *dic* through pre-Teutonic *deik*. The term "teach" is also related to "token"—a sign or symbol. "Token" comes from the Old Teutonic word *taiknom*, a cognitive with *taikjan*, Old English *taecan*, meaning to teach. To teach, according to this derivation, means to show someone something through signs or symbols; to use signs or symbols to evoke responses about events, persons, observations, findings, and so forth. In this derivation, "teach" is associated with the medium in which teaching is carried on.

The conclusion drawn above points to teaching as a symbolic communicative process, i.e. communication directed towards "evoking responses" by using signs or symbols representing something else. In this "teaching as *taecan*" tradition, instruction seems to go back to the activity of a person being able to handle symbols (a priest, a shaman), i.e. a mediator. The emphasis is put on the syntactical aspect of the symbol, i.e. the method of teaching or the how of teaching, not on the content of teaching. It may therefore be interesting to know that the roots of the Finnish word *taika* meaning magic, and the related word *taikuri* meaning magician also go back to the Old German *taikna* and Gothic *taikns* meaning sign (Itkonen & Joki, 1969, pp.1196–1197).

It is useful to contrast this view of teaching with the Middle English *lernen*, German *Lernen* (learning), German *Lehrer* (teacher), German *Lehre* (knowledge). The point is that in the German *Lehren* as well as in the Swedish *lära* and the Finnish *opettaa* the content, i.e. the *what* of teaching, is prominent. The Icelandic word for teacher is in line with this; it is *kennari*, literally meaning a person who knows. In this "teaching as *lernen*" tradition, instruction appears to be more strongly related to the teacher's personal insight into the content than to knowledge of methods.

Smith (1987) has presented a useful overview of definitions of the term teaching, some of which will be pointed out here (see also Smith, 1956). He distinguishes between teaching "in the conventional sense, or the descriptive definition; teaching as success; teaching as an intended activity; teaching as a normative activity; and the emerging scientific notion of teaching" (p.11). Of these the first four will be discussed.

According to Smith, (1987 p.12) an example of a descriptive definition of teaching is that "teaching is imparting knowledge or skill". This is because the definition meets what is typically required of a descriptive definition. Smith (1987, p.11) says that "A statement of the conventional meaning together with an explanation of what the term covers is referred to as a descriptive definition" (see Scheffler, 1960, for an extensive discussion on this topic).

The notion of "Teaching as success", again, implies that teaching always leads to learning. The expression teaching–learning process is often used in order to indicate this. According to Smith (ibid., p.12) "teaching can be defined as an activity such that X learns what Y teaches. If X does not learn, Y has not taught." Dewey (1934) supported this view and Kilpatrick (1926, p.268) argued in the same vein. Ryle (1990) is again mentioned as one of the proponents who argued against this understanding by distinguishing between task verbs and achievement verbs. The point is that while somebody may be engaged in a teaching process without success, it makes less sense to say that somebody has learned something unsuccessfully.

Third, Smith (1987) regards teaching as an intentional activity—"While teaching may not logically implicate learning, it can be anticipated that it will result in learning. A teacher may not succeed, but [ ] is expected to try to teach successfully" (Smith, 1987, p.13). A version of this argumentation is represented by Eisner (1964). Eisner (1964) points to a difference between instruction and teaching. Instruction refers to intentional efforts aimed at supporting student learning but does not require learning to occur. Teaching would again be restricted to those activities that really make learning occur. Similarly Scheffler (1960, pp.60 ff.) in his analysis of teaching distinguishes between teaching as success and teaching as intentional activity.

Finally, teaching is seen as normative behaviour. Teaching is here regarded as a generic term—"It designates a family of activities: training and instruction are primary members and indoctrinating and conditioning are near relatives while propagandizing and intimidation are not family members at all" (Smith, 1987, p.14). This last definition is important, since it makes it possible for us to distinguish educative teaching (*erziehender Unterricht*) from training, indoctrination and conditioning.

Of the above mentioned approaches the view of teaching as an intentional activity is considered fruitful. Yet I would very much like to complete that understanding by stressing the importance of content. Therefore I find Passmore's (1980, p.22) position interesting when he describes teaching as a "covert triadic relation", i.e. a relation including somebody who teaches, something that is taught and somebody who is taught. In German literature this is referred to as the traditional didactic triangle, consisting of the three poles teacher, student and content (see e.g. Diederich, 1988, pp.256–257). However, the fact that teaching is temporally and contextually determined must also be taken into account, especially if we want to understand teaching in schools. Such a view should not be confused with any form of contextual reductionism, according to which teaching is explained by contextual factors.

There are also other ways to approach the problem of teaching. Fenstermacher and Soltis (1986) distinguish between three conceptions of teaching; the executive approach, the therapist approach and the liberationist approach. Various aspects of these conceptions will occur in the discussion of what didactic theory is needed for, what questions it should answer and how the problem of normativity and prescriptivity is handled. However, if the position of this study is to be characterized by one of these approaches, then the liberationist approach is the closest. The difficulty of making use of the descriptions presented by Fenstermacher and Soltis (1986) is that they discuss conceptions of teaching from the practitioner's perspective theoretically in a quite limited sense. The approaches characterized clearly reflect three normative educational philosophies. As we will see, the degrees of freedom with respect to reflection and normative position-taking increase if we adopt a descriptive approach to didactic theory.

Instruction and Teaching

Instruction is conceived of as dealing with all the different ways in which a pedagogical situation helps students to reach or develop certain insights or a certain degree of competence. For example, Gagné and Briggs (1979, p.3) define instruction as "all . . . the events which may have a direct effect on the learning of a human being, not just those set in motion by an individual who is a teacher." This definition naturally means that teaching is seen as only one form of instruction in addition to written instructions and the learner's self-instruction.

The relation between education and instruction may be clarified by introducing the problem of values. Values are connected with the instructional process in different ways; the process may be structured in relation to certain aims (values) or certain values may guide the process as such. Further, since knowledge as such is always value-related on some level, the pedagogical process is connected with values. Reaching insight or acquiring some competence or skill thus includes the internalizing of values connected with a certain field of knowledge; the subject becomes encultured into a belief-system through learning (see e.g. Brown, Collins, & Duguid, 1989). Finally the process of choosing contents to be dealt with in school, the choice of a form of representation and the choice of suitable working methods for the students is in a fundamental sense value-related. In this respect the instructional process is always educating (*bildende*). In this study teaching is understood as one form of educative instruction (Herbart).

Even though instruction and education are two inherent aspects of the same pedagogical process, it is useful to distinguish them for analytical purposes. The distinction between instruction and education allows us to identify situations in the schools that are value-related and primarily educational, not primarily instructional.

If the value-laden, educative dimension is accepted as one dimension present in instruction, then the concept of teaching may be subordinated to instruction. This also means that informing somebody of something is not teaching, since informing is not thought of as including an educative interest. And instruction by indoctrination or by force is not teaching.

Intentionality of Education. It is also important to make a distinction between intentional and unintentional education, or between intentional and functional education. While intentional education is always goal-oriented, this is not the case with functional education. This means that while intentional education is conscious, functional education is not. Here one could ask if it is not possible to distinguish between education or teaching that is consciously intentional and teaching that is consciously unintentional. Yes, it is reasonable to make such a distinction, but it should be observed that when teaching is consciously unintentional this in fact reflects nothing but a very specific intention. Consciously unintentional refers in this case to the teacher's intention not to put up specific goals to be striven for during the instructional process, thus leaving plenty of room to decide upon the goal during the interactive process. Intentionality may also be understood as purposiveness, but this will be discussed in Chapter 8.

As Schröder (1992, p.86) has noted, functional education may sometimes be more effective than intentional education. Intentional education may also functionally lead to other results than those aimed at. Naturally intentional education must be the norm for pedagogical practice in schools. Observe that when we talk about intentional education, it covers the learner's own intentional efforts to reach competence. Thus, self-instruction is included in intentional education. It would be a logical impossibility to create a school following the idea of functional education. In fact, it is not clear that the expression functional education is worth using. Rather the notions of socialization or enculturation might be better expressions for the unintentional and unconscious processes by which an individual is affected (for a discussion of the topic see e.g. Benner 1991, pp.109 ff.; see the section on learning in this chapter).

Thus far we have reflected on how teaching as a phenomenon may be understood preliminarily. However, a description of teaching as a phenomenon is not a theory of the TSL process. We should then ask what such a theory could look like and what such a theory should have to offer.

However, there is reason to define briefly how the concept of education is understood here. Education is conceived of as being synonymous with the German word *Erziehung*, with the Swedish word *fostran* and with the Finnish word *kasvatus*. Education may be defined as the intentional activities through which individuals are intentionally encultured into the practices, norms and values of a society, but in relation to the educated individuals' interests. Thus the pole to education (*Erziehung*) is *Bildung*. This view presupposes the individual's freedom and the possibility of human growth in a wide sense of the word (e.g. *Bildsamkeit*). The practice of education always aims to become something unnecessary: the aim is to support the individual in developing to a point where the educated individual, in a manner of speaking, manages alone. This, again, presupposes that the individual gradually overtakes the responsibility for their own life and growth. This pedagogical process, constituted by education and the human capacity to intentional growth, is always culturally and historically situated.

EDUCATIONAL THEORY AND PEDAGOGICAL PRACTICE

A fundamental question regarding a theory of instruction is why we want to develop such a theory. I want to open the discussion of this issue with Schleiermacher's (1957, p.7) question in his *Lectures on Education* in 1826: What is the object of a theory of education and who needs this theory? Why do we participate in the educational project?

Naturally there are several ways of dealing with this problem. In this study the point of departure is that research on teaching, both conceptual and empirical, should aim at contributing to the development of a conceptual language which enables us to analyse and understand pedagogical reality in a coherent way. In this respect scientific theory is understood in a quite ordinary way. Yet it may be interesting to reflect more precisely on why such a theory is needed. Here two limited perspectives are indicated, i.e. how educational theory is related to teacher education and the practitioners' reflection.

Educational Theory and Teacher Education

In discussing the shaping of a conceptual system it is useful to keep in mind that like so many phenomena, the essence or meaning of the pedagogical reality is partly constituted by our description of it. Educational theory is thus not a copy or picture of pedagogical reality. Precisely because pedagogical reality is constituted of the descriptive activity itself, it is important whose description is counted as normative. Further, when something is valid, it is always valid for somebody for some reason. Thus, in order to decide which model is relevant and which is not, we must also ask for what reason and for whom a model is developed. A common answer is that we want to create knowledge both for active teachers, for the education of teachers and for the administration of schooling. However, it seems that pedagogical theory is sometimes developed more in relation to the needs of teacher education and less in relation to the reality it is thought to describe and explain.

Even though having a developed theory of teaching makes it easier to educate teachers, we should not forget that it is interesting to develop pedagogical theory even if this theory is not used in teacher education. Understanding how a new generation is socialized in a culture by activities within and outside institutionalized schools is of general interest, and should not necessarily be related to the education of teachers.

The relation between pedagogical reality, educational theory and education of teachers may therefore be visualized as follows (Fig. 2.1).

The following points should be noted: (1) The double-ended arrow between Pedagogical Reality and Educational Theory means:

- that educational theory is about pedagogical reality;
- that our way of structuring private and theoretical models partly constitutes what educational reality is, thus making the construction of educational theory important as a process in itself; and
- that educational theory can be developed regardless of teacher education.

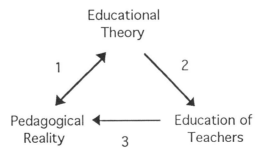

FIG. 2.1. The relations between pedagogical reality, educational theory and teacher education.

(2) The one-headed arrow from Educational Theory to Education of Teachers means two things.

First, the theory of education may be used as content in teacher education. The role of educational theory within the education of teachers is partly dependent on how we define the relation between theory of teaching and reality, since teachers are expected to work within pedagogical reality using educational theory. Therefore the question of how educational theory should be dealt with in teacher education is a separate question; it is the pedagogics of educational theory.

Second, as stated above, our conception of the theory and its relation to practice regulates our way of educating teachers, but the education itself does not necessarily influence our formulation of educational theory.

However, we are naturally free to devote ourselves to the development of the kind of educational theory that is especially useful in teacher education. Indeed much of the theory of didactics seems to have been developed with teacher education in mind.

(3) It is generally assumed that teachers with insight into educational theory are better equipped for pedagogical practice than teachers without such insight.

Educational Theory and the Practitioner's Reflection

A central task for educational theory is to create knowledge of the teaching process from what we could call an ordinary teacher's perspective. Given that this reality is often most complex, it is surprising that many efforts to understand teaching have oversimplified this complexity. I think here of models that address only content and method questions (the what and how questions) as well as of such interpretations of the traditional "didactic triangle" (Diederich, 1988, p.256) which disregard the context or the intentionality of the TSL process. Every effort to structure the pedagogical process raises the question of how the complexity of educational reality should be handled in a non-reductionist way.

An important aim of educational theory is to provide teachers with a conceptual instrument enabling them to reflect on and communicate their pedagogical experiences in a consistent manner. The advantage of scientific language lies in its systematic nature, which makes it an effective tool in communication. And we must not forget that there are several ways of understanding what a scientific theory is and what it allows.

A third role for educational (or didactic) theory is naturally that it should function as a framework for research on teaching. However, if educational theory should be used both as a research model and as an instrument for teachers' pedagogical reflection, we must state under what conditions this is possible. This is an issue to which we will return later.

An obvious additional problem for educational theory is its relation to the value-related dimension of teaching. The question is how a scientific theory handles values. Kansanen (1993b) reminds us of the problem concerning the extent to which a theory of teaching allows for normativity. The question is not whether teaching as such is normative or not; it always is normative and cannot avoid being so. But can a *theory* on teaching be normative? We will return to this question later.

In sum: even though the theory of didactics has been developed to a large extent with a view to educating teachers, we must not forget that didactic theory should do justice to the reality it tries to explicate. The primary problem of a theory of didactics lies in what questions should be posed, and how these questions should be answered in order that the theory is a useful instrument for understanding pedagogical practice. However, since the validity of a theory depends on why and for whom it is developed, it must be said that the model to be presented in this study is a contribution to the development of a theory ultimately aimed at practitioners and researchers in the field.

QUESTIONS TO BE POSED WITHIN A THEORY OF DIDACTICS

In order to move one step forward it is now time to say something about what we are developing a theory about. This is somewhat paradoxical, in that our very way of constructing a theory is partly to define what teaching is. Further, if we say *what* we are going to construct a theory about, then we have already partly constructed that theory. The solution to this problem seems to be to approach the problem stepwise.

We will first pay attention to the concepts of teaching and learning open-mindedly, and start by a speculative discussion on how these concepts might be understood and related to each other. Having done this, we will define the concept of didactics as it offers a conceptual framework and tradition within and in relation to which the ideas of this study have been developed.

Normativity and Prescriptivity as Problems

Some approaches to teaching and education are normative, in the sense that they try to pose questions to be answered in order to support and guide teaching practice. The three main groups of normative approaches are those starting from (a) the content of teaching (subject matter, content theory), (b) the psychology of learning, motivation and development and (c) philosophy of education (the view of man and the world). In the psychologically based theories of instruction it is usually stated that instructional practice must be based on the nature of human learning. In various content-oriented approaches to didactics (*Fachdidaktik*) the argumentation runs similarly—the way teaching is carried out should be based on the nature of the content. This kind of normative argumentation is the oldest when the starting point is philosophy (the view of man, nature and society). All these directions result in normative or prescriptive views regarding the question of how teaching should be carried out.

The positive result of these approaches is that the teacher may get advice on how to choose relevant themes out of a large and complex body of knowledge, as well as how to teach different types of content to different groups of people. Also on a collective (e.g. national) level the normative argumentation is typical; a nation agrees on some principles concerning the content and goals of education that should guide the activities in the schools. All this is quite clear thus far, but the problems begin when normative approaches to teaching, especially those which are based on some world-view, are understood as scientific theories. In other words, the question is the one referred to earlier: can a conceptual system be scientific if it indicates the goals of education?

If an educational theory is based on clear normative values concerning the goals of education, then the difference from educational ideology becomes very unclear. In other words, is a statement concerning the goals of education a scientific statement? This naturally depends on whether our view of scientific theory allows for normativity. Consequently, the problem of normativity is to be clarified by every conceptual system called a model or theory of instruction, didactics or education.

A similar issue is the relation between teaching and education; if every instructional act is always an educational act, it means that every instructional act is a value-related act as well. If so, we may ask whether a theory of didactics must also necessarily be normative since pedagogical practice is by definition normative? Or can educational theory be value-neutral (descriptive) even though its object is a value-laden activity?

A second problem concerning education as a prescriptive doctrine (*Lehre*) is that such a model catches only a limited part of what it is necessary to understand if one wants to understand educational practice; only the practical implications of planning, activity or evaluation are pointed out. The teacher is treated as a technician in this light; as a person who should act as effectively as possible in trying to reach goals put up (not even necessarily internalized by the teacher) by systematically applying accepted instructional principles. In this view teaching is not viewed as a moral craft, as it should be (Uljens, 1994a, pp.123–124).

If the view outlined above is accepted, then what, we may ask, are the questions a theory of didactics or education should actualize? What questions must necessarily be answered if we want to understand educational reality from a teacher's perspective?

Themes to be Acknowledged by Didactic Theory

In one sentence we may define the object of a theory of teaching in the following manner. In teaching there is always somebody (who?) that teaches somebody else (whom?) some subject matter (what?) in some way (how?) some time (when?) somewhere (where?) for some reason (why?) towards some goal (which?) (see Table 2.1).

The definition is inspired by Heimann's (1962) characterization of teaching but tries to develop it and emphasizes the student's intentional, active role for the pedagogical process. Teaching can be briefly defined as a subject's intentional activity carried out in order to facilitate another subject's efforts to reach certain types of competence (e.g. knowledge, insight, skills, etc.).

If we want to understand the pedagogical process, we must accept the legitimacy of all the above-mentioned questions simultaneously. Acceptance of these as legitimate questions is a first step in defining the object of a theory of didactics. The main point here is to show that the object of a theory of didactics is to understand the pedagogical process. The so-called how-question of a *theory* of didactics should thus not primarily be answered in terms of how teachers should act in practice. Rather, a theory of didactics should be an instrument of helping us to *analyse* relevant aspects of educational reality. Having done this, we at least know in what respects normative decisions are required. This position also means that the theory of pedagogical process is not limited to functioning as a predictor of learning results. In this respect Koskenniemi's (1968, 1971) idea of the object of a theory of didactics is supported.

The list of questions in Table 2.1 should not be viewed as being reductionist or deterministic in the sense that the background variables would explain the instructional process. Rather, the questions listed in the table are to be understood as such aspects or dimensions of the instructional process as a theory of didactics should contain. Didactic theory should thus not be reductionist with respect to content theory, psychology, sociology or philosophy. It must be a theory accepting the complexity of pedagogical reality and trying to structure this complexity (Hollo, 1927). Content theory, psychology, sociology and philosophy must thus be aspects of a theory of didactics. Consequently, a theory of didactics cannot be viewed as a theory based on e.g. psychological theory, since the approach is then much too limited.

The previous aspects of the pedagogical process considered essential to didactics are briefly summarized by the following five points: (1) inten-

TABLE 2.1
Aspects of the Phenomenon of Teaching

In teaching there is always

• somebody that	who?
• sometimes and	when?
• somewhere and	where?
• for some reason	why?
• in some way facilitates	how?
• somebody else's	whose?
• efforts to reach	by means of what?
• some kind of competence	what kind?
• in some field of knowledge	what?
• for certain purposes	what?
• that have been agreed upon	by whom?
so that the individual could better realize his interests	

tionality, (2) student–teacher interaction, (3) cultural context, (4) content, (5) methods.

Intentionality

Teaching is always aiming at something that is not present (Stenbäck, 1855). To teach is to try to make real what is ideal. In other words, teaching presupposes an individual who is conscious of what is not present. Thus the fundamental feature of consciousness, i.e. being aware of the non-present as a possibility, is of utmost importance in teaching. The values represented by an individual teacher decisively direct this intentionality. Thus a teacher always enters the TSL situation with certain ideas concerning the learner's future.

In discussing the question of why somebody is teaching somebody else and what this activity is aiming at we must remember that a motive is not a goal. We educate towards something for some reason. Second, if we accept that teaching is directed to some kind of goal, this means that teaching is an intentional activity, a purposeful activity. The teacher would in this view have an idea about an ideal (or rather, potential) order of things towards which he was striving. However, accepting that teaching is a purposeful activity, we must ask what is the nature of this purposiveness. Is it to be understood as just any intentional activity or are there specific features of teachers' pedagogical intentionality?

One answer could be that a teacher by his activity tries to help or make it easier for somebody to reach competence, or simply to intentionally aid someone to learn. A motive for this would be the idea that a teacher believes that it is by the process of learning that e.g. knowledge is reached. A second feature of pedagogical intentionality concerns the ethical aspect of instruction, which involves not only the teacher's but also the learner's rights and obligations in the pedagogical situation.

The Interaction of Two Intentional Subjects

A TSL process requires at least two subjects, a teacher and a student (a learner). The reason motivating the presence of two intentional subjects is naturally that this enables us to talk about the interaction between them. Models of teaching including only the teacher always run into difficulties when it comes to the notion of co-operation or interaction. Such models also represent quite unpleasant pictures of the learner; the learner is a passive receiver of knowledge. Similarly, models of teaching mainly based on the learner's perspective are usually one-sided as well. The interactive nature of the TSL process is a secondary question in such models (Koort, 1974). Thus intention is considered conceptually prior to interaction.

The Teaching-Studying-Learning Process as a Cultural Phenomenon

A pedagogical activity, like every other human activity, takes place in time and space (Andersson, 1995; Bock, 1994). It may be that some human activities may be understood correctly independently of their cultural and temporal embeddedness. However, this seems not to be true of education. This is partly due to the fact that the economic structure in different cultures varies, and while schooling is to a large extent designed to guarantee the continuity of a culture (Habermas, 1987), e.g. by serving the organization of the labour market, it is difficult to understand education as being independent of this (Dale, 1981). Also, when looking at teacher education this becomes evident; every major change of the school system in a country leads to a change in the education of teachers. It is thus important to notice that even though there are similarities in teaching between cultures, teaching practices cannot be understood apart from these cultures (Engeström, 1987; Säljä, 1991).

The Teacher's and Students' Culturally Defined Role. In order to understand what teaching is, it is, among other things, important to understand *who* the teachers are; their personality, their view of mankind and society, and education, what they hold important in life etc. By this we have said nothing about the process of teaching as such, but is it really possible to understand what a teacher does if we do not pay attention to the question of who the teacher is? Is the teacher's personality or ideological conviction completely devoid of interest in this perspective? In other words, is teaching only a commonplace technique of instruction that is first learned and then applied? No, since teaching is an intentional, goal-oriented activity, it is always value-related. Therefore teaching cannot be equated with any kind of technique. Rather, teaching is a moral practice.

This study is directed towards institutionally organized TSL situations, i.e. situations characterized by certain culturally agreed-upon expectations and roles; a teacher is supposed to be able to teach, the students are told to trust the teacher, the students conceive of themselves as learners that must pass exams, etc. In a TSL situation in school, the participants' roles are not solely defined by their intentional interaction in the situations in question but also by the cultural role they have in visiting that institution. Compared to a TSL situation in ordinary life, it is not necessarily the structure of the communicative pattern itself that differs from the pattern in schools, but the conditions circumscribing the situation. One such condition is the curriculum, another is the traditions of a specific school. It is thus impossible to grasp the TSL process in the institutionalized school without viewing it in relation to the curriculum, hidden or not, as well as to many other structural factors constituting this organization (Loser & Terhart, 1994; Lundgren, 1972). Thus learning in schools is one form of contextually embedded learning practice (for a discussion see Mertaniemi & Uljens, 1994; Uljens & Myrskog, 1994).

The Content

Fourth, we have the question of content. If a teacher helps the student to reach some kind of competence, there is always this "something" present in the situation. It is, in fact, very difficult to imagine a pedagogical situation that would not contain any kind of content—there has, it seems, to be some kind of content. Thus, if the content is such a fundamental feature of a pedagogical situation, then this must be acknowledged as a relevant problem in trying to understand teaching. As we will see, several questions are related to content: especially the question of how the content is constructed in an institutionalized educational setting is important (Menck, 1975, 1987).

Methods

The fifth question of relevance in this connection concerns the actual methods that a teacher makes use of in pedagogical work (Schulze, 1993). This includes several sub-questions which will be dealt with in more detail in connection with the theory to be presented later on. In short then, this question involves (a) the methods used to represent the actual content, (b) the working methods used by the students and (c) the instructional and evaluative methods used by the teacher (Terhart, 1989).

Conclusion

In this chapter we have referred to the complexity of pedagogical reality. Questions to be posed in order to grasp this complexity have also been indicated. Yet most problems remain unsolved. One of the first is how the many questions raised above should be related to each other in order to form a structured whole. But before we go that far, it is time for a more elaborate analysis of learning. As teaching is often thought of as something facilitating learning, we must also define the relation between teaching and learning more precisely.

ON LEARNING

Before we can make any suggestions concerning the relation between teaching and learning, we must investigate the phenomenon of learning as such. The motive is twofold—first, practical pedagogical activity is often thought to affect individual learning. Second, the theory of teaching must relate to learning in one way or another.

Thus, what is learning? How should it be limited? What are the basic features of learning? The focus of attention in what follows will be the notion of change. Which changes, we will ask, of all human changes, are identified as learning changes?

The discussion aims at posing questions that will help us to delimit the phenomenon of teaching; if teaching aims at influencing individuals in such a way that changes called learning are brought about, then it may be helpful to understand what is counted as a learning change among different types of human changes.

It should be observed that the present discussion is consciously delimited to only a few issues; (a) the process and result of learning, (b) maturation and learning, (c) experience and learning, (d) learning and invention.

THE PROCESS AND RESULT OF LEARNING

Generally speaking, a common crucial question in theories of learning is how changes occur in the way in which an individual acts or experiences, understands, conceptualizes, approaches, recalls, handles, manipulates, or treats something in his natural and cultural context. Several of the activities mentioned (the list is not meant to be either exhaustive or definitive) can refer either to the process whereby an individual requires a better or new comprehension or skill in some specific matter *or* to a more stable mental state like a present conscious awareness of something or a potentiality to do something. This means that the same terms are, not always but often, used to refer to both the process of learning and the result of learning. In other words, one can learn by acting or by reflecting, and a better ability to act or deeper reflection on something may be the result of a reflective learning process.

A theory of learning should thus not be limited to what is changing in learning, though learning always is a change of something. A theory of learning should explicate both the nature of the process, to the extent that this is possible, and also what is changed by learning (Carey, 1985, p. 200):

> Any theory of learning must have at least two components: a specification of the initial state and a specification of the mechanisms in terms of which that initial state is modified . . . Psychologists who decry the lack of mechanisms of conceptual change focus on only half of the problem.

What is counted as belonging to the process of learning, i.e. leading to some result, and what is called the result of the process, are dependent on e.g. what the goal of learning was. A beginner may identify the mastery of some necessary first step as an important instance of learning, without comprehending that what was learned was almost negligible with respect to the task. A more experienced person who is learning something partly new may have another understanding of what distance must be covered before one has reached a point worth calling a result of learning.

But is it necessary to reach intended knowledge or competence in order to call a change learning? This is a reasonable question since we can easily identify situations where people have tried to reach the mastery of something without succeeding. An individual has, in other words, studied in order to reach some kind of knowledge, but not learned. From a pedagogical perspective there certainly is good reason to keep up this distinction between studying and learning, since teachers are in fact concerned with teaching students how to study, hoping thereby to make learning come about. What we are able to influence in educational situations is precisely how students try to reach a certain degree of competence, i.e. how they study. We may then compare the result of this activity with the study activity itself.

In situations where an individual is intentionally (deliberately) striving towards mastery of x, but without making "any progress at all", this judgement most often stems from the learner and is to be understood against the background of the learner's goals or expectations. The judgement often stems from a learner that is disappointed with the progress made. However, some progress *was* made; in conscious, deliberate learning, progress is *always* made. In this case progress covers a result which implies that an individual found a task too difficult under certain conditions, i.e. that the learner learned that the task was too difficult, or learned what *kind* of task it was etc. We may thus conclude that the reaching of the intended competence is not necessary in order to identify learning.

MATURATION, EXPERIENCE AND LEARNING

Now, can one possess some type of competence or knowledge that is reached by other means than learning? In answering this question we can approach the problem from two perspectives. Firstly, we must decide if competence can be identified with innate abilities or reached through maturation. Secondly, we must deal with the problem concerning the relation between experience and learning.

It is often claimed that individual changes caused by maturation are not counted as learning (Carey & Gelman, 1991; Gibson & Peterson, 1991). The relation between maturation and learning is, however, complex.

In discussing the relation between genetically based development and learning, we must remember that a part of the genetically determined maturation (which develops differently under different conditions), opens possibilities to reach a certain degree of experientially based competence. For example, in considering the example of walking we may say that a child must have reached a certain level of biological maturity in order to succeed; the level of maturity does not however lead to the competence of walking by itself. In a sense biology sets a limit to what can be learned. Our biological constitution provides us with certain capabilities which allow us to develop (learn) different types of culturally based competence. The nativist theory of language learning and cognitive development also argues along these lines, i.e. that individuals are born with a rudimentary innate system which forms the basis for learning a natural language. Then, having learned culturally determined concepts, these gradually become the instruments of reflection (Leontjev, 1977).

Experience and Learning

The term experience has very different meanings. Usually it refers to immediate experience or experiencing, i.e. to the kind of experience that every moment of life is full of, i.e. immediate, engaged beingness or life as lived through. This meaning of experience is close to the German *Erlebnis* (Swedish *upplevelse*). One could say that reflection upon immediate experience, *Erlebnis*, results in experience in the second sense of the word, reflected experience, expressed by the German *Erfahrung* (Swedish *erfarenhet*). Acknowledging the difference between these two senses of experience affects our understanding of what it means to say that learning "must result from some sort of . . . experience" (Shuell, 1986). It can only mean that one refers to the first sense of experience, i.e. immediate experience, since the second sense of experience is a result of reflecting upon the first. We can also identify the difference by saying that even if two persons have experienced a number of equal things, this alone does not entitle us to claim that both are equally experienced. To *be* experienced (generally) requires proper reflection on one's experiences or that an individual has extracted meaning from or given meaning to some experience. Yet all reflection on one's experiences should not be identified with learning.

If changes in our understanding of something occurring without systematic practice, i.e. unintentionally, are included in the concept of learning, then we seem to end up in a situation where every possible change should be called learning. Some of these changes would occur as a result of conscious efforts and others more or less accidentally. From a pedagogical perspective it is natural to concentrate on those changes in competence which occur as a result of systematic reflection on experiences.

Conscious reflection upon one's experiences (that will most likely result in experience) might thus be identifiable with one kind of learning process. However, it seems that this model would require something that is capable of reflecting on experiences, something that may recognize an experience either as something new or as something already known. This ability could be called self-reflection. It may also be possible to view an experience (German *Erlebnis*) as a meaningful sense impression based on a perceptual process. In other words, it means that we have perceptual impressions caused by something else than ourselves. We may be aware of these impressions, yet not understand what they mean. These impressions may thus be given meaning. The meaning of an impression or perception could be established on the basis of earlier experience in the following way.

Previous experience contains a horizon of future possible changes. This horizon would offer us preliminary instruments to establish a meaning. Therefore it is reasonable to talk about something being unexpected. Meeting something unexpected means that an experience is not completely accounted for by one's earlier experiences. It is this gap that results in reflection (not necessarily always but generally). Reflection is thus a way to deal with such a situation.

In accordance with this model, when something incongruous occurs we may ask whether we reflect on our present (new) experiences or on our previous experiences. On none of them solely, I would say. We rather reflect on the fact that something did not work, i.e. both on why our previous experience cannot account for the new experience in a sufficient way *and* on the nature of the new experience. We cannot act otherwise because it is only in relation to our previous experience that a new experience may be called unexpected. And it is only in relation to a new experience that our previous experience is defined as existing.

Learning and Inventing. Another perspective on learning which is important from an educational point of view is whether one can *learn* something that nobody else knows. This might seem obvious—think of researchers, one might argue, are they not a perfect example of what learning new insights means? Yet it seems reasonable to discuss researchers' work in other terms also. One may, for example, say that researchers discover new knowledge, construct new theories and develop things.

The difference between learning in this sense and learning something known becomes even more evident if we notice that some knowledge or skills may be taught to novices in the field. However, nobody can teach researchers new knowledge. General research methods are of course taught, but not what can be found out about the world with the help of these methods. And even though every method or approach points out the limits of what one is most likely to achieve (at least with respect to the type of knowledge), this does not include insight into what will be found. So, we may identify a difference between knowledge that somebody else has in advance and knowledge that nobody is previously familiar with. On the other hand, a counterargument could be presented here: it is correct that there seems to be a difference, but if I, as *learner*, am unaware that somebody else knows what I try to learn then the difference seems to cease. For me as learner it doesn't matter whether anybody who knows exists or if it is only I who am unaware that somebody already knows what I am trying to learn. Only one difference may be noticed; if I know (or have good grounds to believe) that nobody knows what I am trying to learn, this may affect me emotionally or in some other way. The process of learning may appear more exciting if this is the case, or it may be frightening because there is nobody to ask.

The point here is that learning something already known is not the same thing as learning something completely new. This latter activity is often called inventing, discovering or constructing. Plato opened the discussion of this issue of acquiring new knowledge in the *Meno* with a paradox: If one knows what one is trying to learn there is no reason to learn because one already knows it. On the other hand, if one does not know what one is trying to learn one will never be able to decide whether one has been successful or not. However, observe that this paradox makes sense only in talking about acquiring the kind of competence that I call invention (i.e. transcending the known). In the case of known knowledge (i.e. "I know that you know how to do this, though I myself do not know how to do it") the case is different. It is certainly possible to identify knowledge or competence that one would like to reach, but identifying this does not mean that one has reached it. To know what one wants to learn does not mean knowing how to try to learn it. The second half of the paradox ceases to be a problem; in the case of identifiable competence we have a pretty good idea of what is counted as successful.

In Fig. 2.2 learning denotes reaching something which the learner recognizes as something new to them, though it is known by somebody else. In learning something known, i.e. something identified as competence or knowledge by the learner, a fundamental problem is how an individual constructs the initial interpretation or chooses a hypothesis to be tested. One's previous experience seems to contain a limiting horizon of possibilities which are actualized in relation to different experiences. In the same sense as the future is present as potentiality, experiencing actualizes possible interpretations (or definitions of a situation). Some undetermined, round and greyish object in a children's playground may be interpreted as a ball or some construction, whereas the same impression in another context may be identified and acted upon as if it were a dangerous small creature. To explain the limitation of possible interpretations is to explain important aspects of the process of learning.

There is more, however. Having made a first interpretation, after generating a first heuristic model, we also choose criteria to decide when something is achieved, i.e. criteria for when a heuristic (initial) model

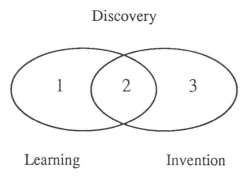

FIG. 2.2. 1. Learning something that the learner is aware that somebody else knows. 2. Discovery. "Learning" something that is recognized (by the learner) as new both to the learner and others, yet, in fact, is known by others. 3. Invention. "Learning" something completely new, not known before either by the learner (subject) or by anybody else.

works. The individual must decide when an understanding of a situation will do, be deep enough, be considered acceptable.

Discovery would again point to learning something that the learner recognizes as previously unknown, not only to themselves but also to others, but which in fact is nevertheless known by others. The point here is that the learner mistakenly believes that she is the only or the first person to know. Inventing would point to something that is new not only to the learner but also to everybody else (in the world). When we identify something as being new, there are several aspects of the problem that we have to pay attention to. Two fundamental aspects are (a) the conceptual field within which something is identified not only as different but also as new, and (b) those individuals who form the "social reference group". Now, from the learner's point of view, learning as Discovery and Invention may be similar; the learner simply does not necessarily know that there *are* people who already have the competence to be reached. This is not a shortcoming of the learner; the distinction between discovery and invention is possible only when some competence is reached and acknowledged.

At this point I would like to remind the reader that I am only trying to point out what is changing in learning, i.e. what kind of changes are counted as learning; I will not go into an analysis of the process of how this change occurs. For example, I do not discuss questions of prior experience or knowledge nor how to generalize context or domain-specific skills or competence, i.e. how competence is de-contextualized or made context-independent.

In a sense one may compare a teacher's knowledge and tasks with a researcher's—they both try to pinpoint a problem. The teacher does this to the student, the researcher to themself. In comparing the student's knowledge with the teacher's, a logical gap may often be identified and a teacher may construct a problem for the student based on this comparison. The researcher asks themself in a sense the same questions as a teacher asks the student; namely those that are confined to what is known and aim at a penetration into the unknown. A question may function as the generative motor in moving from the known into the twilight zone of knowledge.

Reproductive teaching corresponds to learning as described above, while productive (constructive, generative) teaching corresponds to field 2 (a kind of "directed, basic pedagogical practice", simulated as-if-situations). It appears that this is about as far as educational work can go. The last step, invention, definitely touches (in a sense goes beyond) the borders of what is possible in an educational setting.

The educational implication of the distinction between known and unknown is that only invented, discovered or constructed knowledge can be taught; only something discovered can be shown. Something undiscovered cannot be an object of instruction, something unexperienced cannot be explicated.

We can thus see that the concept of teaching may also help us in delimiting the phenomenon of learning. One could, in fact, define learning as achievement of teachable competence, i.e. reaching competence that is possible to achieve by pedagogical means. This definition does not suggest that teaching is a necessary element in reaching a certain degree of competence nor that this must be done in an educational setting. The competence could perfectly well be reached by other means as well (individually, in ordinary activity, unconsciously, by mistake, etc.). The only requirement demanded in this definition is that the process of reaching or moving towards competence must be possible to facilitate through pedagogical efforts.

CONCLUSION

To summarize, one might say that a theory of learning should specify both what is changing through the process of learning and how this change should be described. In this chapter the focus has been on the first of these questions.

From a pedagogical perspective on learning and cognition it appears important to pay attention to the relation between the content of human experience and external (social, cultural) reality as well. How an individual adopts certain cultural ways of acting and how cultural patterns are kept alive by this individual engagement is certainly interesting from a pedagogical perspective. To focus on this relation also directs the attention to the problem of how individuals transcend established cultural patterns.

ON TEACHING, STUDYING AND LEARNING

I will now summarize what has been stated previously, as well as defining more precisely the relation between teaching, studying and learning.

Since education is generally thought to lead to an increase in competence, knowledge, skill, insight or the like and since it is widely held that this process of increase or change may be called learning, it may be useful to start here when we discuss the relation between teaching and learning.

We first get the following relation (Fig. 2.3):

(1)   Learning ($y1$)   ⟶   Competence ($z1$)

FIG. 2.3. Learning as leading to competence.

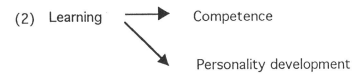

FIG. 2.4. Learning as leading to competence and personality development.

According to proposition (1) learning always leads to competence or the like. However, if learning also leads to changes in personality and if having a personality is not a skill, insight, or competence, then it seems as if learning also leads to changes in things other than competence. Thus the assumption above would not hold true. The first modification to be made on the basis of the analysis above results in Fig. 2.4.

If we accept the figure above, it is time to include teaching in the analysis. Teaching is often defined as intentional activity aiming at supporting someone's learning.

The relation in Fig. 2.5 assumes (a) that teaching always leads to learning and (b) that everything learned is a result of teaching.

With respect to the first assumption, that teaching *in principle* leads to learning, we have already noted that this is not at all the case; a teacher may be teaching without being successful.[2] Further, only because certain types of teaching are often followed by certain types of learning, this is still a probabilistic relationship, not a causal one. Sometimes teaching does not lead to learning at all, and sometimes teaching leads to learning something that was not intended.

Even though teaching may be unsuccessful, that is, even though teaching leads neither to intended learning nor to any other kind of learning, we may ask whether teaching can result in things other than learning. From an educational point of view it is interesting whether or not we agree that competence is possible to reach by means other than learning; as long as teaching is thought to facilitate learning (and nothing else), then reaching the kind of knowledge that is possible to reach by learning becomes interesting from an educational perspective. However, if teaching may also facilitate other means by which competence is reached, then teaching must be understood not only in relation to learning but to these other means by which competence is achieved. For example, biological maturation sometimes facilitates the attainment of competence. If

(3) Teaching (x1) ⟶ Learning (y1)

FIG. 2.5. Teaching as leading to learning.

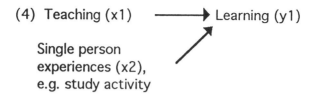

FIG. 2.6. Teaching and study activity as leading to learning.

pedagogical practice aims at effecting such maturing, then it effects the attainment of competence through a process that is not a learning process.

Concerning the second assumption above (proposition b), i.e. whether teaching is a *necessary* element in bringing about learning, the answer is simple—obviously not. Learning can perfectly well occur without teaching, as most learning probably does (Terhart, 1989, p.132). Consequently there are many things in addition to teaching that may facilitate learning. And even if teaching were a necessary element in reaching knowledge, as it may be in some cases, it could not be called a sufficient condition alone; a student has not necessarily learned simply because a teacher has taught. Learning takes more than teaching.

On the question of whether something else than teaching may affect an individual's learning process, the answer is positive—a lot of things may affect the learning process. Here we will limit our attention to only one such factor: the learner's own intentional activity.

We must conclude that the assumptions explicated in the scheme above are not correct. We must therefore complete it. Teaching may thus be unsuccessful, and other things than teaching may affect learning. For example we must recognize the learner's own intentions and study activity as a most crucial factor when attempting to understand the teaching–learning process (see Fig. 2.6).

THE RELATION BETWEEN STUDYING AND LEARNING

How should we understand the relation between learning and studying? First of all we may notice that every student hopefully is a learner, but not all learners are students. Student comes from the verb to study, i.e. refers to a conscious activity directed towards reaching competence. But is it possible to say that learning is an activity in the same sense? Many would probably claim that learning and studying are synonymous, but to me it seems that learning is something that hopefully happens when one consciously *tries* to learn, i.e. when one is studying. Studying is thus always conscious and intentional while learning is not necessarily conscious. Learning therefore covers unintentional acquisition of competence; I may learn something while simply walking down a street, i.e. without trying to learn. In other words, there is a dimension of passivity in the term learning that cannot be found in connection with studying. Studying is thus an intentional activity aimed at bringing about learning. Bereiter and Scardamalia (1989, p.363) have used the expression intentional learning "to refer to cognitive processes that have learning as a goal rather than incidental outcome".

However, saying that "He *learned* X" does not make it clear whether the person in question consciously *tried* to reach X or whether this state was reached more or less by chance, without conscious effort. Thus "He *learned* X" does not tell us about the individual's intentions; we only know that this person really did reach some kind of competence. Thus, to say "He is *learning* X" does not mean that a person really will attain knowledge. It only says that they are engaged in a process. However, the expression "He *was* learning X" seems to imply that the learner had a goal, while "He *learned* X" does not imply this. Therefore there is a certain similarity between "He *was* learning X" and "He *was* studying X". But there is a fundamental difference between saying "He learned X" and "He studied X". From the statement "He studied X" it is not possible to say whether the person actually did reach the desired knowledge. The expression "to study" thus refers primarily to the conscious activity carried out in order to reach knowledge.

As a preliminary conclusion we might say that we need both terms; to study refers only to the intentional activity (the process) of a subject trying to reach competence or insight, while learning may refer both to the process and to a factual change in competence. However, while learning also covers unintentional processes that lead to knowledge, studying only covers intentional processes or efforts. Against this background I refer to the concept of studying instead of intentional learning, as studying is an established term, though not in frequent use (Yrjönsuuri & Yrjönsuuri, 1994). However, it should be observed that the concept of studying should by no means be delimited to such intentional activities aiming at reaching competence as occur in institutionalized schooling. Nor should the concept of studying be related to changes in some specific fields of human competence only. "Studying" as a general concept should thus be used in a content– and context–transcribing sense.

The passive and active dimensions of the terms make it clear why it is necessary to include the learner in a model trying to clarify what teaching is about. In fact, learning is a primary phenomenon in relation to teaching and studying. If there were not such a phenomenon as learning, then activities like studying and teaching would not be meaningful.

Thus it is reasonable to recognize studying even though it does not necessarily lead to actual learning, i.e. to the *reaching* of competence or insight. It is, in other words, not necessary to reach the competence one strives at in order to call something a study process. In this respect learning (reaching knowledge, insight or competence) seems to require more than studying; a study process cannot guarantee that the learning aimed at will occur.

In clarifying the teaching–studying–learning (TSL) process I would now like to refer to one of the conclusions made in the previous chapter ("On learning"). It may be possible to delimit learning on the basis of the relation between teaching and competence. Learning may then partly be understood as the reaching of teachable competence. It may be wise to say that only such human changes aiming at increased competence as are possible to support by teaching or by studying can be called learning. Other forms of learning can be called invention or discovery, etc.

Following the same line of reasoning, we might say that studying (intentional learning) often means trying to reach competence that is identified by the student (the learner). In other words, the student realizes that somebody in his surroundings is capable of something and then tries to reach a similar capacity. However, teaching and studying may also be directed towards a kind of problem solving, i.e. the competence to be reached is not specified in advance. In such a process the result of the process is not identified before the process starts. This was called discovery learning and was connected with productive teaching (in contrast to reproductive teaching, which aims at supporting the acquisition of competence identified in advance). In the first case, attention is directed towards competence as such, in the second case attention is directed towards the process.

A preliminary conclusion is that studying and teaching are two types of intentional human activity aiming at "bringing about learning" (Hirst, 1971). These activities are, however, not necessary prerequisites for learning, i.e. learning can very well occur without intentional studying or teaching. In addition, teaching and studying cannot guarantee learning. The position developed thus far may be visualized by Fig. 2.7.

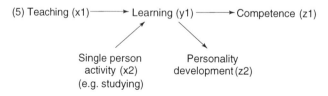

FIG. 2.7. Teaching and studying as leading to competence and personality development through the process of learning.

THE RELATION BETWEEN TEACHING AND STUDYING

Thus both learner and teacher may try to mould the learning process; the teacher does so by teaching and the learner by studying. If we accept this, we may ask what is the relationship between a teacher's teaching and a learner's learning; is it direct or mediated by the learner's study activity?

It could be claimed that teaching indirectly affects the learning process through the student's way of studying. This is not to say that teaching affects a student's study behaviour. Rather, what is claimed is that teaching is conceived cognitively by the student and may then lead to a decision by the student to consciously try to study in a certain way in order to reach some kind of competence.

The point here is that it is not possible to directly affect learning, since the very act of learning is unconscious. Thus I agree with Kansanen (1993b, p.56) when he writes that:

> We cannot get learning to take place by means of will power or by means of a decision on the part of the student. The instructional interaction aims at learning, but it is only possible to steer the activities of students with the purpose of fostering learning, or the student can wish and try to do something that s/he or the teacher thinks will probably lead to learning.

The following figure might therefore be more relevant than the previous one. It does not assume that teaching affects learning directly, but indirectly through the student's own activity (see Fig. 2.8).

The fundamental idea behind Fig. 2.8 is that in intentional teaching a teacher tries to support an individual's study process, not the individual's learning process. This conclusion is supported in the literature. For example, Fenstermacher and Soltis (1986, p.39) claims similarly that "[I]t ... makes more sense to contend that a central task of teaching is to enable the student to perform the tasks of learning."

Matti Koskenniemi (1978, p.73) has argued that in order for the teacher's purposiveness to be successful, this purposiveness must be present as the student's purposiveness. Therefore it may be most practical

FIG. 2.8. Teaching as affecting learning indirectly through the individual's study activity.

for the teacher to try to move towards the goals indirectly via the goals set up and accepted by the students. Accordingly, the process through which students construct their learning goals is most interesting (Wistedt, 1994).

Teaching and studying may thus be called activities supporting individual growth through the process of learning. Learning in itself is therefore a process, among others, through which individual growth is achieved. Competence and changes in one's personality may then be called the results of individual growth.

If learning in the general sense of the word is unconscious, then learning in its active sense, i.e. learning as studying, is conscious. Also teaching must generally be considered a fundamentally conscious activity.

The Learner's Intentions

Teaching is thus an intentional activity aiming at facilitating someone's possibilities of reaching some kind of competence. Primarily, teaching affects the student's study activity. The learner's own activity in this process, i.e. the study activity, is intentional as well; the student has identified some competence and consciously tries to achieve it.

However, assuming that both the student's and the teacher's activities are intentional, we have made the picture more complex, especially as these intentions may differ from each other.

We could now imagine a situation where the learner (student, pupil) has *tried* to reach what was agreed upon together with the teacher, but failed. In this case we would have one subject who has tried to teach, another subject who tried to learn but did not reach competence. Now, was teaching present in this case? Yes, I think so. If the teacher tries to teach in a situation where the learner tries to study, then teaching is present.

The next question is whether a teacher has taught if the student does not try to learn, i.e. study? Some researchers give a negative answer (e.g. Yrjönsuuri, 1994, p.103). The argument is that if the student's intention has not been to learn the content presented and taught by the teacher, then teaching has not occurred. The teacher has been doing something else. I disagree with such a conclusion on the following grounds.

I do not require that the learner in the institutionalized school necessarily strives or tries to learn in order to recognize a teacher's intentional activity to support the study process as teaching. Otherwise it could be said that a teacher teaches only those children in a classroom that at that moment intend to learn, and that the teacher does not teach those in a classroom who do not intend to learn. This is obviously false. Naturally the teacher normally tries to teach all students in a classroom.

Sometimes, of course, the teacher focuses attention explicitly on one student, thus disregarding for a moment the rest of the class. In fact, a teacher quite often pays attention to and tries to teach those who do *not* intend to learn.[3]

Further, the content in a TSL situation is not one and the same thing for the different participants. The teacher can by no means guarantee that the content will be understood in the same way by all the students (Marton, 1981). Therefore a student may be engaged in trying to solve a completely different problem from the one that was meant to be solved, because they understood the task differently from what the teacher intended. Thus, even though students would *try* to reach a kind of competence, i.e. *try* to work through a problem, they may still be solving *different* problems. This also calls in question the idea of using the student's conscious effort as a criterion for identifying teaching.

However, I do require that the teacher understands himself as a teacher, i.e. the teacher's explicit intention must be to support (but not to force) another person to reach competence in order that his activity should qualify as teaching. This means (a) that the teacher (ideally) must try to be aware of what their intention is, and (b) that the teacher believes that the student intends to learn or that the teacher is aware that the student may be expected to intend to learn (study). By saying this we also avoid the unpleasant conclusion that activities forcing individuals to change could be called teaching.

THE SOCIO-CULTURAL SITUATION

An additional way of clarifying this position is to acknowledge the social agreement concerning the TSL situation. If teaching, as described above, occurs in a social institution like a school, then the activity of facilitating the learner's acquisition of competence may clearly be called teaching, even though the learner has not tried to learn what the teacher honestly tried to teach. If this position is rejected, we run the risk of applying a kind of reductionism in our argumentation as indicated above; the teacher's activity would be made dependent on the student's intentions.

There is also a risk of making the opposite mistake; it would be wrong to say that the student is engaged in an active learning process each time a teacher is teaching (in the teacher's own opinion). The student's activity cannot thus be made dependent on the teacher's intentions, nor can the teacher's activity be made dependent on the student's intentions. The kernel of the problem is thus to what extent both these parties' intentions must be in existence in order for teaching to occur. I have claimed that the teacher's intention is always required and that it is reasonable to require that a teacher should have good reasons at least to expect that the student intends to learn, in order that we may call an activity teaching.

It is also suggested that the situation or context framing the intentional TSL process must be acknowledged in order to identify teaching. If both the teacher's and the student's understanding of a situation is that they participate in a common TSL process (with the intention to teach and to learn) then this is enough to make teaching occur. An activity identified as teaching should not be made dependent on individual student's intentions or the result of the process in terms of learning achievements. Making teaching dependent on student's intentions would lead, in a classroom, to the conclusion that whether the teacher is teaching or not depends on from which student's perspective the classroom reality is described. Therefore we must remember that the *social contract* in a school assumes that even the uninterested subject is an intentional learner; even though the subject is uninterested, the teacher has the right to expect an interested attitude from the student. In some cases the teacher can refer to the student's parents, whose intentions are often regarded as more decisive than the student's. One might even say, in some cases, that the student's intentionality is replaced by the parents' intentionality. The structure of the school as a social institution thus gives the teacher the right to assume intentional efforts to learn on the part of the students. If this were not the case, evaluation of students' achievements would solely be an evaluation of the teacher's ability to teach and not of the individual student's ability, efforts and achievements.

To acknowledge the social contract agreed upon between the participants in the TSL process helps us to understand the conditions on which the participants are present in the TSL situation. The social contract is of importance not only in order to identify something as teaching, but more generally in order to understand institutionalized education (Bergqvist, 1990; Mercer, 1995).

CONCLUSION

As has been stated, one of the aims of this study is to investigate the pedagogical implications of learning theory. The previous analysis suggests that the instructional implications of learning theory consist of prescriptive claims concerning how teachers should assist the learner's intentional study activities in order for learning to occur.

It is also important to recognize that when the relation between teaching and learning has been discussed thus far, it has not been done within the theory of didactics. Rather, the previous analysis may be characterized as an ontological reflection on teaching, studying and learning and the relations between these phenomena.

One of the most important results of the previous discussion is that when the theory of didactics is developed, one must necessarily pay attention to the intentions and the intentional activities of the teacher and the learner. The intended results of the TSL process cannot be the sole fundamental criterion when trying to identify the phenomenon of teaching; the intentions of the interacting subjects must be acknowledged as well.

The remaining question is what role the process of learning as such plays in a theory of didactics. In other words, as we can meaningfully claim that a teacher has taught even though a learner has not learned, it is reasonable to question the role of learning in understanding teaching. Only one answer has been given so far: the learner's study process is important. But as has been shown above—as studying should not be confused with learning, and the question remains partly unanswered.

Even if teaching is logically independent of learning, teaching practice always *intends* to influence learning. This intentionality has to do with teachers' reflection on how they could facilitate the study process in order to affect learning. As a theory of didactics is assumed to be an instrument in teachers' pedagogical reflection, this theory must be explicit concerning what role learning theory has in the theory of didactics.

If the instructional implications of learning theory are prescriptive propositions concerning how teachers should act, then a theory or model of didactics should be clear with respect to what role prescriptive and normative propositions have in the theory or model in question. We will return to this question in the next section.

DIDACTICS AS THE SCIENCE OF THE TEACHING-STUDYING-LEARNING PROCESS

Thus far the expressions educational theory, instructional theory and theory of didactics have been used when talking about theoretical conceptualization of pedagogical practice. While the present study partly has primarily Nordic and continental pedagogical theory as its frame of reference, the concept of didactics must be commented upon especially.[4] Didactics may preliminarily be defined as the science of the teaching–studying–learning (TSL) process, as long as this process is understood as previously described.

In clarifying the concept of didactics, it should be noted that there is no possibility in the present context of going into a detailed historical analysis of the concept, its origin and development. Nor will there be any attempt to present a complete overview of the contemporary usage of the term.

There are several reasons for these decisions. Firstly, an analysis or even a description of the historical development of the term and a description of its contemporary use would each require extensive studies. Since there is no reason to describe the tradition of didactics as such in this study, there is no reason to repeat in a condensed form what has been said in numerous previous publications in the field.[5] Secondly, since the focus of this study is primarily on how one may deal with learning within the theory of didactics, attention is mainly focused on this question. In addition, one section is devoted to relating the presented model to some influential German schools of thought. Also, the question of normativity is regarded as a central issue and is dealt with in a section of its own (see Chapter 3).

The motive for clarifying didactics in this context is thus to communicate the nature of the model proposed in this study. It is easier to understand the didactic model that will be presented later by having a general understanding of what is meant by didactics. To clarify and understand the features of the model is important, especially since it will be used as the pedagogical frame of reference for the subsequent analysis of learning theory.

THE CONCEPT OF DIDACTICS

The etymology of the German and Swedish word *Didaktik* shows that it originates from the Greek verb διδασκειν (*didáskein*). In its active form it refers to teaching, presentation, clarification, and instruction. In its passive form it means to learn, to become taught. In addition, there is a mediating meaning of the term; to learn by oneself, to adopt, i.e. *aus sich selbst lernen, sich aneignen*. Further the noun derived from the verb is διδαξισ (*didaxis*), which means teaching, instruction. In addition there is the expression art of teaching (διδακτικε τεχηνε, i.e. *didaktiké téchne*) referring to the practice of teaching. Finally *didaskaleion* meant a school (see Heursen, 1994, p.307).

Didactics should not be confused with the French *didactique*, a term still used today for a specific kind of instructional literature (Blankertz, 1987, p.21). This usage has its roots in Greek literature. According to Herwig Blankertz, didactic literature comprised various kinds of instructional poems which existed side by side with the heroic and historical poems.

As was noted above, the term didactics has already appeared in Greek literature and even in the Old Testament (Knecht-von Martial, 1985; Kroksmark, 1993). It is, however, common to connect the first modern use of the term with Wolfgang Ratke (1571–1635), who presented a reform programme, the so-called *Frankfurter Memorial* for schools in 1612 (Kansanen, 1992, p.5). In those days didactics was primarily understood as the *art* of teaching (Lehrkunst). For Johan Amos Comenius, i.e. Jan Komensky (1592–1670), didactics was an art. It was the art of "teaching everything to everybody". In his *Didactica Magna* of 1657 Comenius expounded his views (Comenius, 1990).

In clarifying terminological differences between didactics and some Swedish, Finnish and German terms, I will rely on previous explications of didactics. But the conceptual analysis of the field is also approached by proposing a model developed in order to deal with pedagogical activities in the institutionalized school.

Even though the concept of didactics is one of the most central in continental educational research, there is no single specific definition one could refer to. This has led to a continuous need for clarification of the concept.

One way of starting the discussion is to take a look at how textbooks on didactics deal with the different schools of didactics. Memmert (1991, p.9), for example, lists four ways of defining didactics:

1. *Didaktik* is the science of teaching and learning;
2. *Didaktik* is the science of teaching (*Wissenschaft vom Unterricht*). When *Unterricht* is used in order to define *Didaktik*, the term *Unterricht* is often understood as an institutionalized teaching–learning process in a wider sense of the word;
3. *Didaktik* is curriculum theory (*Curriculum Forschung*) or human-science theory of education (*Geisteswissenschaftliche Didaktik*) i.e. a difference is usually made between didactics in a narrower sense, including curriculum theory only (*Didaktik im engeren Sinne*), and didactics in a broader or wider sense (*Didaktik im weiteren Sinne*), including both curriculum theory and instructional methods;
4. *Didaktik* is the science of behavioural changes (*Wissenschaft von der Verhaltensänderung*).

Schröder (1992, p.60) supports the second delimitation mentioned above. He writes that: "In its widest sense, didactics can be defined as the science of teaching [*Unterricht*]".[6] Schröder (1992, p.61) then mentions the following contemporary German approaches to didactics (see also Gudjons, Teske, & Winkel, 1980):

- Erudition-centred didactics within the framework of critical-constructive science of education (Klafki);
- Instructional-theoretical didactics (Schulz);
- Cybernetic information-theoretical didactics (v. Cube);
- Curricular didactics (Möller);
- Critical-communicative didactics (Winkel)[7].

Of the approaches mentioned above the first two will be discussed in Chapter 3 in relation to the model put forth in this study. When using the term didactics in an English text like the present one, we must try to relate it to existing English terminology. There is, however, no possibility in this context of going into a detailed discussion of how the concept of didactics should be translated into English. I will only point out some important features that may be helpful in comparing the Anglo-American and the continental traditions.

The Continental v. the Anglo-American Approach to Research on Teaching

We will now turn our attention to the relation between the continental use of the term and what it could be taken to mean in the Anglo-American research community.

First of all there is reason to notice the recent and growing interest in instituting a discussion between representatives of the Anglo-American, Nordic and the continental tradition concerning research on teaching, curriculum and didactics. The recent interest has been called the Didaktik-Renaissance and has manifested itself in both meetings and numerous publications (see e.g. Doyle & Westbury, 1992; Gudmundsdottir & Granqvist, 1992; Gundem 1980, 1992a; Hopmann, Klafki, Krapp, & Riquarts, 1995; Hopmann & Künzli, 1992; Hopmann & Riquarts, 1992, 1995; Kansanen, 1987, 1989, 1991, 1992, 1993b, 1993d, 1995a; Kansanen & Uljens, 1995c, 1996; Kroksmark, 1989; Marton, 1986a; Stormbom, 1986; Uljens, 1993b, 1994c, 1995a, 1995b, 1995d, 1995e, 1996, in press; Westbury, Hopmann, Künzli, & Riquarts, 1995).[8] Parallel to this interest, a new subfield of didactics seems to be emerging: comparative didactics (Hopmann, 1994).

The Nordic discussion on didactics has also been very lively during the last decade. In Finland the debate was revitalized in the late 60s and at the beginning of the 70s especially in relation to the school reform and the radical development of teacher education in the country (Koskenniemi, 1968; Koskenniemi & Hälinen, 1970; Lahdes, 1986). Faculties of education were established and many new professorships in general education and associate professorships in didactics were created (see Kansanen & Uljens, 1990, 1995a,b).

In Sweden a debate on didactics started at the beginning of the 1980s. Discussion was also connected with reforms in teacher education and developed largely in the form of an exchange of opinions between the phenomenographic group in Göteborg around Professor Ference Marton emphasizing the individual student's understanding of the subject matter (Kroksmark & Marton, 1988; Marton, 1986a) and the curriculum theory group in Stockholm around Professor Ulf P. Lundgren (Arfwedson, 1994a; Englund, 1984; Lundgren, 1986, 1987; Wallin, 1988a, 1988b). For the development in Norway see Engelsen (1990) and Gundem (1991, 1992a, 1992b).[1] See also Biørndal & Lieberg (1979). Nordenbo (1993) has presented an analysis of the development and current situation of didactics in Denmark. Curriculum history from the perspective of specific school subjects has simultaneously been an object of growing interest in the Nordic countries (see, for example, Andersson, 1979; Englund, 1986, 1990; Gundem, 1989).

Pertti Kansanen (1989, 1995a,b,c) has presented a useful and clarifying overview of the differences between the Anglo-American and the continental approaches to research on teaching (didactics). Among other things he has pointed out that English textbooks in educational psychology often contain two different but complementary parts: educational psychology as such and a normative part aiming to guide educational practice. This latter part of British and American educational psychology is very close to what is recognized as normative didactics. Kansanen (1995c) summarizes the position well in the following words and is therefore cited at length:

> In the American literature of research on teaching, the problems of teaching and learning are usually held together without any theoretical model building. Attention is paid to the methodological problems, and there the various background principles can be seen. In German educational literature, didactic problems define an independent subdiscipline of education which really is quite the same as general education, however, with its own point of view. The area of Didaktik is mainly larger than educational psychology and it includes much philosophical and theoretical thinking. In German literature Didaktik and educational psychology are clearly separate fields with different representatives. The situation in Great Britain and the US is quite the contrary; the same people are working in this common area.

It is also usual to understand didactics as covering both problems in relation to the process of teaching and to the selection of content (Klafki, 1991). If traditional educational psychology covers the normative or prescriptive dimension of didactics dealing with the process of teaching (i.e. how one should teach), then one might say that the term curriculum or curriculum theory refers to the process of selecting contents for schools on a collective level.

A great deal of empirical research has, however, been carried out concerning both the teaching process as such and teachers' selection of content within the Anglo-American tradition. This is normally identified as research on teaching.[9] But what is less developed is the *theory* of teaching as such; empirical research is not always analyzed in order to develop, or contribute to, some conceptual system in the field. When this is the case, i.e. when efforts to build up models of teaching are made (e.g. Shulman, 1987), then research on teaching comes closer to the German descriptive version of didactics.

However, in the continental tradition, empirical research alone is not often the basis for constructing theories of didactics. Instead, researchers refer to a cultural heritage of practical pedagogical experience. One should, however, be careful not to generalize too much in this context since many continental models represent different combinations of normative and analytic aspects. In addition it is possible to identify different levels of didactical theory; there are both the ordinary level of theory in which the aim is to conceptualize and explain something and also the meta-theoretical levels (Knecht-von Martial, 1986).

The relation between German Didaktik and curriculum theory is more complicated and cannot be discussed in detail within the framework of the present study (see Blankertz, 1987; Hameyer, Frey, & Haft, 1983; Hopmann, 1992; Kansanen, 1995a).

If we wanted to continue the discussion, i.e. to clarify how the different schools of didactics arose in Europe and how they developed especially during and after the 19th century on the basis of the thoughts of Pestalozzi (1746–1827), Fichte (1762–1814), Herbart[10] (1776–1841), Schleiermacher[11] (1768–1834), and Dilthey[12] (1833–1911), a second study would be required. Therefore, in order to avoid an inadequate history of the use of the term didactics and its content I will now instead take up some problems that I consider important from the point of view of the model I will present later. Having presented the model for school didactics, I will return to two different ways in which German didactics have been understood. Such a comparison makes it easier to understand the present model in relation to the current approaches to didactics.

DIDACTICS AS THEORY AND DOCTRINE

A first necessary clarification before we explain the model that will be presented concerns the nature of didactic propositions.

Two different ways of approaching the pedagogical process involve asking the following two questions: (a) how should a teacher act in order to be a good teacher? and (b) how should we act in order to understand or explain pedagogical activity? Every answer to the first question will be normative or prescriptive. The answer depends on what standards should be met for it to be accepted and why.

In answering the second question, i.e. what is required in order to understand or explain a pedagogical process, we do not have to find a normative solution, but we must have some idea of what the fundamental characteristics of teaching are. We must also say for whom and for what reasons we develop our theory. In doing so we are making value-based decisions. However, saying how teaching in schools is constituted and how it should be analysed is not to say *what* this teaching should aim at. Nor is it to say how this teaching should be carried out. Therefore answers to the second question can be regarded as descriptive or analytic. The distinction between the answers to these two questions may also be kept up by talking about didactics as doctrine and didactics as theory, respectively.

Didactics as doctrine is equal to normative didactics, covering pedagogical schools of thought stating how teaching *should* be carried out. These norms and prescriptions emanate from everyday experience, psychology, sociology, philosophy and subject knowledge or theory. The norms developed on the basis of some view of man, society and nature are primarily connected with values while prescriptions guiding practice usually emanate from learning theory. The difference between prescriptive and normative propositions is, however, not always easy to maintain.

From history we know that complete pedagogical programmes have been developed solely on the basis of normative arguments derived from philosophy (Steiner, Makarenko). Prescriptive perspectives on learning, motivation and development have also resulted in many instructional programmes (e.g. Aebli, 1983).

Didactics as a theory is equal to descriptive didactics, which agrees with the analytic function an educational theory may have. Through this function educational theory offers us an instrument by which we may actualize varying dimensions of pedagogical practice in order to understand that practice better. As far as I understand, descriptive didactics does not contain direct norms for action. It mainly poses relevant questions requiring answers in order that we may understand the TSL process. Descriptive theory helps us to handle normative and prescriptive principles created on the basis of subject knowledge, psychology or philosophy within an educational frame of reference.

DIDACTICS, INSTRUCTION AND EDUCATION

Having defined didactics as theory and doctrine, the next step in our analysis will be to relate these two aspects of didactics to instruction and education. This may be seen as one preparatory step towards solving the problem of in what sense a descriptive theory is value-related.

In analysing how didactics should be related to instruction and education, the following typology was developed (see Fig. 2.9).

	Didactics as doctrine	Didactics as theory
Instruction (Unterricht)	**1** Prescriptive principles guiding instruction. Answers based on psychology, content theory and philosophy.	**2** Theory of instruction based on empirical research on instruction, philosophical reflection.
Education (Erziehung)	**3** Normative standards concerning what values education should realize. Answers based on analysis of the view of man, society and nature.	**4** Philosophical reflection and analysis of educational philosophies (partly done within curriculum theory).

FIG. 2.9. Didactics as doctrine and theory in relation to instruction and education.

The main idea of distinguishing between instruction and education is that the concept of "educative teaching" advocated by Herbart is considered fruitful (Herbart, 1895/1993). In this way we can distinguish teaching from such concepts as indoctrination and training since the concept of education implies that the educated individual (learner) participates in decisions on what parts of a culture (values, practices, norms, etc.) they will try to reach. Educative teaching constitutes a significant part of the process of intentional enculturation. Through this process the individual is supported in her own intentional efforts to develop into a socially, intellectually, and personally mature member of society.

Didactics as doctrine covers fields 1 and 3. The first field (1) refers to what has previously been defined as the development of instructional principles based on psychology and content theory. In the third field we find educational doctrines based on some view of man, society and nature (3). Educational history is full of pedagogical schools of thought telling teachers how they should act (e.g. Makarenko, Montessori, Steiner, etc.).

The second field (2) refers to theory of instruction. A descriptive theory of instruction does not tell us how we should teach, although it considers the development of instructional principles as something to be dealt with. Finally (4) we have the philosophy of education aiming at reflection on and analysis of educational norms and goals. Curriculum theory also partly falls within this field.

Didactics as descriptive theory covers fields 2 and 4. It should also offer a conceptual framework for developing instructional principles.

Education and Individual Growth—Erziehung and Bildung

Education (*Erziehung*) is often understood as a collective concept including all those conscious activities which aim at affecting other individuals' competence, knowledge, personality and value-system.

But sometimes the term education is used in a restricted sense, i.e. to refer to the intentional influence on the development of somebody else's personality (Schröder, 1992, p.85)[13]:

> Education can be described as an influence on the individual development of the individual to a personality. This definition concerns the process as well as the goal of education. The process of education can be characterized as influence. The influence can originate from fellow human beings . . ., from oneself . . ., but also from cultural matters, values, etc.

Accepting that one can not meaningfully talk about instruction as separate from the process of education (*Erziehungsprozess*) means here that every instructional act is necessarily also value-laden and therefore an educating act. Thus, a theory proposing to offer conceptual tools for dealing with pedagogical practice must acknowledge both instruction and education as related to each other. If every instructional act is simultaneously an educating act, it is also true that education is most often, though not always, realized through instruction. This means that even though we may analytically define instruction as the enhancing of learning, whereas education would be directed towards the development of the learner's personality or an individual's identity, we must remember that when we develop a theory about pedagogical practice, both dimensions must be covered. In this study educative instruction is therefore identical with teaching.

In the typology above, didactics as theory is defined so as to cover both instruction and education, i.e. teaching. Understanding didactics as theory in this way also means that it is descriptive; it does not provide any solution regarding what the goals of education should be, nor does a descriptive theory indicate what contents should be included in education or what methods should be used. In this sense didactics is limited to being an analytical instrument helping us to structure and understand pedagogical practice. It is thought that a scientific theory should not answer questions requiring normative answers like the ones above. This does not mean that one could not investigate what values are realized in some specific educational setting or programme or why certain teaching methods or contents are chosen.

Even though it was said above that teaching is seen as educative instruction, didactics is not equated with any theory of teaching only. As shown before, didactics is seen as the science of the TSL process. In other words the learner's intentional activity is stressed.

Finally, when theory of education (i.e. *Theorie der Erziehung*) primarily refers to the process of influencing the subject, the concept of *Bildung* or theory of *Bildung* is understood as referring to the individual's growth as such. Therefore a comprehensive theory of pedagogics covers both the process of education (*Erziehungsprozess*) and the process of individual growth (*Bildungsprozess*) (see e.g. Benner, 1991). We could conclude by saying that while general education discusses the nature, possibilities and limits of the pedagogical process in general terms, the theory of didactics, being a subfield of general education, approaches the pedagogical process in terms of teaching, studying and learning.

Different Types of Value-relatedness

It is not argued that a theory of didactics developed within fields 2 and 4 is value-neutral in every sense of the word. Every scientific theory within the humanities and within social and cultural sciences is value-laden, and that is also the case with every didactic theory at some level. Therefore it is necessary to identify the difference between two ways in which a theory of didactics can be related to values. First, in accordance with so-called normative approaches to didactics, normativity usually refers to propositions concerning *what* teachers should teach as well as *how* this should be done.

Normativity in the second sense refers to the values behind scientific theory in general. This means that didactics as a theory may avoid being normative in respect of pedagogical practice but never to be value-neutral in the second sense. One such question of values behind didactic theory concerns what the theory in question should be used for. In other words, while the first level of value-relatedness is connected with the goals and means of education, the second level is not connected with goals or methods but with what the theory should be used for and whom it is intended for. This second level of value-relatedness thus concerns the knowledge interest represented by the theory itself. Descriptive theories of didactics are value-neutral with respect to the first case of value-relatedness, but not with respect to the second type.

DIDACTICS AND LEARNING THEORY

The descriptive and the normative or prescriptive approaches to educational conceptual systems are related to learning in two different ways. The descriptive approach makes it possible for us to include the problem of human learning as one of many questions to be acknowledged by educational theory. Descriptive theories thus treat learning theory as a question subordinated to educational theory. In addition, descriptive theory does not aim at laying down pedagogical principles for practice based on learning.

When psychological theory is used as the point of departure in the construction of educational principles, we may, at best, reach predictive, hypothetical theories, i.e. prescriptive propositions. These propositions would suggest certain practical pedagogical procedures, that is, instructional or pedagogical principles aimed at guiding practice in terms of stating how an individual should act in order to teach successfully.[14] However, if we were to accept that not only prescriptive principles, but also didactical theory could be developed from psychology, it would mean an absurdly limited view of instructional knowledge. This is not to say that such principles should not be developed. It is only made clear that descriptive didactic theory should not be equated with prescriptive principles guiding teaching.

It may be relevant to note that when instructional principles are developed in relation to a specific psychological school of thought, this developmental work cannot consist of a logical deduction of instructional principles from psychological theory (Hollo, 1927; James, 1958). The role of psychological theory in this developmental work is instead that it defines the *type* of knowledge that a student may be aiming at in a pedagogical situation as well as how this knowledge should be reached.[15] Further, even though psychological theory may have quite clear general pedagogical implications, these implications must always be developed in relation to a presumptive pedagogical context.

If we were to accept the idea that educational theory may be developed with learning theory as a point of departure, it would mean reducing educational theory to an application of psychological knowledge, which is a very narrow, though quite widespread, conception of the role of didactics (cf. Rein 1912, p.102).

It may also be noted that even though William James (1958) was right in his conclusion that it is not possible to develop teaching methods solely on the basis of psychology, his opinion was that teaching was an art and that it is not possible to use scientific knowledge as the basis for something that is an art. The position represented by this study is that James' argument was right, but his motive was not. The reason why psychology cannot be used as the foundation for developing teaching methods is not that teaching is an art, but that psychology offers far too narrow an approach in trying to understand what teaching is about. However, it is clear that no didactic theory can ever offer solutions for every situation in the teaching process; reality is too complex for this.

In other words—questions of human learning are naturally central in didactics, but the question concerning human learning should be actualized *within* a pedagogical conceptual structure. It must also be evident that educational research must be interested in what *determines* our possibilities of reaching competence. In other words, the question must be how the teacher *gets* the learner to learn rather than how the learner learns, as Koskenniemi (1978, p.71) has emphasized.

Research on teaching should thus develop a *theory* of didactics, not be limited to developing instructional principles which guide practice. These two different ways of approaching pedagogical-educational reality can be visualized by Fig. 2.10.

The point of departure of this model is pedagogical practice.

The first relation (1) in the figure refers to what has been called the descriptive or analytic theory of didactics as already explained.

The second relation (2) between psychological theory and pedagogical practice is an example of prescriptive or normative didactics. Research into this relation usually leads to principles which guide practice, i.e. principles of how teachers should act in order to be good teachers. Even though such principles may be used as analytic instruments as well, i.e. in order to investigate to what extent teachers follow these principles, they are, as such, all too narrow to function as theories of teaching. Sometimes instructional psychology is used as a term denoting the field of research which identifies relations between learning theory and instructional theory (Glaser, 1987).

The third relation (3) in Fig. 2.10 concerns the relation between educational and psychological theory. The view adopted in the present study is that pedagogical principles developed on the basis of psychological theory must be handled by educational theory. This means that educational theory may incorporate the kind of pedagogical developmental work that

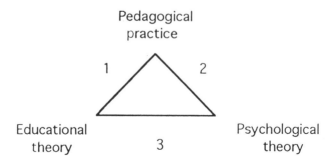

FIG. 2.10. Two different perspectives on pedagogical practice: educational theory and psychological theory.

aims at the development of principles for instruction. Educational research is thus not limited to constructing conceptual systems aimed at analysing pedagogical reality. In order to carry out such developmental work, the theory of didactics must contain conceptual instruments for showing what role such developmental work may have for educational theory and what role these principles may have with respect to pedagogical practice. According to this view educational research includes research-based developmental work which aims at creating principles for teaching. The third relation in Fig. 2.10 should be understood to indicate that psychological questions constitute a part of educational research. How psychological questions are to be dealt with must, however, be decided within the framework of educational theory (Harva, 1965, p.21).

A fundamental question is thus what a didactic theory should be like, in order to create possibilities for both (a) analysis of and reflection on the constituents of pedagogical reality and (b) the creation of pedagogical principles aimed at guiding practice based on e.g. psychology. The kernel of this problem is that of normativity; since a principle guiding practice is always normative or prescriptive in nature, we must ask how such a principle can be related to analytic or descriptive theory. Is it thus possible for an educational theory to be analytic and normative at the same time? Or is educational theory always normative? If educational theory is normative, then the question is whether it can be accepted as a scientific theory. Should we, in other words, accept a position like Brezinka's (1978), according to which the normative ideological part of education belongs to philosophy and the pedagogical practice is always non-theoretical practice, i.e. that only the *description* of the pedagogical reality is science? It must be evident from the previous discussion that such an understanding is not accepted in this study. To say that practice is non-theoretical by definition is a mistake; practical action may be founded on some more or less developed understanding of the pedagogical process. This means that pedagogical practice can be non-scientific, but can also be scientific in the sense that it is reflected upon in a certain way. If pedagogical practice includes both reflection and action, then at least the reflective part of practice may be scientific reflection. But what about didactics as theory—can a scientific theory of didactics be normative? The position adopted in this study is explicated in Chapter 3.

CONCLUSION

An educational theory should acknowledge many more questions than the problem of learning in order to be valid for the pedagogical reality in schools. Therefore a descriptive approach to educational theory seems to be more powerful than prescriptive programmes. A descriptive theory of education is not reductionist in character as are some normative approaches.

However, even though we accept a descriptive approach as a useful point of departure because of its readiness to accept the complexity of the pedagogical reality, it is not necessary to try to avoid normative and prescriptive propositions. Such propositions can in fact be developed on the basis of questions acknowledged by descriptive theory.

Also, from the practitioner's perspective, the normative and descriptive aspects of educational theory are relevant. The teacher reflects in a normative fashion in the pedagogical situation as well as in planning and evaluating a pedagogical sequence and how a specific TSL process should be organized. But in order to understand what they are doing, teachers need to get a perspective on this activity. A descriptive theory of education offers such a perspective. Descriptive theory may be used as an instrument focusing on problems which require normative reflection and decisions. This is the main function of a descriptive theory of didactics in relation to teaching practice. The teacher is thus both an acting and a reflecting subject. In fact, pedagogical practice is characterized by these very aspects—a continuous shifting between reflection and decision-making, planning and action, evaluation and action.

Having identified the two principal approaches of didactics, the normative and the descriptive approach, the time has come to put forth the elements of a descriptive, analytical theory of pedagogical practice. The conceptual model discussed in Chapter 3, the descriptive school didactic theory, is designed primarily to be valid for teaching and education in institutionalized schools. Therefore it is called a model of school didactics. Having presented the model I will return to the question of why it is called a model of school didactics, i.e. how that field of research is delimited. I will also clarify how the model is related to normative problems.

The idea of presenting this model is twofold. First, the model as such has been developed within the framework of the present project and may thus be considered as a result in itself. Indeed it is a central result of this study. Second, the conceptual structure of the model follows the principles outlined above. This means that the model gives us the means of handling the construction of pedagogical principles based on learning theory within a pedagogical framework. The model is thus used as the framework for the second part of the study, which is an analysis of the pedagogical implications of the cognitivist approach to learning.

NOTES

1. "Teaching" is here understood as a synonym of the German word *Unterricht*, the Swedish word *undervisning*, and the Finnish word *opetus*.
2. Fenstermacher and Soltis (1986, p.38) conclude: "It makes no more sense to require learning in order to be teaching than it does to require winning in order to be racing, or finding in order to be looking."
3. The reason why Yrjönsuuri (1994) has reached another conclusion in his definition of teaching may be that he problematizes teaching generally speaking while I limit my attention to the TSL process in institutionalized education. In other respects we seem to represent quite similar positions in the way we understand the pedagogical process. I especially appreciate the fact that Yrjönsuuri and Yrjönsuuri (1994) also emphasize the learner's intentional study process as a key-concept.
4. Hopmann (1992) has suggested that the word "didactics" should be written with a "k" also in English instead of with a "c" following the German spelling, i.e. "Didaktik" instead of "didactics" in order to indicate the continental tradition from which it stems. This spelling is however not used in this study. Instead it is hoped that a renewed usage of the English word will gradually change the general sense and understanding of it.
5. Overviews of the contemporary traditions of didactics have been presented, for example, by Kansanen (1989, 1992, 1995a), Arfwedson (1995a,b) and Gundem (1980, 1991, 1992a,b). In German numerous overviews are available, e.g. Menck (1975), Blankertz (1987), Adl-Amini and Künzli (1991), Knecht-vonMartial (1985) and Jank and Meyer (1991). An investigation of the theory of science of didactics has been carried out by Knecht-vonMartial (1986), see also Hopmann and Riquarts (1995).
6. "In ihrer weitesten Fassung kann Didaktik definiert werden als Wissenschaft vom Unterricht" (Schröder, 1992, p.60).
7. • die bildungstheoretische Didaktik im Rahmen kritisch-konstruktive Erziehungswissenschaft (Klafki);
   • die lehrtheoretische Didaktik (Schulz);
   • die kybernetisch-informationstheoretische Didaktik (v. Cube);
   • die curriculare Didaktik (Möller);
   • die kritisch-kommunikative Didaktik (Winkel).
8. In October 1991 an international symposium addressing the theme was arranged in Aarau, Switzerland. In 1992 a symposium on this theme was arranged at the AERA conference in San Francisco (Hopmann, 1992). On October 5–8, 1993, the international symposium *Didaktik and/or Curriculum* was arranged at the IPN at the Christian Albrecht Universität Kiel by Dr. Stefan Hopmann and Dr. Kurt Riquarts, bringing together researchers from North America, the Nordic countries, Britain, Germany and Switzerland. This symposium was followed up with a conference in Oslo in August 1995.
9. Isberg (1994) has neatly summarized (in Swedish) a large body of recent relevant empirical research findings which fall within research on teaching. Chapters 2, 3 and 4 of Isberg's report are explicitly devoted to research findings on the planning, carrying out and evaluation of teaching. A great many of these research findings could well be included in the present study but are deliberately left out in order to avoid a too extensive report. For a comparable overview see Arfwedson (1994b). I also refer to Wittrock's (1986) *Handbook on Research on Teaching* for an overview of empirical findings.
10. Umriss pädagogischer Vorlesungen (1835), see Herbart (1993).
11. Vorlesungen über Pädagogik (1826), see Schleiermacher (1957).
12. Über die Möglichkeit einer allgemeinen pädagogischen Wissenschaft (1888), see Dilthey (1958).

58 SCHOOL DIDACTICS AND LEARNING

13. "Erziehung kann beschrieben werden als eine Einwirkung auf die Individuelle Entfaltung der Person zur Persönlichkeit. In dieser Definition wird sowohl der Prozess als auch das Ziel der Erziehung angesprochen. Der Prozess der Erziehung wird gekennzeichnet als Einwirkung. Diese kann von Mitmenschen..., von sich selbst..., aber auch von Kulturgütern, Werten u.ä. ausgehen." (Schröder, 1992, p.85)
14. In this view psychology has been considered a science and teaching an art (see e.g. Skinner, 1954).
15. I am grateful for discussions with Ference Marton on this topic in October 1993.

3 A Model of School Didactics

FORMS, LEVELS AND CONTEXTS OF PEDAGOGICAL ACTIVITY

A very general model of human intentional activity, of which teaching and studying are examples, is constituted by the concepts of intention, action and reflection. In teaching this is taken to mean (a) that teaching activities are considered as intentional, (b) that these activities or the results of them must be reflected upon in order to determine their pedagogical meaningfulness and (c) that the result of such evaluative reflection normally affects the subsequent intentions. On a general level many researchers on teaching and learning accept this point of departure (e.g. Bennett, Carré & Dunne, 1993; Bereiter & Scardamalia, 1989; Gudmundsdottir & Shulman, 1987; Kansanen & Uusikylä, 1983; Kaufmann, 1966; Klafki, 1994a; Kolb, 1984; Koskenniemi, 1968; Norman, 1980; Shulman, 1987; Winne & Marx, 1977). This general position must therefore be specified in order to communicate the features of the model to be advanced.

Pedagogical Intentionality

The view presented suggests that in order for something to be pedagogical it must be intentional in terms of being goal-directed (Stenbäck, 1855). However, when mentioning the concept of intentionality, we must make a distinction between its phenomenological use denoting the fundamental feature of the human mind as always being directed towards something. Pedagogical intentions are always oriented towards something considered meaningful in the pedagogical process (e.g. the student, context, content, resources, curriculum, etc.). When we discuss teachers' intentions in relation to a future or ongoing pedagogical process, it may be valuable to try and determine the teacher's type of purposiveness and degree of awareness.

Type of purposiveness refers to what the teacher is directed to in the pedagogical process. The type of purposiveness may partly be understood in terms of the choices a teacher has to make before, during and after a pedagogical situation. In making these decisions the teacher may be directed towards the goals, the content, form of representation, instructional method, the students efforts to reach competence of some kind, working methods used, resources available, organization, curriculum, different contexts and many other things. However, the expression "type of purposiveness" is also related to notions like the teacher's personal view of education and knowledge, rights and obligations towards the individual and collective i.e. ethical reasoning, view of mankind etc.

Given that teaching is a purposive activity in the above described sense, being directed to a variety of factors of importance in the pedagogical situation we may ask about the extent to which the teacher is aware of the content of his own awareness. This may be called degree of awareness. Degree of awareness means that individuals are not always equally aware of their own understanding as well as of their motives or reasons for doing something. In other words this awareness varies. These two aspects, i.e. the type of purposiveness and degree of awareness of pedagogically relevant questions, are fundamental features of the teachers' pedagogical intentionality.

However, as teaching is purposive in nature it also represents a kind of teleological activity. As teaching thus includes some idea of a future state, the goals have a special role in pedagogical intentionality in relation to other issues. This immediately calls to mind von Wright's (1971) model of explaining intentional acts by referring to an individual's intentions. An intention is the internal aspect of an act and constitutes its cause. This refers more or less equal to the conative dimension of activity. Consequently, in order to understand instruction, we must have knowledge of these intentions, i.e. knowledge about what the teacher intends to reach through their acts and why these acts are considered necessary (not only sufficient) in order to reach what was intended (von Wright, 1985, pp.51 ff.). An Aristotelian, teleological model of explaining instructional activity is thus accepted as a fundamental point of departure. Intentionality as goal-directedness may thus be considered as a special case of the phenomenological use referring to intentionality as directedness in general.

In this study I will not, however, discuss the different aspects constituting the concept of teachers' pedagogical intentionality in greater detail or how this type of intentionality is related to the general structure of human consciousness. I only emphasize that if one wants to structure teachers' pedagogical reflection, it is obviously necessary to relate the concept of intentionality to how the structure of consciousness is understood (Uljens, 1995c).

The most fundamental reason why teaching requires evaluative reflection is that this activity as such does not guarantee learning. Therefore pedagogical planning and teaching are rather meaningless without evaluation. This being the case, every model, theory or paradigm of teaching must include these three fundamental phases of the pedagogical process. However, a model aimed at structuring the pedagogical process as a whole must simultaneously acknowledge the learners' intentions. Only by acknowledging two intentional subjects in the above mentioned sense may we understand the interactive nature of the pedagogical process.

Levels of Pedagogical Activity

The second fundamental assumption accepted as a point of departure is that the pedagogical activities indicated above may be planned, carried out and evaluated on different levels (Klafki, 1994b, pp.35–36). We can distinguish a collective level, an individual teacher level, an interactional level, and a student level.

The collective level may in turn be divided into a societal–national level, a community level, and a school level (Dahllöf, 1967). There are also other ways of characterizing what is here identified as the collective level. For example, Gundem (1993, p.130) has divided the collective dimension of the curriculum level into five levels: a national, regional, community, institutional, and classroom level. Leino (1985) again pays attention not only to levels but to different constituents of the curriculum in discussing its levels. He distinguishes between an ideal or intended curriculum, the official and written document, the curriculum as realized by teaching materials and, finally, the curriculum as experienced by the students. We thus see that all divisions of the collective level are relative; *how* the collective level is structured must be understood in relation to the actual culture. The only distinctions valid for every culture are: (a) the division between the individual teacher's intentional planning and the regulating collective frames or contextual factors, and (b) the division between the individual teacher's intentions and the interactional process carried out by teacher and students together.

The individual teacher level of the pedagogical planning refers to the individual teacher's planning. Also the fact that teachers' planning itself can be temporally differentiated in various ways supports the idea of a fundamental division between planning on a collective and on an individual teacher level. Teachers plan their teaching in various temporal perspectives, from planning specific operations during a lesson to planning a school year. For example, Clark and Yinger (1979) differentiate between eight different types of temporal planning. In the present model the main distinction concerning teachers' planning is laid on planning before an educational situation and planning during the pedagogical process. This is not contradictory to Clark and Yinger's (1979) findings, quite the contrary, but it is again argued that as we are probably able to discern teachers' temporal planning in an even more detailed fashion than Clark and Yinger (1979), this road has no end. It is considered more important to focus attention on the distinction already made between planning before an educational process and during such a process. In making this distinction we also enhance the possibility of handling the distinction between what is called individual teacher planning, and interactional planning done by teachers and students together. Secondly, as this reality is complex, it is wise to pay attention only to the main distinctions in a model comprising so many different aspects.

The interactional level of planning is constituted by the pedagogical meeting of at least two individuals, a teacher and a student (learner). This level is different from the other two levels in that the pedagogical activity is realized here. It is the kernel of pedagogical reality.

The individual student level. When discussing how the curriculum is realized in the Finnish comprehensive school, Uusikylä and Kansanen (1988) distinguish between three levels of the curriculum; the curriculum made up in advance, the activities carried out to realize the curriculum and finally the curriculum as experienced by students. This division is supported here. The only difference is that concerning Uusikylä and Kansanen's first point, planning in advance, the difference between collective planning in advance and an individual teacher's planning in advance is explicitly emphasized here. The similarity between the present division and Uusikylä and Kansanen's (1988) division is the emphasis on the curriculum as experienced. In the present model it is considered relevant to point out this individual level as the learner ultimately controls what is intended to be learned. According to this structure, the individual teacher's intentionality is in a mediating position between the collective curriculum and the students' intentions.

However, even though the individual learner often is seen as responsible for how the curriculum is realized, i.e. for what is learned, the learner has usually very limited freedom to plan and evaluate their own study activities and success. Given this, the position taken in this study is that the learner is not made solely responsible for the learning results. The teacher and the instructional system must share this responsibility as they also have the right to decide upon the aims, content and evaluation of the TSL process.

We have thus identified different forms of pedagogical activity and different levels on which these activities may take place. These two fundamental aspects of pedagogical reality, forms and levels of activity, are illustrated in Fig. 3.1.

The number of X's in the figure indicates where the emphasis is laid on each of the four levels. On the collective level the focus is on planning and evaluation. This level is only indirectly related to the TSL process. Even though the ultimate responsibility of the planning for e.g. the Nordic comprehensive school system may be seen as a formal responsibility, it is still on the collective level that the degrees of freedom are spelled out.

The responsibility for the realization of the pedagogical process, on the other hand, is to be found on the individual teacher level (on the level of pedagogical activity). Although the teacher is concerned with planning and evaluation as well, i.e. with a kind of curricular work, these activities usually, though not necessarily, take place within the boundaries specified on the collective level. Figure 3.1 shows that the teacher's freedom to plan is subordinated to the collective level but superordinated with respect to the individual student's interests. The same relation holds true for evaluation; the degrees of freedom for how teachers should evaluate the process and results are explicated on the collective level while the individual student is in a weak position with respect to the teacher.

On the other hand, with regard to the realization and carrying out of

	Forms of activity		
Levels of activity	Planning	Teaching-Studying-Learning in the Classrooms	Evaluation
Collective level	xxxx	x	xxxx
Individual teacher level	xxx	xx	xxx
Interactional level	xx	xxx	xx
Student level	x	xxxx	x

FIG. 3.1. The forms and levels of pedagogical activity. Number of X's indicates the emphasis on each different level.

the pedagogical process, the collective level is weak for understandable reasons. The teacher has an unquestionable role to play in this respect. The reason why the interactional level and the student level are emphasized is naturally that this interaction *is* the pedagogical process but also that the individual student is the one ultimately doing the learning through intentional study activity.

One could thus say that teaching in the institutionalized school system must be understood both in relation to the task every single teacher has been given by the community, and in relation to the individual student's needs and interests. This mediating role of the teacher is a specific landmark when discussing the teacher's work as a profession.[1]

It is thought that the levels of pedagogical activity presented are consistent with Egglestone's (1977) view of how the curriculum is related to the teacher's work. Egglestone distinguishes between a received perspective on the curriculum, a reflexive perspective and a restructuring perspective. The received perspective is handled by maintaining the distinction between the teacher's and the community's planning in advance. The very same distinction enables us to discuss the reflexive perspective considering that different teachers interpret the same document differently and have different ideas of how it may be realized. Finally, the restructuring perspective is acknowledged by including the interactive and student level in the model above. In other words, the present model offers a framework for understanding and analysing different perspectives on how a collective curriculum is related to the pedagogical work in schools.

The third point of departure in the model to be developed is that the TSL process in a school is to be understood in relation to the cultural and historical context in which it exists and which it partly constitutes. This will be discussed in more detail in the next section.

A SCHOOL DIDACTIC MODEL

Having actualized the three different assumptions indicated earlier (forms of activity, levels of activity and contexts of pedagogical activity), we are ready to introduce a model that is thought to reflect the main ideas of the school didactic model I want to put forth.[2] The following presentation refers to the visual model in Fig. 3.2.

The reasons for identifying the model as a school didactic model have been touched upon previously but will be explained in detail later in this chapter.

The figure consists of four main components. They refer, respectively, to the planning, realization and evaluation of the pedagogical process, as well as to the contexts providing the framework for the pedagogical

3. A MODEL OF SCHOOL DIDACTICS   65

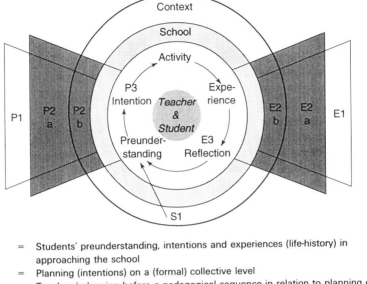

S1	=	Students' preunderstanding, intentions and experiences (life-history) in approaching the school
P1	=	Planning (intentions) on a (formal) collective level
P2(a)	=	Teachers' planning before a pedagogical sequence in relation to planning on a collective level
P2(b)	=	Teachers' planning before a pedagogical sequence in relation to the individual, local culture and the school as context
P3	=	Teachers' and students' continuous situated intentional planning
E3	=	Teachers' and students' continuous situated evaluative reflection of their teaching and learning experiences
E2(b)	=	Teachers' evaluation of process and results after a pedagogical sequence in relation to the individual, local culture and the school as context
E2(a)	=	Teachers' evaluation after a pedagogical sequence in relation to curriculas and evaluation on a collective level
E1	=	Evaluation on a formal, collective level
School	=	The classroom and local school as context
Context	=	Non-formal cultural context of education

• The dark field in the centre of the figure refers to the intended and experienced content in the TSL process.
• The inner circle describes the dynamic developmental process of teachers' and students' individual and shared intentions, activities, experiences, reflection and their situated teaching, studying and learning experiences

FIG. 3.2.   The levels and forms of pedagogical activity in terms of a reflective model of school didactics.

activity. The model thus identifies the constitutive elements of the teachers' pedagogical work (planning, teaching and evaluation). Concerning the context, a major distinction is the one between the school as context and the local society as context for the pedagogical work.

Before a more detailed discussion of the model the following points should be noted:

1. Intentionality is a key concept in the model. The model acknowledges both the learner and teacher as intentionally acting and reflecting subjects. Only by accepting two authentically acting, intentional subjects makes it possible to discuss pedagogical *inter*-action as shared activity on a specific content aiming at reaching a goal commonly agreed upon.
2. The model acknowledges both the planning, the TSL process (defined in Chapter 2) and the evaluative phase on different levels. This is the thesis of perspectual complementarity of the model, i.e. that all these forms and levels of activities are accepted but that they are approached from the perspective of the unique pedagogical meeting in e.g. a classroom.
3. When discussing several subjects' intentional interaction we can not avoid the ethical dimension of this interaction. This holds especially true for education. The simple reason is that the ethical problems in educational matters concern the acting participants' intentions and the normative system regulating this activity. The following questions indicate the relevance of the ethical question. Towards what should we educate people? Who has the right to decide upon questions concerning goals, content and methods of teaching? On what conditions do different interest groups participate in the construction of goals, contents and methods of education? The model makes a distinction between normative questions concerning the goals for education, prescriptive questions concerning methods used and the value-related knowledge interest concerning in whose interest the theory is developed. Concerning the normative question of towards what we should educate the present model is descriptive in nature, although it is value-related in other respects.
4. The idea advocated here is that the role of didactics as a subfield of general education is to point out what levels are needed, as well as to keep together these levels in a coherent system in order to give a picture of the pedagogical reality.

The idea is that different levels and perspectives (e.g. philosophical, curricular, sociological, psychological, subject-matter based, methodical, contextual etc.) should not be reduced to, or explained on, another level. Nor should they be regarded as equally valid for approaching every possible question raised. Different perspectives may be more or less appropriate for dealing with different sub-problems. Accordingly, didactics should not be reduced to an application of philosophy, psychology, sociology or content theory. The role of didactics is to help us to decide to what extent different disciplines are relevant to understanding the pedagogical process. This is called the thesis of school didactic autonomy.

5. This model emphasizes that the above-mentioned forms of pedagogical activity are to be understood in relation to the socio-cultural, economical and historical context within which they are embedded. This is the contextual thesis of school didactics.
6. In addition it must be acknowledged that institutionalized education following a collective curriculum is a special form of educational activity requiring a model of its own. This is why the model is called a school didactic model and not a model of e.g. general didactics. Thus, it should be observed that school didactics is recognized as a field of research covering the TSL process in institutionalized education and that the model presented is one model trying to explicate this field of research.
7. The conceptual model visualized in the figure includes both a temporal and a structural dimension. Its temporal dimension is constituted by the relation between the different types of activities the teacher is expected to carry out. The structural dimension is constituted of identifying components or aspects of importance for understanding the pedagogical reality as well as of the logical relations between these.
8. The complementarity thesis concerning the theory of didactics described above is related to the thesis of interdependence concerning decisions in the practical pedagogical situation, i.e. content, method, media and goals.
9. The school didactic model may be used both as a research model and a model for reflection on the pedagogical process and its frameworks.

PLANNING—A NETWORK OF PEDAGOGICAL INTENTIONS

The left wing of the model consists of two parts, P1 and P2. P1 is planning on the collective level and P2 planning on the teacher's level. As noted above, the collective level, P1, may be divided into different levels. The planning activity on these levels may be discussed in terms of different curriculums, which presupposes that several curriculums exist simultaneously, but each with a different function and status. As Gundem

(1993) points out, there is reason to remember the difference between the ideas behind an official curriculum and the actual document produced. The original ideas and thoughts represented by those who participated in the making of the curriculum do not disappear when the document is written. And they do not always correlate with the final content. In addition, the document is often experienced and interpreted very differently by different interest groups—politicians, teachers, parents, and school administrators.[3] This is one reason why the model of school didactics above accepts a differentiation between teachers' personal understanding of the curriculum and teachers' belief in what the official, collective interpretation of it is (Engelsen, 1995).[4] The teachers' planning is thus divided into two related fields—planning in relation to different types of collective curriculums (P2a) and planning in relation to the local school and culture as contexts (P2b).

We thus see that planning on the collective level (P1) reaches the classroom reality only indirectly through the teachers' own planning. In this sense the teachers control how and to what extent the curriculum is realized at the classroom level. Although it is clear that a teacher in a school financed by the state or community is expected to follow the curriculum, this is not necessarily always the case; a teacher may very well deviate from the collective (e.g. national) curriculum or follow it only partly. Because of this the left wing indicating teachers' planning (P2) transcends planning on the collective level (P1) in the figure.

The teacher's planning of activities *before* a pedagogical sequence P2 (a school year, monthly or weekly planning or planning before one lesson) and *during* a pedagogical process (P3), contain several central questions (Clandinin, 1986). These questions may be exhibited in four fields on which a teacher makes decisions. These concern the choice of the goals for education, the choice of relevant content, the choice of a relevant form of representation and finally the choice of an instructional method to be followed as well as the choice of relevant working methods for the students. These four fields are briefly characterized below.

At the very outset it should be emphasized that these aspects are considered as closely interrelated. Because of this it might be more accurate to talk about the teacher's network of pedagogical intentions than about goal-oriented planning.

Choice of Goals

Concerning the *goals* of teaching, each teacher must relate the general goals of the curriculum to their own goal-setting and personal educational philosophy. But when teachers make decisions concerning the goals they are forced to pay attention not only to (a) the collective curriculum but also to (b) the subject matter, (c) the students and (d) the resources available.

The teacher's beliefs concerning knowledge and ideas about acquiring knowledge of different subjects affect the choice of goals. The teacher thus asks about the nature of e.g. mathematical knowledge and historical understanding, i.e. about what kind of goals it is meaningful to set up on the basis of the nature of some specific subject matter. The relation between subject matter and goals is therefore reciprocal (e.g. Heimann, 1962, p.418).

Second, when goals are set up, attention is also paid to the individual's needs and interests. In fact, these interests may be understood as a curriculum as such; the students' intentions affect what collective goals it is reasonable to set up (Peterson, Marx & Clark, 1978). But naturally other psychological aspects connected with the learner also influence the goal-setting.

A further question to be considered is the relation between the teacher's way of working in the classroom and the goals. Normally both the collective goals and the teacher's personal goals determine how the content is dealt with. Ethical norms, for example, regulate the social interaction. Again the situation is reciprocal; the possibilities available also affect what goals and norms are considered meaningful by the teacher.

To sum up: ideally the goals regulate what items the teacher should deal with and how this should be done. The teacher's understanding of the real situation again affects what ideal collective goals are accepted and realized. The concrete school reality thus partly determines the teacher's interpretation of how the collective norms and goals should be realized. Even though a reciprocal relationship exists between the goals and other factors of educational reality, it is nevertheless true that we may find a general goal-orientation of teaching more fundamental than many other aspects. In this respect it is relevant to discriminate between several types of goal-setting. The model emphasizes especially the teacher's interpretation of the collective goals and therefore the teacher's general goal orientation.

That a reciprocal relationship between different aspects and levels of planning is supported naturally means that a linear model of planning is not supported. Instead of talking about teachers' goal-orientation, it is reasonable to discuss the interrelated aspects described above in terms of the teacher's network of pedagogical intentions.

In addition—and this is important—only because intentionality is accepted as a fundamental category in this model, the social, cultural and historical dimensions of the TSL process in schools are by no means overlooked. On the contrary, one of the fundamental ideas in the present school didactic approach is the conviction that the school forms a very special context for teaching and studying. Teaching and studying in schools should thus not be viewed in a decontextualized perspective (Simola, 1995, pp.123–128).

Choice of Content

Another matter dependent on the teachers' planning is the choice of relevant content. In making this choice the teacher reflects on several sub-questions.

We may begin with the goals of education on the curricular level. Teachers cannot choose to deal with just any content in the schools; their freedom is clearly limited by external factors such as the curriculum.

In addition the choice of relevant subject matter must be made in relation to the students to be taught. This may be done in at least two different ways. Firstly, the students' cultural background and heritage must be recognized. Secondly, the psychology of the students must be taken into account.

When these two questions are considered, we may ask what it means for an individual to have these insights. What kind of knowledge do we have when, for example, we are able to perform gymnastic movements? What is the difference between reasoning within mathematics and ethical reasoning? And finally, how do we learn these different things? In answering such questions both the teacher and the researcher reflect in terms of epistemology and learning theory.

Concerning the cultural aspect, we may refer, for example, to Wolfgang Klafki (1963), who emphasizes the necessity of paying attention to the students' reality. We may also refer to the phenomenological concept of lifeworld, discussed in a pedagogical context by, for example, Meyer-Drawe (1984) and Lippitz (1984). Both stress the necessity of analysing and understanding the overall circumstances under which a child or a student lives outside the educational institution in order to be able to choose meaningful contents and in order to arrange meaningful occasions for learning.

The second dimension is the psychological, which in turn may be divided into three sub-problems. The first is a psychological learning problem (how students learn). The second problem belongs to the psychology of development. Finally, there is the problem of the psychology of personality. This last problem constitutes of the student's personal and cultural identity and in educational terms of the teacher's educating activities.

Third, the choice of content is to be made in relation to the field of knowledge to be represented, i.e. how it comes about that a chosen subject matter represents the field generally (Menck, 1993; Menck & Wierichs, 1991). This aspect is closely related to the teacher's knowledge of the subject matter. But it has also an epistemological dimension; there is reason to distinguish between the structure of different school subjects in principle as well. Traditionally we distinguish between aesthetic subjects (music, arts), ethical subjects (religion), practical subjects (handicraft, gymnastics) and theoretical subjects (e.g. biology, mathematics and history). The mother tongue and the study of languages might be identified as communicative subjects. Other divisions are also possible. Furthermore it is clear that all subjects contain ethical and aesthetic dimensions. Willman's (1903) idea of the educative dimension as a criterion for choosing contents is also accepted as fundamental. One must thus focus on the content from the individual's perspective and from that of the collective field of knowledge it represents.

Choice of Instructional Methods and Working Methods

The third matter requiring explicit decision-making from the teacher concerns instructional methods. When discussing methods of instruction within didactics it should be borne in mind that there is no generally accepted definition of method today (Terhart, 1989).

In trying to delimit what is covered by research on instructional method (German *Methodik*) we have many possibilities. However, the concept of method cannot be defined without reference to one individual's activity to support another individual's efforts to reach competence through the process of learning.

Perhaps it would suffice here to say that as the aim of didactics is to understand and structure the overall educational situation with intentionality as one of the fundamental notions, the object of instructional method (*Methodik*) is reflection on what activities are required in order to support an individual's learning. To support learning does not necessarily mean to think of methods as techniques. If we understand Dewey's ideas as proposals for new teaching methods, we see that methods can cover decisions concerning the goals as well as the contents of education.

It is, however, interesting to notice a continuous concern with the problem of what a method is (see e.g. Adl-Amini, 1993; Kansanen, 1992; Meyer, 1987; Schulze, 1978, 1993; Schulze & Terhart, 1993; Terhart, 1983, 1989). Yet the question of teaching method has received relatively little attention from a theoretical standpoint compared with questions of goal, media and contents (Adl-Amini, 1993, p.83).[5] Terhart (1989) belongs to the didacticians who have dealt extensively with the question of method. Among the many issues relating to methods, he distinguishes four of special importance. These are (a) the question of reaching goals by applying methods, (b) the relation between content and methods, (c) the relation between methods and theory, and (d) the institutional dimension of methods.

The first of these relations, between methods and goals, as well as that dealing with the relation between contents and methods, have been briefly commented on previously. In part two of this study the third will be discussed by investigating methodical implications of cognitivist learning theory. The final aspect pointed out by Terhart (1989), concerning methods in an institutional perspective, is also conceived of as an especially important issue. From the perspective of the present school didactic model it is easy to argue that methods are partially to be understood as being embedded in a socio-historical and institutional tradition. It is almost impossible to understand teachers' instructional practice and choice of methods without acknowledging this fact. Many structural features determine to some extent what methods teachers choose.

As was previously noted, there is a reciprocal relation between many factors in an instructional situation. This is also the case with instructional principles and students' working methods in relation to other important features of the instructional setting. For example, there is a reciprocal relation between working methods and content; the content regulates how it should be dealt with in a pedagogical setting.

This means that the method as such is not conceived of as something principally subordinated to the what- and why-questions of teaching. This position disagrees with the view expressed by Weniger (1952, p.18) when he writes that: "In reality methodical arrangements can never be made, rules can never be proposed, until the didactic questions have been decided. Thus method is always something secondary"[6] (see also Koskenniemi, 1968, p.11).

It is true that (1) the teacher's personal competence determines the choice of instructional method and that the *goals* of the pedagogical situation affect this choice as well. But (2) the teacher's familiarity with certain methods of teaching affects both what content is chosen and what goals are set up. Further (3) the working methods as such may also be viewed as a goal; if the goal is to train students to cooperate, then group work is a relevant way of trying to reach that goal regardless of what a group is working on (also Adl-Amini, 1993, pp.95 ff.).

It should also be noticed that if the notion of method is given an independent position in relation to didactics, then didactics is limited to curriculum theory (*Lehrplantheorie*). Such an understanding of didactics would primarily refer to Weniger's (1963) position. Didactics in a narrower sense was for Weniger a theory of the content of education and curriculum (*Theorie der Bildungsinhalte und des Lehrplans*) while didactics in a wider sense included the problem of method in teaching (*Methodik des Unterrichts und der Schularbeit*).

Sometimes when methods have been considered almost identical with didactics, this confusion may be seen as a result of terminological problems as Schulze (1993, p.145) has noted.

In this study, theory of instructional methods is seen as a part of the theory of didactics. However, this is not to say that instructional decisions may be made apart from the goals, content and context of the educational situation. The notion of method should not be emphasized too much, because of the risk of making it a technological concept which may lead to an oversimplification of educational activity (see Schulze, 1993, p.141). And didactics should not be mixed up with *allgemeine Methodik* (Aebli, Herbart, Pestalozzi, Rein).

By approaching the pedagogical process from the perspective of method, Terhart (1989) succeeds in showing that the relation between methods and the instructional context has been a neglected issue. In addition he argues that teachers may play a more central part with respect to the research process if the concept of method is used as a key concept. In other words, to use methods as a central concept in trying to understand the TSL process correlates clearly with teachers' knowledge interest. In this respect Terhart's (1989) position is supported although the concept of method has not been given a central position in the present study as it has in Terhart's (1989) model.

Form of Representation

One aspect of the reciprocal relation between content and method consists in the choice of a relevant form of representation in representing the chosen subject matter. The question then is how knowledge is represented within the schools and classrooms. In addition it should be noted that in classrooms the real reality is seldom present. Most often what is being studied is a constructed representation (Menck, 1987). The most traditional method has been to use the written language, especially after the technical revolutions in the 17th century that made this possible, but different types of symbolic or pictorial presentation are also usual. Thus the subject matter determined is constituted in the classroom by how it is physically presented and how it is psychologically represented by teachers and students.

An important factor determining how knowledge is represented is the teacher's personal competence. Especially from a teacher-education perspective, it is necessary to reflect on and decide about the competence the teachers must represent personally.

Generally speaking, the question of representation is a vital problem in all pedagogical contexts. The choice of a relevant form of representation is to be made in relation to both the learners and the content and often to the resources available.[7]

It is doubtful whether or not the question of representation should be regarded as a problem apart. On good grounds we may ask if it should not be counted as belonging to instructional methods. The reason why the question of representation is considered central in this present study is that the model developed is considered relevant to institutionalized education. The point is that a major part of the work done in these institutions is concerned with the study of a *represented* world. The question of how reality is represented in the classroom is a most important question since insights reached in the classroom are expected to be valid outside the classroom too. In other words; the problem here is *how* the reality to be instructionally elaborated on is constructed in a classroom.

The fundamental problem in all representation is how a sign refers to its content and possible object. This problem is fundamental in pedagogical situations since knowledge, regardless of how it is defined, is also understood as being represented in the classroom by some individual or by some medium (see Schnotz, 1993).

By understanding the problem of representation as construction of the content in the classroom (Menck, 1987), it becomes a much more complex problem than the question of techniques of presentation.

CONCLUSION

The intentional dimensions of the pedagogical process have been discussed on the basis of a division into various structural levels of planning. In addition the temporal aspects of instructional planning were considered important in understanding the process. Special attention was paid to teachers' preparatory planning. This planning phase of the pedagogical process has been discussed following a traditional division between goals, subject matter, methods and media.

The interdependence of these aspects has been emphasized. This also means that in their intentional planning a teacher may approach the actual pedagogical process from any of the above-mentioned points of view, as they are organically related to each other and occur simultaneously. In addition, many of the aspects discussed were considered to be related to the learners' intentions, personality, learning, and previous knowledge as well as to different curriculums and contextual dimensions.

THE INTERACTIVE TEACHING-STUDYING-LEARNING PROCESS

It is considered necessary to distinguish between the teacher's preparatory planning (P2) and the teacher's situated planning (P3), which goes right to the heart of the model. It is relevant to distinguish between these two forms of planning because of the difference in their character previously discussed (Clark & Yinger, 1979).

This means that one phase of teachers' individual pedagogical planning (P3) takes us into the actual pedagogical process. The model explicates the pedagogical process itself in terms of what has been called the pedagogical meeting (*Begegnung*, Weniger). Here the teachers' and students' intentions, activities and reflections meet (Suortti, 1981).

Two aspects of this process have already been pointed out: the teacher's situated planning and evaluation. How are these two aspects of the teacher's activity related? It seems that a relatively simple model of human action may serve as a point of departure in this matter. The structure of the process is considered analogical to the model as a whole. Namely, the actual process also follows the structure intention–action–reflection. The teacher's situated planning is conceived of as a special case of human planning or intentionality in general.

The following schema describes the reflective process:

1. A teacher has continuous experiences in a pedagogical situation;
2. Parallel to these experiences the teacher has specific intentions (one or several);
3. As a result of continuous comparison of past or present experiences with a potential future state of affairs, the teacher tries to realize her intentions through continuous pedagogical acts;
4. The student experiences the teacher's activities and acts in relation to them on the basis of their own understanding of the situation and their own intentions;
5. The teacher experiences the student's activities;
6. The teacher evaluates their experience of the student's activity in relation to their understanding of the situation and their own intentions;
7. The result of this process may, according to the standpoint of the teacher, be called the *Situated Didactic Experience*. The resulting experience for the learner may be called *Situated Learning Experience*. This experience constitutes the preunderstanding from which the teacher continues intentional and reflective activity.

This model (intention–activity–experience/impression–reflection–didactic experience) of institutionalized intentional interactional instructional activity, belongs to the family of approaches using the concept of intentionality in explaining activity (von Wright, 1971; 1985, pp.51 ff.). Notice that this intentional activity is to be understood as culturally embedded and that it should not be understood as representing a mechanistic view of man.

This model works not only for describing the teacher's situated activity (P3–E3 level) but also for describing the teacher's planning before and evaluation after the pedagogical process (P2–E2 level). In this second case the teacher's reflection is focused on the process as a whole (i.e. a pedagogical sequence like an hour, a day, a week, a project).

In changing the object of reflection from reflection during a process in which the teacher is involved to a future or past process, the context in relation to which the reflection is made varies. In situated reflection the context is primarily constituted of the immediate situation with its unique demands and characteristics. In reflection on the process as a whole, the context may consist both of the teacher's overall pedagogical aims and ideas about possibilities of realizing them. Planning and evaluation on the collective level may function as the context for both forms of teacher reflection.

It should clearly be observed that when the teacher evaluates students' performance it is as a reflection on the *experience* of these performances, not on the performances as such. The same holds true for the students' reflection—when students evaluate how useful a teacher's efforts have been for their study process the students reflect upon how they have experienced the teacher's activities.

The Student's Intentional Activity

It is most important to notice that the model contains a similar cycle from intention to situated experience both for the student and for the teacher. The student has also specific intentions in the TSL situation which, naturally, result in specific activities (Koskenniemi, 1946, pp.78 ff.). And like the teacher, students also have experiences (*Erlebnisse*) which are considered to result from reflection connected with their study activities. The student, like the teacher, reflects on these experiences and the result may be called the *Situated Learning Experience*. As the reader can see, this is clearly indicated in the previous visual model in that the student is included in the centre of the figure illustrating the descriptive model (Fig. 3.2). One important aim of this model is thus a clarification of the pedagogical process in order to capture the dynamics of interaction in a pedagogical situation.

The Student as Teacher—The Teacher as Student. When it is claimed that students are intentional individuals it means that the students can educate the teacher—through their intentional study activity, and otherwise, they can express in what respect they themselves think they need support in order to learn. The students teach the teacher to teach them. This can happen intentionally and unintentionally. Similarly the teacher can adopt the role of an intentional learner in trying to figure out how best to help the students in their efforts to reach competence. The teacher is thus also a student in teaching—a real educator continuously grows in this respect. A teacher who does not conceive of themselves simultaneously as being a learner with the students as teachers is not an educator in any deep sense of the word (Hollo, 1927, p.78).

In order to be entitled to call a model of the TSL process genuinely interactional the assumptions described above must be accepted. Many models of the pedagogical process do not, however, understand the student as a teacher and the teacher as a learner—the student remains a student and the teacher a teacher. However, when this is argued for it is clear that the content of what is taught varies with the interacting subjects' changing roles—they teach and learn completely different things.

In an interactional perspective it is relevant to ask what understanding teachers have concerning teaching, studying and learning as well as concerning their role as learners in teaching. Similarly it is important to actualize:

1. The students' views of what learning is (e.g. Marton, Dall'Alba & Beaty, 1993);
2. How students think learning can be promoted by study–activity, i.e their epistemic attitudes (Dweck & Bempechat, 1983);
3. How students think that teachers can help them in their studying–learning process (Mertaniemi, 1990, pp.64–68) and;
4. How students and teachers relate emotionally to the content and to the pedagogical process (Ginsburg & Allardice, 1984; Francis, 1982).

Perspectives on Pedagogical Interaction

We have already pointed out the importance of including the students in a model of didactics by referring to the concept of interaction, i.e. we stressed that the identification of two subjects' intentional activities gives us the possibility of understanding the pedagogical process in a truly interactionist sense.

The next step is to ask about the nature of this interaction. What is it like? What must we understand in order to capture its essence? In contemporary literature there exist models for "teacher's interactive thoughts" (Leinhardt & Greeno, 1986; Shavelson, 1973). The main differences between these models and the present one is that this model:

1. Includes two intentional and interacting subjects, the teacher and the learner;
2. The social and historical context framing the process is emphasized;
3. Teachers' and students' reflection is not conceived of in terms of information processing psychology; and finally,
4. Teaching is (also) seen as a moral craft.

Some further features concerning the interactive nature of the process will be discussed later.

Among others, Doyle (1986) has characterized the classroom as the working place for teachers and students (see also Mehan, 1979 and Weinstein, 1991). The classroom is conceived of as a microcontext having at least the following features. Multidimensionality refers to the fact that in a room where dozens of people meet, many different and divergent interests are expressed. Decision-making in this complex environment is not a simple straightforward process. Parallelity is connected with multidimensionality and refers to the many parallel sequences of activities occurring in classrooms. Further Doyle (1986) emphasizes unpredictability as a typical feature—even though teaching is generally considered intentional, it is still not possible to plan everything in advance as the situation may radically change. In addition, the classroom is, from the teachers' and to some extent from the learners' perspective, a kind of public sphere. The fact that teachers and students regularly meet over a rather long period of time constitutes a specific historical dimension of teaching and learning in classrooms. The participants are able to construct common practical, social and ethical conventions and rules. In addition to these aspects pointed out by Doyle (1986) I would also like to draw attention to the following questions considered useful in trying to understand interactional dimensions of instructional processes in institutionalized education.

The Teacher's Responsibility Towards the Student. The student's participation in the pedagogical process always has a different status and role compared to that of the teacher—it is always asymmetrical. The first is the difference between the teacher's and the learner's experience and competence in a certain field.

A second question concerning the subjects' (teacher and learner) interaction in an educational situation is the seemingly simple question of *why* they participate at all. Is it of their own free will or are they obliged? It is important to remember that the condition on which the actors are present is a key question in understanding the difference between different types of pedagogical situations. The reasons why teachers appear as teachers in public schools, as soccer trainers or as leaders of religious groups are generally different. In the institutionalized school, but also elsewhere, this is related to the teachers' formal position as gatekeepers; they have been given the right and responsibility to examine whether or not an individual has reached a certain standard or type of competence.

A third, related difference (or absence of difference) is age. The difference concerning experience and competence is hopefully always present. All of the implications of the difference in age cannot be discussed here; it is only acknowledged that the teacher's educative role diminishes in proportion to the student's increasing age. The ethics of this relation include the optimization of the student's participation in relation to their interests, abilities, motivation and personality (see Kansanen & Uusikylä, 1983).

The heart of this problem lies in the fact that the teacher in an institutionalized school is an employee who is in charge of the community. Teachers have to decide the extent to which they are ready to accept the values behind the curriculum. The collective, responsible for the national curriculum, must in turn decide what kind and what degree of deviation is accepted. In other words, as long as teachers operate between the curriculum and the individual, teachers are responsible to both, but for different reasons. A fundamental question then is to what extent teachers accept the collective goals, as well as to what extent and on what conditions students accept or internalize the goals set up by the teacher and the collective (Koskenniemi & Hälinen, 1970, p.92).[8]

The Existential Dimension. The nature of interaction is constitutive of the social climate in a pedagogical situation and is in itself educating. This is something which can only partially be planned, and is even more seldom explicitly evaluated, but which often belongs to the experiences students are affected by for the rest of their lives. Van Manen (1991) has shown that an essential dimension of the student–teacher interaction may be approached through the concept of pedagogical tact (also Ottelin, 1931, p.70). His understanding of the notion offers possibilities of handling the existential dimensions of the pedagogical process.[9] Pedagogical tact is partly constituted of a teacher's sensibility to and respect for the growing child's personal integrity and the teacher's ability to act so that this is not violated during the process or as a consequence of the pedagogical process (Lehtovaara, 1992). It may also be that some aesthetic concepts can be used in order to capture this existential dimension of the pedagogical meeting.[10]

The existential aspect of the model is influenced by humanistic psychology (Rogers, 1969) and its view of education. This branch of psychology offers us possibilities for reflecting on the existential dimensions of the participating individuals' experiences. The existential view supports the view of the learner and teacher as intentional subjects. However, even though the teacher's role is to support an individual's personal growth, the present position does not accept a therapist approach to describing the pedagogical process. The reason is that the teacher in the institutionalized school represents the collective in the pedagogical process. Naturally the teacher has a considerable degree of freedom, but to imagine that she could act as the students' advocate with respect to the interests expressed by the community or the state is pedagogical naivety.

A final aspect of interaction is related to how teachers' and students' intentional and interactional activity can lead to the desired goal. The relation between student and teacher activity was discussed in some detail with respect to learning in Chapter 2. Some of the main conclusions were:

1. It is relevant to call an activity teaching even though it does not result in learning;
2. It is possible to identify study activity even if learning does not occur as a result of this process;
3. The effect of a teacher's instructional activity is mediated by the learner's conceptualization of the process and their intentional activity;
4. The cultural and social contract concerning instructional activity in the institutionalized school partly defines the participants' roles in the process. This presupposes that the uninterested learner is sometimes treated as an intentional learner;
5. A teacher's activity cannot be made empirically dependent on a student's intentions as this would lead to the conclusion that a teacher teaches only those learners who intend to learn;
6. Nor can students' study activity be made dependent on the teacher's intentions and activities as it is not reasonable to say that only those students that are being taught are the ones engaged in an intentional studying process. In addition, the learner's intentions may differ from the teacher's, consciously or by mistake, and, second, the student can try to learn without being taught, i.e. by being engaged in a self-directed study process.

The intentional and interactional features of the pedagogical process are also brought to mind by the fact that the participating subjects in a pedagogical process, the teacher and the learner, may be described in similar terms. Both carry out intentional acts and these acts are determined by the participants' rights, obligations, wishes and abilities, etc. In this respect the TSL process is a "dialogical" one (Hintikka, 1982).

EVALUATION

In the present model evaluation is given a quite distinctive role. The reason for this is the descriptive nature of the model—it aims at being valid for the institutionalized TSL process. This pedagogical reality cannot be truly understood without accepting evaluation as a fundamental category. However, a problematic question is whether the concept of evaluation should be equated with concepts like intention and interaction as they are understood in this model. The problem is whether evaluation can be seen as an independent concept or whether it should be subordinated with respect to intentionality. The position taken in this study is that the concept of pedagogical intentionality cannot be correctly understood without reference to evaluation. It may thus be that the concept of intentionality may sometimes be correctly understood irrespective of evaluative reflection, though it appears that this aspect is not dispensable in understanding pedagogical intentionality.

Some further notes concerning how evaluation is understood here are adduced.

A differentiation similar to that in planning (P) can be made with respect to evaluative activities (E). First there is the continuous situated evaluation during the teaching process (E3). Second there is the teacher's evaluation after different kinds of pedagogical sequences in relation to the classroom and school as contexts (E2b) and in relation to the evaluation on the collective level (E2a). Evaluation after a sequence covers both evaluation of the students' results in relation to the goals and the teacher's evaluation of their own activities for instance regarding the choice of relevant content, form of representation, etc. Finally, E1 refers to evaluation on the collective level (e.g. national evaluation of school achievement).

As in the case of teachers' planning, there is reason to make a distinction between the *kind* of evaluation teachers make continuously as a part of the instructional or educational process (E3) and the kind of evaluation teachers make after having finished a pedagogical sequence (E2a,b). It might be reasonable to talk about teachers' formative evaluative activity during the process and their summing-up evaluation after having finished the process.

With regard to the teacher, we may say that not only the teacher's own evaluation of the students' achievements influence the teacher's activities, but naturally also systematic evaluations made on the collective level may have the same function. The impact of external evaluative activities varies along with the type of external evaluation. For example, in cases where the possibility of a student continuing his education is regulated by success in external tests, teachers' evaluative activity plays a subordinate role.

When strict external evaluation is carried out, it is likely that the teacher brings the teaching into line with the standards imposed by external authorities. This is also the reason why teachers' professional status partly depends on what success the students have in collective annual tests carried out by an authority outside the school. External evaluation therefore naturally affects the school culture.

This clearly shows that the pedagogical work in a school is affected by the cultural function the grades have outside the school. The more important the grades are outside the school, the more the teacher is controlled. This mechanism also gives teachers instruments to control students by reminding them that the teacher is the collective's representative in the classroom.

Concerning evaluation on the collective level, we can distinguish between systematic and occasional evaluation. Occasional evaluation refers to national or international summing-up evaluations of students' academic achievements or the like made for some specific casual reason. An example of systematic evaluation is the annual Finnish matriculation examination at the end of upper secondary school (gymnasium). The content of this examination is decided by a special national committee which is appointed for this purpose and also evaluates the results.

Finally we have the students' evaluation and self-evaluation of their activities and the teachers' support, goals, contents, etc. However, the students' evaluative reflection primarily occurs on the E3-level, but also outside the school. This is pedagogically relevant as the students' evaluation outside the school in fact may influence future pedagogical activity indirectly, in that parents or the community are made aware of how the pedagogical activities have appeared to the students.

In sum, there are (at least) five important perspectives on evaluation which are of importance to the pedagogical situation: (a) the teachers' different forms of evaluation, (b) the collective evaluation of achievements, (c) the function of grading in the culture outside the school community, including continuing education and the labour market and finally, (d) the social psychological function of grading (Kallós, 1989; Lundgren, 1989) and (e) the students' evaluation.

The final comment concerning evaluation of the pedagogical process is related to the individual student's rights and obligations to participate in this process. In the figure presented earlier concerning the forms and levels of pedagogical activity, it was claimed that students in institutional school settings often are in a quite weak position with respect to evaluation of their own achievements.

In the present model, both students and teachers, as well as the instructional organization as a whole, are conceived of as responsible for the students' achievements. It should be obvious to everybody that if students are made partly responsible for the learning outcomes, they must necessarily be conceived of as intentional learners. It makes no sense to conceive of the relation between teaching and learning as a causal relation and then hold only students responsible for the results of the TSL process. Thus, when students are given the responsibility for their success, this includes a view of the learner as an intentional subject.

CONTEXTS

In the present model the learners are identified not only as active intentional subjects in the pedagogical situation but also as subjects representing part of the local community surrounding the school. This fact is thus an additional way in which the local context is acknowledged by the teacher. The students simply bring the local context into the classroom.

It is also useful to reflect on the context within which the students act because it is radically different from the teacher's context. The students' context is constituted of those possibilities and limitations that delimit the students' learning space in the school situation. The organization of the school, the local school culture as well as the individual teachers define this space (Arfwedson, 1986; Mercer, 1993, 1995). The classroom and school as a learning environment should not be overlooked as a historically developed context defining the individual student's possibilities of participation in different pedagogical processes (including choosing content, working methods, planning the school year, etc.) (Simola, 1995, pp.108, 114; Terhart, 1989, pp.57–60). Observe, however, that even though the historicity of the TSL process is emphasized, this does not in any way reduce the student's role in constructing the context for themself. In an important respect the meaning of the context is constructed by the student although it is first shaped by tradition and the teacher.

In an institutionalized pedagogical process the student steps, in a manner of speaking, into an intended context. But the experienced context does not have to coincide with the intended context. We will return to this question in discussing the curriculum as intended and experienced.

The local school culture in turn is affected by the traditions of the school and teachers' beliefs concerning education and values. As Koskenniemi and Hälinen (1970, p.92) remind us, it is also important to acknowledge the peer students as a most influential factor in this respect.

The second self-evident context for the students is the local culture and the home background. As numerous empirical studies have shown, this context is of great educational importance and must therefore be considered important from a pedagogical perspective, even though its impact is indirect. On a general level, and with reservations that cannot be discussed here, the phenomenological concept of lifeworld may be used in discussing the student's context (Lippitz, 1984; Uljens, 1992a, pp.29–31).

When didactics is discussed the didactic triangle (*das didaktische Dreieck*) constituted of the three relations between the content, the teacher and the student is the most frequently used model (see e.g. Diederich, 1988, pp.256–257). Without mentioning here the positive sides of the didactic triangle, its fundamental problem is that it actualizes the context of teaching in a very limited sense. The present model is to some extent a reaction against the didactic triangle models because of the contextual limitation they suffer from.

Second, the intentional dimensions of teaching are also extremely crucial in the presented model, but this aspect is also invisible as a constitutive factor in the didactic triangle. Of course, if it is argued in some didactic triangle models that intentions determine the relation between the content and the teacher, then intentions are accounted for.

Returning to the question of the teacher's relation to context, one might think that the teacher's preparatory planning (P2) always occurs within the limits of the planning on the collective level (P1). This, however, is not always the case since the teacher may move beyond or even oppose the national (collective) curriculum. This is the reason for extending the field of P2 beyond the field of P1 in the school didactic model presented. Because of this the effects of planning on the collective level are dependent on the teacher's sanctioning of this planning. Yet my impression is that the curriculum is not so effective in general. The teacher's understanding of the more immediate cultural context is a context that probably influences the teacher's activities much more directly.

The local culture is also brought into the schools by the students. In the figure presented earlier, the local culture is indicated by the outer circle surrounding the process. Acknowledging this dimension allows us to handle that aspect of a school's curriculum which regulates who is granted admission to the school.

It is also important to pay attention to the existing educational interests expressed e.g. in mass media and by other pressure groups surrounding the school. This should be more central in pedagogical reflection since students not only bring this context into the school but partly constitute this very context.

We may thus identify both a cultural and a curricular context for teachers' pedagogical activity. The curricular context may be divided into different levels as has been noted (i.e. a national, a local, and a school level). The cultural and curricular contexts motivate a corresponding division of teachers' planning. Fig. 3.2 on p. 65, this is indicated by the fact that the field P2 is divided into two subfields. Let us call them P2(a) and P2(b), where P2(a) refers to teachers' planning in relation to the curriculum on all collective levels (both to national and local curriculums) and P2(b) refers to teachers' planning in relation to other than curricular interests. This means that the national level is represented by the national curriculum, whereas the local level is represented both in the form of a local curriculum (part of P1) and the local community (informal context). Thus the local community has both a formal (curricular) and an informal impact on the teachers' work.

In assessing the impact of the curriculum on classroom activities we should remember that the collective, formal and institutionalized regulating activities are not limited to this form of mediated regulation through the curriculum. Decisions concerning, for example, the economic resources the teacher has access to are also made on the collective level. Nor is it up to the teacher (or the students) to decide what subjects should be taught or studied or how much time should be devoted to the different subjects. And it is not the teachers who decide about the content of the final examination in the upper secondary school (gymnasium in Finland). In this sense the collective levels interfere quite directly with the level of pedagogical action. In other words, when discussing how the formal collective level regulates educational reality, it may turn out to be more through these kinds of pattern than through the curriculum. The curriculum should perhaps rather be viewed as a political document conveying general signals to the field.

Finally, there is the school as context. The conditions for the pedagogical activities taking place within an institutionalized school are special because of the organizational structure of this type of educational setting. Also the material resources of the school, as well as the relations a school has both to the formal local context (the local board of education on the municipal level) and the informal context (the local culture) define the school as the context for teachers' pedagogical work (Arfwedson, 1986).

It is possible to identify specific dimensions of each *type* of context, i.e. the school as context, the local society as context, the formal local context, and the national context. Three dimensions of each context are identified; a curriculum dimension, an organizational dimension and a resource dimension. Relating the contexts to these dimensions result in the following typology (see Fig. 3.3). Figure 3.3 completes the model

	Dimension		
Type of context	Organization	Resources	Curriculum
School as context	Organization of the school	Buildings, technical aids, materials	The curriculum of the school
The local culture as context	The local culture generally	Parental participation, commercial interests	Educational ideals of home
The formal local context	Board of education, local school-administration	Economical resources, continuing education	Municipal curriculum
The national context	Legislation, disposition of time	Primary education, teaching materials	National curriculum, school subjects

FIG. 3.3. Four contexts and their dimensions framing the teaching–studying–learning process in classrooms in the institutionalized school.

presented earlier in several respects. First, not all of the dimensions pointed out in the figure were included in the previous model. For example the school as context was identified only on a general level; its different dimensions were not mentioned. Concerning the national context, again, only the curricular dimension was previously discussed. It is, however, clear that the resources and national legislation also affect the teachers' educational practices both directly and indirectly. By resources on the national level we mean both the pre-service teacher education usually financed by the state and the acceptance of teaching materials used in the schools. By organization on the national level again we mean both the laws regulating activities in the schools and the regulation concerning which subjects should be included in the weekly schedule and the time allocated to the different subjects. A second major difference between the previous model and this typology is that the local culture is divided into two different types of contexts: (a) there is the local culture in a wide sense and (b) the formal local context, i.e. the local way of organizing educational activities (school administration).

However, there is no reason to articulate the differences between the contexts and dimensions in any detail in the present study. It serves the purpose of this study to identify the contexts and their dimensions at this general level. It should be mentioned that there are other ways of differentiating the culture surrounding the institutionalized school. For example, Lundgren (1972, 1980) presented a model for analysing factors of importance in understanding how decisions are made concerning teaching and teaching content in schools. He noted the difference between curriculum as a governing goal system, the administrative apparatus as a constraining frame system and the juridical apparatus as a regulating formal rule system. Arfwedson & Arfwedson (1991, pp.41 ff.) in turn have distinguished between an outer and an inner frame system; the outer system refers to contextual factors outside the school as an institution and the inner system to the school as an institution, including its inner life. There are also obvious similarities between the present way of structuring the outer context and those presented by Fend (1980). The major difference is that the present model distinguishes between three dimensions typical of each context, i.e. the organization, resources and curriculum of each context. Making the above-mentioned distinction between the dimensions in question is considered valuable in that it offers a refined way of structuring the very important context. The fundamental difference is, however, that the approaches mentioned above are primarily theories or models of frame factors (curriculum theory) affecting the teaching process while the present model puts the pedagogical activity in the centre. In trying to understand teaching, studying and learning in schools, it seems impossible to neglect these contextual frames.

WHY SCHOOL DIDACTICS?

During the development of the present model, I gave much consideration to the question of how the conceptual system was to be characterized to fit a suitable label. At first it appeared that many terms could have been used. After closer consideration this was not the case and I will now try to show why.

General Didactics

The first reflection concerning the present model is its character as a general model for education in institutionalized schools. The model focuses on the different phases of the pedagogical process, and does not take the content or the population as its point of departure. In other words, it is not a model of subject didactics or a model of special education or adult education. However, even though the main structural elements are valid for all forms of education, the model is still not a model of general didactics. It is primarily aimed at helping to understand the pedagogical process in the institutionalized school.

The orientation of this study is thus similar to that of many other didacticians like Menck (1975). His definition is: "I will use 'didactics' for every consideration, proposition and theory concerning 'teaching in schools' (*Unterricht in der Schule*)". The only difference between my position and Menck's (1975) definition is that when Menck says that he will use didactics for every consideration, proposition and theory concerning teaching in schools, I choose the expression school didactics to reflect this interest.

The actual descriptive model cannot thus be called a model of general didactics since the aim of general didactics must be to present thoughts relevant to any pedagogical situation (see e.g. Diederich, 1988; Kansanen, 1993a). Thus the scope of general didactics is broader than that covered by the present model; general didactics covers the TSL process anywhere, whereas school didactics is limited to these processes as they occur in schools.

The model developed here is primarily constructed for analysing education in institutionalized education, i.e. schools. The expression "institutionalized education" refers to schools financed and governed by e.g. the state or some other collective. The main difference between the TSL process in schools and learning in many other educational situations is the decisions made on a collective level regulating pedagogical activities. Concerning the comprehensive school, for example, the parents of the children attending these schools participate in the political process defining how the schools are to function. The result of this process is stated in political documents (curriculums). Thus the students (or their representatives, i.e. parents) participate in this process, which is not the case when education takes place in companies or religious organizations. The employees/members do not constitute the group which ultimately decides the educational curriculum of a company; often there is no curriculum to agree upon.

Instructional Science?

A further possibility in determining what the model should be called is the German notion of *Unterrichtswissenschaft* or *Wissenschaft vom Unterricht*, (e.g. Adl-Amini, 1993). This term is not easy to translate into English. With reservations we can translate it by the expressions science of teaching or instructional science. It seems, however, that *Unterrichtswissenschaft* in one sense is too narrow and in another sense too wide. It is too narrow in that it is sometimes limited to the instructional-communicative dimension of the pedagogical process without recognizing the contextual questions included in the model discussed.

On the other hand, it may be understood as being too wide in order to correctly reflect the model presented in this study in that it is contextually neutral; *Unterrichtswissenschaft* is about *Unterricht* occurring anywhere (Benner, 1991, p.206). However this is not always the case. Schröder

(1992), for example, not only says that "Unterricht ist organisiertes Lehren und Lernen", but also that *Unterricht* is institutionalized by localizing *Unterricht* as an activity going on in "schools". However, the notion of school is extremely wide:

> The concept of school is here taken in its very widest sense, not only including public and private educational institutions but also, in addition, school-like activities (driving school, skiing school, sailing school, etc.) and the school-like contribution of mass media (school radio, school film, school-TV). All these orientations [Einrichtungen] represent an institutionalized form of teaching and learning; that is to say, instruction.[11]

The model presented in this study does not primarily make use of such a wide notion of school or institutionalized teaching and learning. The model was primarily aimed to be used for institutionalized education in schools following a collectively agreed-upon curriculum, where the students or their representatives were assumed to participate in the development of the curriculum regulating educational activities.

Theory of Instruction?

On the other hand, the German term (*Unterrichtstheorie*), approximately "theory of teaching and learning" or "instructional theory", is sometimes used synonymously with *Didaktik* (see Glöckel, 1992, pp.316 ff.). For example Klafki (1980, 1991) uses the terms *Unterrichtstheorie* and *Didaktik* as synonyms, both including curriculum theory. As long as curriculum theory is placed within *Unterrichtstheorie*, this label is not suitable for the present model. A more important problem with the general notion of *Unterrichtstheorie* is that such a theory should, again, be valid for *any* TSL process, i.e. irrespective of context.

A feature of the model presented here is that it acknowledges teachers' critical reflection concerning both goals, contents and methods in education. However, the present model does not aim at an analysis of how the goals are formulated on the collective level. It is limited to teachers' critical reflection concerning goals. In this respect there is a difference between this model and curriculum theory.

School Pedagogics?

If the model cannot be called a model of general didactics, we may reflect on the possibility of turning to the concept of school pedagogics (German *Schulpädagogik*, Swedish *skolpedagogik*, Finnish *koulupedagogiikka*), which is well established in German educational literature (e.g. Steindorf, 1972; Einsiedler, 1978; Benner, 1995, pp.47ff.). Perhaps it could be translated as school education or school pedagogics. In Finland the term school pedagogics has a long history (see e.g. Cleve, 1884; Lilius, 1945; Salomaa, 1947). Having been out of use for about 40 years there is a renewed interest in the concept in Finland (Kansanen, 1992, 1995b). An argument supporting the choice of the concept of *Schulpädagogik* would be that the present model identifies the school, with its organizational structure and culture, as one of the most important contextual aspects affecting all phases of the pedagogical process. However, since several writers conceive of this term as a rather wide concept including a theory of school (*Theorie der Schule*), it may be misleading to use this term for the model presented in this book (see Apel, 1993). Beckman (1981) also includes politics of school (*Schulpolitik*) and legal questions connected to the school (*Schulrecht*) in *Schulpädagogik*. Schröder (1992), again, mentions the following fields as the most important in *Schulpädagogik*:

The most important problem areas of school pedagogics are therefore:
- the theory of school, including legal and organizational questions in connection with schools as well as problems related to the form of school life and school hygiene,
- theory of instruction, including curricular problems, forms and princles of instruction as well as instructional technology and media didactics,
- teaching practice with special reference to effective instructional planning and organization, including effectivity control.[12]
  (p.311, bold-faced printing in the original not marked here)

Schröder's (1992) description is quite close to that represented by Cleve's book from 1884. The present model is not developed in order to conceptualize what role the school has in society as a cultural institution. Nor is it aimed to cover school legislation and organization. Rather, it aims at offering tools for handling the TSL process within the institutionalized school. Under such circumstances the present model cannot be identified as a model of school pedagogics (*Schulpädagogik*).

This is not to say that the model is ideologically uncritical. First, the values behind the model may and will be explicated. Second, the teacher's critical role in relation to the values regulating the pedagogical work is pointed out as an important aspect of teachers' work. In this sense the present model falls within school pedagogics as well as within general didactics. However, having said this, it is necessary to clarify the internal relation between school pedagogics and general didactics. Kansanen's (1989, p.13) argument is relevant in this context. He shows that school pedagogics may, first of all, be considered as a part of general education (*Allgemeine Pädagogik*). Second, as an explanatory framework general didactics transcends the pedagogical practice of schools. This means that general didactics goes beyond school pedagogics because of two facts. First, general didactics is about teaching wherever it occurs while school pedagogics covers only educational issues related to schools. Second, general didactics covers curriculum theory. Thus general didactics has a partly independent role in relation to school pedagogics. Against this background the field uniting school pedagogics (*Schulpädagogik*) and general didactics may be called school didactics (*Schuldidaktik*).

School Didactics

Since the model developed here is primarily directed towards an understanding of pedagogical activity within schools, the term school didactics (*Schuldidaktik*) was finally chosen as the most appropriate. It is not as broad as general didactics; it is limited to teaching and educating activities in the institutionalized school. It is not as wide as *Schulpädagogik* either; school didactics is not the theory of school or schooling in general. Finally, it is not limited to the methods of instruction as such.

The aim of school didactics is to provide a conceptual language by which we may talk about educational reality in the institutionalized school. The expression institutionalized school refers to such educational organizations as arrange learning environments regulated by a collectively agreed curriculum. Schooling is seen as a compromise between the individual student's needs and interests and the collective's interest.

Traditionally many didacticians have worked with problems explicitly related to teaching and learning in schools. In contemporary educational research, schools appear as only one of many pedagogical settings investigated. This change in the educational field has motivated a division of general didactics into different subfields. In talking about school didactics it must be noted that it is not the same as "didactics for a certain level" (German *Stufendidaktik*, Swedish *stadiedidaktik*) exemplified by pre-school didactics, compulsory school didactics[13], university didactics etc. (German *Grundschuldidaktik Hochschuldidaktik*). The present notion of school didactics incorporates all these levels as long as they function as institutionalized educational systems following a collective curriculum.

The following model can be used to visualize the relations between general education, school pedagogics, school didactics, general didactics, and subject didactics (see Fig. 3.4).

Figure 3.4 shows that school didactics falls within school pedagogics, which in turn falls within general education. It was previously pointed out that general didactics goes beyond school pedagogics. School didactics is thus the field which unites general didactics and school pedagogics.

92 SCHOOL DIDACTICS AND LEARNING

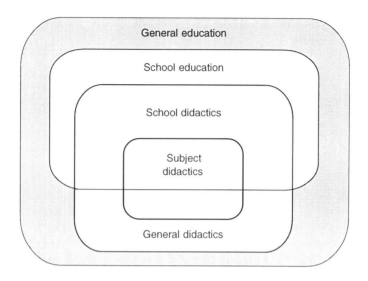

FIG. 3.4. A model visualizing logical relations between school didactics and related concepts. Explanations:
General education = *Allgemeine Pädagogik*
School education = *Schulpädagogik*
School didactics = *Schuldidaktik*
Subject didactics = *Fachdidaktik*
General didactics = *Allgemeine Didaktik*

The situation is analogous to that of subject didactics (*Fachdidaktik*). First, it goes beyond teaching in schools; in principle it deals with teaching different subjects anywhere. Second, it is connected with school pedagogics through school didactics. Further, it may be noted that subject matter didactics does not reach beyond general didactics; as such they are both valid for any type of pedagogical setting.

The model does not say much about how curriculum theory should be placed.[14] What has been said is that curriculum theory goes beyond school didactics. A further motive for placing curriculum theory outside *Schulpädagogik* as well is that *Schulpädagogik* may be seen as a field of research and not as a general theory. However, curriculum theory may also be placed within *Schulpädagogik* since curriculums are almost exclusively constructed for institutionalized schools. But it would probably also be possible to find arguments for letting general didactics include curriculum theory.

The second conscious limitation of the model is that it leaves out didactics for special groups (adult education, special education), i.e.

models using the population as the criterion. It would however be easy to include such a field in the model above; didactics for special groups would (a) fall within general education and (b) cover all fields apart from subject didactics.

The position presented here is supported by Scholz and Bielefeldt's (1978) delimitation. Also Klafki (1984) has used the term *Schuldidaktik* in relation to *Freizeitdidaktik*. It should be noted that the notion of *Schuldidaktik* is not in frequent use in the contemporary literature, for example Schröder's (1992) dictionary of educational terminology does not contain *Schuldidaktik*, only *Schulpädagogik*. In Finland Bruhn (1935, p.190) has used the concept, but not in a systematic way.

Yet many researchers in general didactics regard themselves as primarily concerned with didactics for the comprehensive school. In Finland this is true for both Soininen (1901, 1906), Koskenniemi (1946), Bruhn (1953), Koskenniemi and Hälinen (1970) and for Lahdes (1986). It is true also for German didactics (e.g. Heimann, Klafki).

As the difference between school pedagogics and school didactics is justified, it is suggested that school didactics should be conceived of as a specific field of research within general education. Observe however that the expression *field of research* is not an argument for introducing a new subdiscipline under general education. Thus we avoid a further unhealthy differentiation of education as a discipline (Macke, 1990; Sjöberg, 1994).

With this explanation the first problem posed in this study may be regarded as solved, at least tentatively. A field of research within general education called school didactics has been presented. Second, a descriptive-analytical conceptual model (also called *The School Didactic Fly* referring to the visual shape of the model) within the frames of this field has been explicated.

However, thus far the conceptual structure developed has been called a model, not a theory. What then is the difference between a model and a theory? This is the question to be answered in the following section, then the presented model will be related to some influential German schools of didactics. Finally the problem of normativity is reflected upon, and the position of the present model in this respect is explicated.

A MODEL OR A THEORY OF SCHOOL DIDACTICS?

Conceptual didactic structures have been called models, theories, theoretical models, thought models, etc. In this study the expression didactic model has been used for the developed conceptual structure.

Jank and Meyer (1991, p.92) have suggested the following definition of a didactic model:

1. A didactic model is a theoretical construction within educational sciences for the analysis and modelling of didactic activity in contexts in and out of school;
2. A didactic model claims, in a theoretically comprehensive and practically consistent manner, to explain the prerequisites, possibilities and limits of teaching and learning;
3. A didactic model will, with regard to its theoretical core, generally be delegated to some scientific-theoretical position (often more than one).[15]

With regard to the first item we can say that the present model is developed to analyse pedagogical activity in institutionalized schools conceptually.

Second, the aim of the present model is to systematically understand the preconditions, possibilities and limits of teaching and learning. Finally, the fundamental assumptions concerning the theory of science of the present model have been discussed. Thus the present study shares the definition of a didactic model presented by Jank and Meyer (1991).

But how is the difference between models and theories defined? One approach is to say that theories are the final result of scientific endeavour while models reflect steps towards a final theory (see Knecht-vonMartial, 1986, p.8). This difference between a model and theory is only terminological and functional, not essential.

Didactic models have also been categorized with regard to which level in the school system they describe or explain (the collective-individual level) or with respect to which phase of the pedagogical process they try to understand (process and product models). The present model describes both different levels and phases of the pedagogical reality—a point of departure which is not unique (see e.g. Adl-Amini, 1993).

Still another way of categorizing models in didactics has been presented by Knecht-vonMartial (1986). Knecht-vonMartial distinguishes between two groups of theories; object-theories and metatheories. Object-theories consist of propositions delimiting the object of research of a discipline: "Die Objekttheorie bestäht auf den Sätzen über den Gegenstand einer Theorie" (ibid., p.27). The object of metatheories again is one of several object-theories. Within both groups or levels, normative and descriptive theories are discerned. For example, a descriptive object theory is a description of teaching methods while normative object theories dictate under what conditions certain methods should be used (ibid., p.28). For example, investigations into the principles of how object theories are constructed belong to descriptive metatheories. Heimann's work *Didaktik als Theorie und Lehre* (1962) exemplifies what is meant by descriptive metatheory. Finally, normative metatheories cover all propositions concerning what the rules building up object theories should look like. As Kansanen (1989, p.78) points out, it easily happens that a metatheoretical description of a rule is used as a norm for how one should construct theories. Thus it is not always easy to keep descriptive and normative metatheories apart.

If we use this method of structuring didactic theories in order to place the actual descriptive model, we can see that the model as such may be regarded as a descriptive metatheoretical construct. However, during the process of constructing the model and in explaining why it is constructed as it is, clear normative metatheoretical argumentation was used.

It is also obvious that the construction presented does not have predictive value; there are no direct hypotheses to be tested. However, by using the model as a point of departure for empirical research, such hypotheses could very well be formulated in relation to existing empirical research.

COMPARISON OF THE SCHOOL DIDACTIC MODEL AND SOME GERMAN APPROACHES

Since the theory of didactics has been developed to a very advanced state in Germany, it will be useful to point out some connections between the present model and parts of the German tradition, especially since it became obvious during the development of the model that such similarities exist. At the same time this comparative analysis helps us to understand the specific features of the model in question. This phase exemplifies the hermeneutical dimension of the study.

Attention is limited to two schools of thought; the human-science theory of education as understood by Wolfgang Klafki, and the *lerntheoretische* approach represented by Paul Heimann. These two were considered to represent acknowledged schools of thought and were both considered relevant because of the similarities between them and the present model.

ERUDITION-CENTRED THEORY OF DIDACTICS

One of the most influential schools of thought in German didactics is the so called *bildungstheoretische* tradition or the *geisteswissenschaftliche Bildungstheorie* (here called the human-science theory of education).

It must be said from the start that there is no well established English term for German *Bildung* (Swedish *bildning*). Hopmann (1992, p.7) suggests that *bildungstheoretischer Didaktik* should be translated erudition-centred didactics. He justifies his choice as follows:

I prefer the ancient term *erudition* to translate the German concept of *Bildung*, because it seems to have some of the ancient flavour of the self-development and scholarship affiliated with this central piece of German pedagogy, developed by Herder, Goethe, Schiller, Humboldt, and others in late 18th and early 19th century. The modern use of the term Bildung came into being by the translation and modernization of the latin concept of *eruditio* (as used by Comenius, for instance). Other common translations like *formation* or, worst of all, *education* tend to provoke misleading connotations. Erziehung—the direct translation of education—is in fact a corollary to *Bildung*, normally meaning the external side of the personal development called *Bildung*. In German the process of (a) becoming *erudite* by (b) help of others (i.e. education) is termed in the combination of both as *Bildung and Erziehung*. Finally, *Bildung* means both, the process (erudition) and the product (eruditeness) . . ."

When education is used in this study it refers both to the process of *Bildung*, becoming erudite, and to *Erziehung* (Swedish *fostran*) as the intentional process of education (cf. Benner, 1991, pp.47–106). Human-science may be conceived as an acceptable translation of German *Geisteswissenschaft geisteswissenschaftliche Bildungstheorie* but could also be translated human-science theory of education. However, in order to avoid many parallel interpretations, Hopmann's (1992) suggestion is adopted in this study; erudition-centred theory of didactics refers to German *bildungstheoretischer Didaktik*.

In its modern version the erudition-centred theory of didactics was founded by Erich Weniger (1930, 1952, 1963) and Nohl (1949) and was later developed by Wolfgang Klafki (1964, 1994). Klafki writes that in his early works he "drew on and developed the theory of education (*Bildungstheorie*) from the human-science pedagogy (*Geisteswissenschaftliche Pädagogik*), especially didactics, the theory of content and curriculum (*Theorie der Bildungsinhalte and des Lehrplans*)" (Klafki, 1995).

Some of the fundamental and generally accepted features of the *bildungstheoretischer Didaktik*, i.e. erudition-centred theory of didactics are discussed here. The point of departure methodologically is the pedagogical reality, i.e. the factual educational reality. Secondly, any conceptual system of didactics should be developed in relation to practice. In other words, it should do justice to the practitioners' way of understanding pedagogical reality. Thirdly, a historical perspective is adopted in understanding educational reality, i.e. a pedagogical situation is historically given and must be conceived of as such. Finally, the complexity of pedagogical reality is accepted. This means that no solutions of pedagogical problems may be deduced from any set of general norms or principles (see e.g. Blankertz, 1987, pp.35, 122).

3. A MODEL OF SCHOOL DIDACTICS

On this general level it is not problematic to accept these positions from the perspective of the previously presented model. Firstly, the complexity of the pedagogical reality has been accepted as a point of departure. Not only were the parallel questions many, but the relations between them have been shown to be complex.

Secondly, the point of departure taken in educational reality as such was accepted in saying that precisely this reality and nothing else should be the object of didactics. For example, when the relations between educational reality, teacher education and didactics as scientific theory were discussed, it was claimed that the relation between theory and pedagogical reality is the primary one. The secondary relation is the one between teacher education and didactics as theory; having such a theory makes it easier for us to educate teachers. When educational theory (didactics) is made the content of teacher education, we may in fact talk about the didactics of educational theory or *die Fachdidaktik der Didaktik*.

Thirdly, the claim that the conceptual language developed should be close to the language used by practitioners is also accepted. It was claimed that the aim of didactics must be to offer teachers a language with which they can explicate their pedagogically relevant experiences in a coherent manner. This has been the aim of the present model.

Finally, the demand that a pedagogical situation should be understood as historically developed is accepted by acknowledging the social, political and historical context within which the single teacher operates. Since the model presented is primarily limited to education within schools regulated by a curriculum, it is natural to accept the historical demand; the school as a cultural institution is a historically developed institution. It cannot be understood separately from its historical origin and the tradition from which it has grown. Nor is it possible to understand it as separate from contemporary society and culture within which it exists and which it partly constitutes. However, even if this is accepted, the main emphasis is not laid on an analysis of the historical or cultural dimension of the TSL process, although the model does offer opportunities for such an analysis. The cultural–historical aspect is also accepted, in the sense that the presented approach is not understood as a universal theory valid for every form of schooling in the world. In this sense the approach is also empirical; its validity for different contexts must be tested.

To conclude, the main features of the erudition-centred theory of didactics (*Bildungstheoretische Didaktik*) are accepted and followed on a general level. This does not mean that there are no differences between this theory of education and the present school didactic model. Several differences may be noted.

The main difference is the way in which the question of *content* is treated, i.e. what position it is given.

One way of opening the issue of content in the human-science theory of didactics is the widely recognized five questions put forward by Wolfgang Klafki at the end of the 50s in his *Didaktische Analyse*.[16] This analysis was conceived as the fundamental core of planning instruction. The questions raised at that time were:

1. What wider or general sense or reality do these contents exemplify and open up to the learner? What basic phenomenon or fundamental principle, what law, criterion, problem, method, technique or attitude can be grasped by dealing with these contents as examples
2. What significance does the content in question or the experience, knowledge, ability or skill to be acquired through this topic already possess in the minds of the children in my class? What significance should it have from a pedagogical point of view?
3. What constitutes the topic's significance for the children's future?
4. How are the contents structured (which have been placed in a specifically pedagogical perspective by questions 1, 2, and 3)?
5. (a) What facts, phenomena, situations, experiments, controversies, etc. in other words what intuitions, are appropriate to induce the child to ask questions directed at the essence and structure of the content in question?
   (b) What pictures, hints, situations, observations, accounts, experiments, models, etc. are appropriate in helping children to answer, as independently as possible, their questions directed at the essentials of the matter?
   (c) What situations and tasks are appropriate for helping the principle to be grasped by means of an example of elementary case, or the structure of a content, to become of real benefit to the students, helping to consolidate it by application and practice it (immanent repetition)?

These questions should not be conceived as being in a certain significant order. They were intended to function as conceptual instruments, laying a foundation for methodical decisions.[17] It is obvious that these questions are most relevant to any teacher. To my understanding they do not contain anything that is not acceptable from the perspective of the present model—quite the contrary. The question is only what role or position this set of questions is given. In relation to the model presented in this study, the five groups of questions may well be integrated in the fields P2 and P3, i.e. teachers' planning of instruction before and during a

3. A MODEL OF SCHOOL DIDACTICS 99

pedagogical sequence. In the present study didactic analysis is not, however, limited to reflection related to the planning phase of education.

It is evident that the kernel of Klafki's way of reasoning is the content and the notion of *Bildung*. Therefore we will now take a brief look at how the concept of *Bildung* is understood.[18]

A widely accepted and general understanding of the term is to be found in Schröder's (1992) dictionary. Schröder (1992, p.37) refers to Henz's (1991) definition: "[*Bildung*] is the increasing participation in the culture in order to form a value-oriented, harmonious personality." (p.126). *Bildung* would thus refer to a subject's increasing participation in a culture aiming at including the development of a harmonious personality, in short, the development of a personal cultural identity. Four fundamental features of this process are pointed out (referring to Henz, 1991, pp.126ff.):

- Dynamics (through the adjective "growing"), with the comment that [Bildung] cannot be finished and never be an established final state.
- Participation (through taking part), where "part-taking" as participation in the fundamental properties of Being is something relatively permanent and more than occasional.
- Cultural identity (through increasing participation in the culture), by which is meant the feeling and consciousness of being a part of the culture.
- Goal-orientation (defined as "personality"), assessed in terms of the maturity of the developed individual, by which personality stands out for instance through balanced development, through an active relationship with cultural values, through orientation towards values and through humaneness.[19]

Further, Schröder (1992, p.36) understands the theory of "Bildung" in the following way:

> Erudition centred approaches in modern times emphasize the individual's interaction with her surrounding world through [Bildung], the coping with tensions and conflicts, and the self-determination of human beings.[20]

In discussing the concept of *Bildung* Wolfgang Klafki (1986, p.461) puts the emphasis on content. In his critical-constructive understanding of the erudition-centred theory of didactics the leading question is the following:

> With what content and circumstances must young people interact in order to arrive at a state of self-determination and a rational way of life, in humaneness, in mutual recognition, in freedom, happiness, and self-fulfilment?[21]

A general answer within this tradition would be that education should help individuals to develop into independent and mature subjects, i.e. that education should support young people to achieve *Mündigkeit*.
 A key question in this approach is what are the contents of education (*Bildungsinhalt*)? Naturally these contents have been decided by the collective (the community) and are explicated in the curriculum.[22] But how are they chosen? The notion of *Bildungsgehalt* is used in describing this process. A fundamental part of every teacher's work is to analyse the contents of education from the perspective of its educative value, i.e. to analyse the *Bildungsgehalt*. This selection procedure constitutes the kernel of what Klafki calls didactic analysis. This analysis is specifically focused on what qualities of the content are thought of as educational in a certain situation. Klafki (1995, p.21) writes:

> Curriculum designers assume that these contents, once the children and adolescents have internalized and thus acquired them, will enable the young people, in themselves and at the same time in their relation to the world, "to produce a certain order" (Litt) in themselves and at the same time in their relation to the world, to "assume responsibility" (Weniger), and to cope with the requirements of life. The contents of teaching and learning will represent such order, or possibilities for such order, such responsibilities, inevitable requirements and opportunities, and that means at the same time opening up the young people to systems of order (legal, social, moral, etc.), responsibilities (such as human welfare or politics), necessities (such as the mastery of cultural skills, a minimum of vital knowledge, etc.), and human opportunities (e.g. to enjoy and be active in leisure time, for example, in the arts, in the choice of profession, etc.).

When the subject matter is analysed, this analysis should be made from a pedagogical perspective: "[T]his 'matter' is from the very beginning an 'object' seen through a pedagogical lens which a young person's mind is to 'possess': it is in short content of education." (ibid. p.15).
 Klafki calls Otto Willman's work *Didaktik als Bildungslehre* a fundamental step in the history of didactics since the distinction between *Bildungsinhalt* and *Bildungsgehalt* was introduced here (Willman, 1903). For Willman the contents of education comprise "something invisible yet tangible which needs to be grasped if the matter is to be mastered" (Klafki, 1995). He cites Willman's point of view: "From among the whole of an object of instruction, we distinguish its educational substance (*Bildungsgehalt*) and comprehend the latter as those elements of the former [*Bildungsinhalt*] where the subject matter can begin to take root and to be internalized, and on whose retention the value of learning and the practising essentially depends."

Klafki points to Herman Nohl and Erich Weniger as those who came to develop Willman's position. Willman was criticized for representing a kind of objectivism; it was argued that the educational value of the subject matter existed in the content as such. Nohl in turn emphasized that the educational value of a content was to be determined in relation to the subjects that were to be educated and the historical situation within which they live ("a definite, historical-spiritual situation with the past clinging to it and the future opening up before it" Klafki, 1963, p.132). This was identified as the pedagogical criterion (*das pädagogische Kriterium*) by Nohl (1949, p.427):

> Whatever demands are made upon the child by the objective culture and the social relationships, they must tolerate a transformation which proceeds from the question: what is the sense of this requirement in the context of the child's life, for its development and the increase of its faculties, and what potential does the child have for coping with the demands?[23]

Klafki (1963) relies on Weniger (1952) when he develops his view of the historical relativity of education. Weniger's historicity points both backwards in time and towards the future. Klafki's conclusion is that "whatever claims to form the content of education, must at the same time pay heed to the future of the subject of education" (Klafki, 1963 p.133, see also pp.22 f.).

The other fundamental aspect of historicity may be explicated in existential terms; what *meaning* does the content or subject matter have for the individual? An individual is able to make cultural contents their own personal property. Through this process they become a member of a certain culture and carry it further.[24]

Finally the concept of *kategoriale Bildung* must be acknowledged. The point of departure for traditional *objectivistic* or so-called *materiale Bildungstheorien* is the content as such; it is asked what contents of all possible contents of a culture are so valuable that they should be taught. The formal, functional or *subjective* approaches (*formale Bildungstheorien*) again emphasize students' capacities, which are conceived of as possible to develop by means of certain cultural contents. For Klafki (1963, pp.43–44) "categorial education" means that both the cultural and the subjective aspects must be present in order to identify a phenomenon as educative (eruditive):

> By erudition [*Bildung*] we mean every phenomenon in which—through our own experience or through other people's understanding—we become directly aware of the unity of an objective (material) and subjective (formal) entity. Erudition [Bildung] is the opening-up of a concrete and spiritual

reality to one human being—that is the objective or material aspect; but at the same time it [also] signifies the opening-up of this human being to the reality he perceives—that is the subjective or formal aspect in at once both the "functional" and the "methodical" sense . . . Erudition [*Bildung*] is *categorial erudition* in the double sense that a reality has been opened up to him and that, as a result of this, he has himself been opened up to this reality.[25]

To sum up what has been said about the difference between human-science theory of education and the present model thus far.

In contrast to the erudition-centred theory of didactics, the present model took as its point of departure not the content as such but the pedagogical process thus emphasizing the question of intention; towards what do we want to educate? The fundamental idea was to start from the rather general concepts of intention, action and reflection, in terms of pedagogical planning, instruction and evaluation. Klafki's (1995) five questions concerning content would thus fall within the P2 and P3 fields in the model in Fig. 3.2.

One similarity between Klafki's (1963) position and the present school didactic model is that both emphasize the individual teacher's continuous alternation between didactic and methodical analysis, i.e. between analysis of the subject matter and reflection on how education should be carried out in concrete terms (instructional planning). In the 1958 article (*Didaktische Analyse*, here referred to as Klafki, 1995) Klafki clearly proposes a two-step analysis; first didactic analysis, then methodical planning. Later he emphasized the reciprocal relation between didactic analysis and methodical planning.

Conceptually, the present model is not limited to what was previously understood as *Didaktik im engeren Sinne* (didactics in the narrower sense). Rather this model accepts the idea of interdependent relations between intentions, content, method (and media) within a curricular and cultural context. It may thus be understood as part of *Didaktik im weiteren Sinne* and is functionally seen as closer to Klafki's (1985, 1994a) position.

The present model thus has a double function. Firstly, it may be understood as a result of an ontological analysis of the nature and conditions of the intentional TSL process in institutionalized schools. Secondly, by using the model as a conceptual instrument, the teacher is expected to be able not only to analyse the pedagogical reality but is also reminded of what questions require normative as well as prescriptive decisions in the phase of planning teaching. In this sense the model may be used for two purposes—as a research model and as a model for pedagogical reflection.

The present model acknowledges the process as well as the evaluative phase of the pedagogical process. The advantages of acknowledging these parts of the process are several:

- We are able to discuss the intentional and interactive relationship between the teacher and the student;
- The result of the TSL process in terms of learning results can be discussed and related to the teacher's, the student's and the collective's intentions and expectations and finally;
- We better understand how the teacher's pedagogical work is embedded in a cultural context in which the curriculum and the local culture are of fundamental importance.

From the perspective of the present model it is easy to empathize with Wolfgang Klafki's (1976, 1985, 1994) present-day critical-constructive position. The main difference from Klafki's previously held position is that he now tries to unite ideas from the traditional erudition-centred theory of didactics with the critical theory developed by the Frankfurter school. The critical dimension of his position thus relates to the goals of pedagogical activity; this activity cannot be limited to the transfer of selected cultural contents to the next generation. Education must retain the possibility of changing society. By critical Klafki (1993a, p.5) means that the theory of didactics should as far as possible contribute to eliminating barriers to the attainment of values embodied in his model:

> This didaktik aims at enabling children and adolescents to orient themselves towards more self-determination, more co-determination and more solidarity. At the same time it takes the fact that the reality of society and educational institutions does not correspond to this goal seriously ... Therefore, didaktik must ... investigate barriers and the reasons for them that face teachers trying to bring about the above.

By constructive he refers to "the continual reference to practice, the interest in acting, structuring and changing" (ibid. p.5) the educational reality.

In his move towards critical-constructive didactics, Klafki (1976, 1994) emphasizes the role of contents less. Instead the intentional character of teaching is placed to the fore. In this respect the present model is closer to Klafki's (present-day) position compared with the earlier approach.

A difference between Klafki's critical-constructive approach and the present school didactic model is that the aims of education are explicit in the tradition represented by Klafki. The model presented in this study does not take a stand in a similar way with regard to what goals education should aim at. According to this way of reasoning, a descriptive or analytic theory does not necessarily have to formulate what education should aim at. Rather it is claimed that it is reasonable to limit interest to an identification of central dimensions, in order to understand the pedagogical process. This, however, is not to say that a theory of didactics could be value-neutral. But it does not mean that an information-theoretical model (cybernetics) is accepted. There is a position between pure cybernetic and emancipatoric positions.

The problem with accepting a normative perspective is that a didactic approach may be considered an ideological programme which may compete with the ideas expressed in the national curriculum. The scientist thus competes with the political process in society in putting up goals for education. Should a scientist do this? We may, in fact, ask whether such a position would not rule out the democratic process of decision-making? This may be to push the interpretation too far, since a researcher cannot possibly decide that the goals of the research should be realized. But the question must be asked as a matter of principle. Even though we accept that the researcher does not possess the power to decide that their values really should be realized, there is reason to pose an additional question: "What function would an ideological theory of didactics have if its goals were realized, e.g. accepted as the norm for a national curriculum?" Would a normative theory, one can ask, have *any* function in such a situation, i.e. any function that goes beyond a scientific support of an ideological programme? Obviously the critical power of the theory would be eliminated if the values of normative didactics were accepted.

However, Klafki (1985) *does* accept that the teacher works *for* a collective and does not put the teacher above this collective concerning the choice of goals to be realized in the schools. But when he gives the teacher the right to criticize the collective goals he also suggests *what* position the teacher should take in his criticism. Klafki (1985, p.256) writes:

> The general definition of an instructional goal can here be seen in the fact of helping learners to develop their capacity for self-determination and solidarity, one element of which is capacity for co-determination. Self-determination and solidarity include, as constitutive element, rational capacity for discourse, that is, ability to justify and reflect, for developed emotionality and for ability to act, that is, ability to influence actively one's own relationships with natural and social reality in terms of reasoned goalsetting.[26]

As distinct from the school didactic model, Klafki suggests which values should be guiding ones. The school didactic model advocated in this study leaves the question of what the guiding values should be open to the teacher. That this question is left open means that teachers are explicitly required to take a stand; as critical and independent intellectuals, they must themselves decide what position should be taken with regard to value-related questions. The present school didactic model may hopefully function as a thought model or as an instrument in this process, but it does not suggest any solutions (see the later text on descriptive models).

Wolfgang Klafki has presented his thoughts in the form of a scheme for instructional planning (*Perspektivenschema zur Unterrichtsplanung*, 1985, p.215; 1991, p.30). This model is very comprehensive. It is difficult to find anything connected with teaching and learning that would not be included in the model. Here it differs from the present model, which is limited to understanding the TSL process in the institutionalized school.

Functionally the use of that scheme and the present model are identical; and they are thought to be used in the same manner. They do not offer checklists for teachers' planning, rather they are what Klafki calls *Problematisierungsraster*, instruments to investigate educational practice. In other words the model is helpful in making different aspects of this reality visible by asking certain questions. Phenomenologically we may talk of using didactics to structure our pre-scientific pedagogical experiences. The theory may thus help us to specify our noematic aspect of the pedagogical object of our consciousness (Uljens, 1995c).

The process through which a teacher makes a didactic conceptual system his own personal property reminds us of the dialectic relation offered by Klafki's *Kategoriale Bildung*. In this process, the theory of didactics as a conceptual system may remain unchanged; it may be experienced again. To express it differently, one may construct one's experiences a second time with the help of the model. But it is also possible to claim that the teacher's original pedagogical experience remains to some extent unchanged. The evidence for this is that the teacher may change their understanding of the pedagogical reality; a theory used for organizing one's experiences may be abandoned after having been accepted for a while. What makes this possible is the individual's ability to relate an original experience to the new conceptual system. This is one of the main roles educational theory can have for the teacher.

However, even though we may identify a kind of functional similarity between the models, the difference is, as mentioned, a difference concerning normativity. The present model is to be understood as an analytical tool to be used by the teacher (a thought model) as well as to function as a research model. The teacher in his turn decides what values should be realized.

Like Klafki's (1985), the model presented in this study does not discriminate between didactics in the narrow and the wide sense. The choice of goals and contents, as well as the choice of methods and forms of representation, are questions to be considered in relation to each other. Yet the intentionality concerning goals is given a more important role compared with the other dimensions. Thus Klafki's position concerning the primacy of goal decisions is supported. In fact the structure of the present model conceives of intentionality on the individual and on the collective level as a fundamental concept. This means that even though an interdependent relation between the goals, content, methods and media is accepted, the goal of the pedagogical activity is of fundamental importance.[27]

However, the school didactic model presented in this study does not comprise curriculum theory; it is more limited in its approach. Although it is not always easy to clarify how curriculum theory should be defined, it may suffice to say that the present model takes the teachers' perspective into account in investigating institutionalized education.

A final difference is that the school didactic model emphasizes the evaluative phase of teaching. The result of the TSL process is considered important, since teaching cannot guarantee that learning will occur. This is a fundamental reason why the evaluative phase must be included in a model emphasizing teaching and studying as intentional activities.

THE BERLIN MODEL

The school didactic model will be briefly compared with the so-called Berlin model of didactics developed by Paul Heimann and later by Wolfgang Schulz (Heimann, 1962, 1976; Schulz, 1980, 1991). When I speak of the Berlin model, I refer primarily to Paul Heimann's *lerntheoretische Didaktik*, not so much to Schulz's *lehrtheoretische Didaktik* or his *kritische Didaktik*, although there are many similarities between Schulz (1980) and the school didactic model as it is presented in this study.

Generally speaking Heimann (1962) understood didactics as a theory of teaching. His approach included an analysis of the method, media, content and goals of education as well as the socio-cultural and individual conditions for the teaching process. In other words, a broad approach to understanding the TSL process was advocated. According to Blankertz (1987, p.91), the position was partly developed as a reaction against the erudition-centred theory of education already discussed which, among other things, was considered so general that it lacked applications in practice.

The model presented by Paul Heimann, which was later developed on many occasions by Wolfgang Schulz, consisted primarily of two dimensions; (a) a structural analysis (*Strukturanalyse*) and (b) an analysis of the conditions for the teaching process (*Faktorenanalyse, Bedingungsprüfung*) (see Fig. 3.5). The Berlin model was also visualized by Blankertz (1987, p.101).

As the model has been both described and discussed in numerous previous publications and books on didactics, it is not felt to be necessary to describe it in detail here (see Blankertz, 1987; Gundem, 1980;

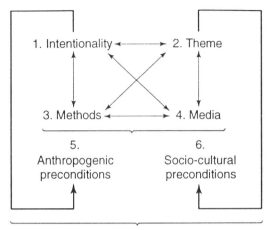

FIG. 3.5. The Berlin model developed by Paul Heimann and Woflgang Schulz presented in accordance with Blankertz (1987, p. 101).

Heimann, 1962, 1976; Jank & Meyer, 1991; and Schulz, 1980). Only the main features of the model will be commented upon, paying special attention to similarities and differences with respect to the model presented in this study.

A very clear way of presenting the fundamental points of departure for this model is the following summary by Heimann (1962):

In instruction [*Unterrich*] the following always takes place:
a) there is someone who has a very definite intention.
b) To achieve this end he brings some matter
c) within the horizon of a definite group of people.
d) He does this in a very definite manner,
e) using very definite aids, which we call media,
f) and he also does this in a quite definite situation.

In other words, in every pedagogical process there is somebody who has a clear intention. With this intention some content or object is established for a special group of people in some way, by using some kind of media, and all this is done in a special situation. Even though neither Heimann nor Schulz explicitly makes use of the notion of school didactics (*Schuldi-*

daktik), it is obvious that their pedagogical models were developed for analysing instruction in institutionalized schools.

In delimiting the object of research, many similar questions are posed in the Berlin model and the school didactic model in this study. Both models emphasize the situation as an important question. The context of the teaching process, i.e. the *Sozialkulturelle Voraussetzungen*, is defined both in terms of classroom situation, school, and wider contemporary socio-cultural context (*der sozialkulturellen Gesamtsituation unserer Zeit*). These levels are also identified as central in the school didactic model. In addition, many other types, levels and aspects of contexts are identified in the school didactic model. Heimann's first level, the classroom level with its social climate, was illustrated in the centre of the school didactic model. The school as context was also clearly pointed out in the visual model. The other contexts were then presented in a separate table and were analysed in terms of an organizational, resource and curricular dimension.

Another feature closely related to one presented in the school didactic model is that the four aspects of the first level of didactic reflection (intention, content, method, media) are interrelated. They cannot be viewed as fundamentally independent of each other; a change in one of them affects the other aspects. The first level of didactic reflection shows that Heimann's model is not limited to a description of the instructional process, or that the method is seen in isolation from the other aspects.

Even though it is admitted that all the aspects mentioned affect each other, intentionality still gets a somewhat different position in relation to the other aspects (content, method, media) in the school didactic model. It is clear that all these four aspects are present in every TSL situation, but so are many others. The reason for the primacy of intentionality in the school didactic model is that through this concept the kernel of teaching is accepted; teaching is seen as a goal-oriented, conscious effort to enable somebody to reach some type of competence. Intentionality also reflects the future orientation of teaching.

In the school didactic model intentionality has both a temporal and a non-temporal dimension. The temporal dimension is emphasized in that the collective dimension always exists before an individual teacher begins to plan a pedagogical situation. Second, there is a temporal difference between planning before and planning during a process. Finally the temporal character is present in the differentiation between the phase of planning, the process and the evaluative phase.

The non-temporal or logical dimension of intentionality is reflected by the structurally defined relations between intentions, contents, methods and media; the teacher's goal-setting is primary with respect to the factors mentioned. Also, in agreement with Klafki, it is not considered possible to deduce norms for educational practice from the accepted goals. Thus a closed normative system is strongly opposed. Even if the school didactic model may be normatively subordinated to the national curriculum, this does not mean that the curriculum must be interpreted as a closed normative system. Subordination does not mean acceptance. It has been clearly pointed out that the teacher may depart from the goal-setting on the collective level. But, unlike Klafki's model, the school didactic model does not show how this departure should be accomplished. A fundamental problem with Klafki's position is thereby avoided; if the collective level were to accept the values advocated by a specific theory of didactics, then that theory would have no function. It would in a sense be tied to the values presented; how could one claim the importance of the criticism of the national system if the values considered important in the topical model are identical with those at the national level? In other words, when a normative model is realized within a specific culture, the critical power of the model ceases to exist. The school didactic model again emphasizes that the individual teacher must load the model with ideological gunpowder. As the school didactic model developed in this study is descriptive in nature, it does not offer goals for education.

Observe however that this is also an ideological position—teachers are given both the freedom and the responsibility to decide how they relate themselves to the values accepted on a collective level. The teachers' value-decisions cannot thus be subordinated to the school didactic model as a didactic model.

The four interrelated aspects are in the school didactic model placed within the fields P1, P2 and P3. A difference with respect to Heimann's model is that the school didactic model emphasizes the importance of acknowledging the four interrelated aspects (intention, content/theme, method, medium) on four different levels (collective, teacher, interactional, student).

Heimann's anthropogenic preconditions, i.e. the psychology of individual learning and development, are partly included within these fields and partly within the dimension called the local cultural context since the educated individuals partly constitute the very culture within which the school functions.

The decision to place learning here emphasizes that the teacher's planning is situated between the collective curriculum and the cultural context on the one hand and the individual's needs and interests on the other; the collective goals exist prior to the individual teacher's planning, and the planning is directed towards a pedagogical meeting with a specific group of students. Naturally the teacher here analyses both how human learning is constituted generally and what this view of learning means for the specific group. A teacher may thus make decisions concerning teaching and study methods on the basis of their understanding of learning and the type of knowledge it may lead to.

It is, in fact, quite common to view the psychology of learning as a basis of the choice of methods of teaching and working, of relevant media, contents and even goals. One could imagine a teacher viewing learning in a hierarchical way similar to Gagné's (1965) typology of learning from simpler to more complex forms. But we should not forget that the relation can be the opposite as well; some of these factors (media, contents, etc) may also affect the teacher's understanding of what the student's learning is about. Limited available resources may also lead to a change of opinion on the part of the teacher as too how the individual is expected to learn some specific items or reach some specific goal. There is thus no simple relation between anthropogenic preconditions and the other factors demanding decisions.

Perhaps one could say that the school didactic model distributes the anthropogenic preconditions over several different fields, while Heimann gives them a very distinct position. In the school didactic model, learning psychology is seen much more in relation to the didactic aspects content and methods of teaching.

Another feature that makes the school didactic model similar to the Berlin model is that both are neutral with respect to explicit goals or values. In neither of the models are the goals of education explicitly formulated. Both models emphasize instead that education in schools occurs in a social and cultural context which largely determines its contents and goals. This also means that the teacher acts under quite specific conditions. The teacher cannot decide upon the goals of the school without considering collective expectations.

The instruments offered by Heimann in this respect are criticism of norms and evaluation of facts and forms of teaching (*Formenanalyse*).[28] The structural similarity between Heimann's two levels and the school didactic model is that both accept a distinction between the analysis of the pedagogical situation and a value-related level concerning decisions on different fields.

According to the school didactic model the normative decisions made by the teacher thus go beyond didactics as theory. These decisions are made on a normative basis (values, political orientation, world view, etc).

However, in the school didactic model a pure positivistic position is avoided by explicitly admitting that certain values lie behind it. For example, one motive for developing this model was to increase the teacher's possibilities of paying attention to the individual student's needs and interests. Such an increase of awareness was thought to be supported by offering the teacher tools in terms of a theory of didactics. The analytical model offered is thus developed for certain purposes but is still

3. A MODEL OF SCHOOL DIDACTICS   111

not committed to specific values to be realized. The teacher may thus reflect conceptually in analysing and planning a pedagogical situation, but becomes a political subject in making the decisions as to what will be taught, towards what goals to strive with the students and how this should be done.

Like every human purposeful activity the development of the school didactic model is also bound to certain values and interests. But still, the model may be called a descriptive model in that it does not suggest what values the teacher or school-system should realize.

As with Heimann, a critical attitude towards norms and values is supported, but the present model naturally does not offer any instruments to evaluate which norms should be followed and which not. Nor does the model as such offer criteria for what methods should be chosen by the teacher in a specific situation.

Instead, a critical attitude towards ideologies means (in the school didactic model), analysing the contents of ideological propositions conceptually and paying attention to what the ideological layer of descriptive propositions looks like. The representatives of an ideology are then identified as those groups in society which have the power to affect the choice of content and the setting of goals in schools (Blankertz, 1987, p.110, see also Bourdieu, 1991, pp.289–293).

The reason behind this position is that the school didactic model aims at being valid for the TSL process in the institutionalized school, which follows a politically and collectively agreed-upon system of goals. Because of this, the socio-cultural context surrounding the school is acknowledged as very important. This dimension thus binds the pedagogical situation to a certain culture. The school didactic model is therefore not understood as a universal theory of education valid for any contemporary culture. It is a culturally and historically regional theory of the TSL process, primarily thought of as being valid for countries following collective curriculums.

A clear difference between the models is that while it appears that Heimann has been oriented towards the education of teachers in developing the conceptual system, this has not been the case in developing the school didactic model.[29] This may be the reason for the difference in how the actual TSL process is emphasized; in the present model the difference between a teacher's planning before a pedagogical situation and during an ongoing process is identified as central. The same argument is valid for evaluation; it is important to emphasize the difference between continuous situated evaluation and evaluation taking place after a finished sequence. The distinction presented also makes it obvious that the teacher reflects during the teaching process itself and that this is something very different from reflection before and after a teaching sequence.

The context of the teaching situation is also more prominent in the present model since it is important to understand under what circumstances a teacher works; the socio-cultural sphere is more developed in the present model compared with Heimann's position.

A DESCRIPTIVE MODEL, A NORMATIVE MODEL, OR BOTH?

It was previously claimed that descriptive theory here refers to the analytic function of a didactic model. Such a conceptual system may be used in order to actualize varying fundamental features of the pedagogical process in order to understand it better and act within it. In fact we may say that it is this analytical function that makes it possible to discuss didactics in terms of theory, not only in terms of ideology or in terms of doctrines guiding pedagogical practice. In other words, a descriptive theory of didactics does not say how teachers should act but it helps teachers to recognize dimensions demanding explicit reflection, decision-making and position-taking. Yet, the actual model itself is not value-neutral even though it is descriptive in nature. The sense in which the model is value-laden is explained in this section.

Firstly, the model is developed for certain purposes; the knowledge interest is to develop a language of didactics that teachers may use as an instrument in order to reflect on their own pedagogical practice (emancipatory knowledge interest, Habermas).

The use of the model is not however limited only to teachers. A researcher may also use the model as a conceptual frame of reference in carrying out empirical research. This means that one and the same model may be used both by practitioners and researchers in education. In this respect the model is a research model, though not a typical one since it is not based on empirical research findings. However, it may be changed on the basis of such findings.

Secondly, the model is value-laden in that it emphasizes the individual student's right to have their needs and interests accepted and satisfied in the school. The idea behind this position is the following. The extent to which teachers may act in line with the student's interests and needs is proportional to the autonomy the teachers have in relation to the collective—if the teacher is considered only as an instrument in the realization of the collective aims, there are less opportunities for the teacher to pay attention to the individual student's interests. In order to make it possible to act as the student's lawyer, the teacher must be seen as relatively autonomous when it comes to goals, contents, methods and evaluation of instruction. In line with this, the student's interests are emphasized as a normative frame for the teacher.

The extent to which the teacher is given the right to decide how the collective goals should be fulfilled partly regulates teachers' possibilities of attending to the students' interests and needs. Increasing freedom for teachers in this respect leads to increasing ability to take the individual's needs into account in the pedagogical process.

In the above-mentioned sense the presented model is value-bound but not necessarily normative; it does not require the teacher to use his freedom in the sense described above. Instead it requires the teacher to reflect on his personal values in relation to the collective curriculum.

It is in fact reasonable to ask whether there would be any merit in developing an explicitly normative model in order to understand the pedagogical process in a school following the national curriculum, as a normative model would only compete with the national curriculum (Kansanen, 1989, p.122).

TWO WAYS OF UNDERSTANDING VALUE-RELATEDNESS IN DIDACTICS

Open and Closed Normative Models

In contrast to closed normative systems, i.e. educative systems or programmes starting from fundamental coherent value systems or a given view of man, open systems are characterized by leaving possibilities open to the teacher, for instance concerning goals (Kansanen, 1989, p.98).

The question then is how "open" is the present model? A totally open system excludes normative decisions from didactics as a science. For example, in cybernetic models normative decisions do not belong to didactics as a science (Blankertz, 1987, p.62).

The problem is then whether a model of didactics can be considered as a scientific model if normative decisions are made within the framework of that model. In other words, can a normative model be scientific? A positive answer to this question must naturally accept normativity as a part of scientific reasoning. A negative answer again would imply that normative decisions do not belong to didactics as a science but e.g. to the philosophy of education (Brezinka, 1978). Yet this does not necessarily mean that philosophy is not science. As long as education is understood as the science of enlightened discussion, the philosophy of education is naturally a science. However, if by philosophy of education we only refer to normative propositions concerning ideals towards which we should strive in education, then it is questionable if it is a science.

But we may also admit a third possibility—normative problems may be accepted within didactics as a science in terms of problems to be solved. Indeed, identifying a problem as normative by nature may very well be done within an analytic model. This does not mean that one must also solve a normative problem within the framework of didactics as science, i.e. that the model identifying the problem would also have to contain the right answers. This is precisely the position of this study; didactics as scientific theory cannot decide on values that some educational system or individual should try to realize. Yet didactics as a science may contain instruments for analysing normative and prescriptive problems within education but not necessarily the standards for deciding whether norms should be accepted or not. In the second part of this study for example, pedagogical implications of human learning will be investigated. This is an example of how prescriptive problems may be dealt with within a descriptive model.

That a descriptive model is pedagogically non-prescriptive does not mean that it is completely value-neutral in every other respect. For example the present model is not neutral when it comes to the teacher's role in relation to the educated individual and the collective.

This position supports the idea that an explicit and reflective process preceding normative decisions is more valuable than a non-reflective and uncritical acceptance of norms. Such a process increases the subject's self-awareness, which in itself is a positive value. It also leads to more conscious decisions on the teacher's part. In Koskenniemi's (1968, pp.223–224; 1978, p.197) terms the teacher becomes a didactically thinking professional. To reflect systematically on one's work may also be conceived of as one version of investigating one's own work (Kansanen, 1993c). As the present model is not purely descriptive or normative, it may be called *a reflective theory of didactics*.

Two Value-dimensions of Didactics

In an analysis of several German schools of didactics, Kansanen (1989, p.134) suggests how these theories could be related to each other. Two axes are suggested; one referring to whether the approaches are normative concerning the goals of education and a second referring to whether they are prescriptive with regards to the methods to be used in practice. This leads to four fields; a theory can be (a) both normative and prescriptive (e.g. normative didactics, human-science pedagogy (Klafki, the Hamburg model), (b) normative but not prescriptive (curriculum development), (c) not normative but prescriptive (cybernetic models, goal-oriented didactics) and finally (d) neither normative nor prescriptive (descriptive didactics).

Using Kansanen's (1989) analysis, the present model belongs to the last group, descriptive didactics. This school didactic model does not contain norms indicating what teachers should teach. Nor is the model

TABLE 3.1.
The school didactic model in relation to (a) values behind the model, and (b) how the descriptive and normative aspects of the model are understood in relation to research and to pedagogical practice.

---

1 Values and motives behind the development of the model
 (a) To develop a conceptual model of didactics valid for the complexity of intentional, interactional, institutionalized, instructional activity as,
 (b) such a model is considered as a useful instrument for teachers by increasing their possibilities of reflecting on:
  • how their pedagogical practice should be organized and carried out, as well as on
  • what values this practice should be based on in relation to the collectively accepted norms
 (c) This (b) in turn helps teachers to take better account of the interests and needs of the individual student.

---

2 The model
The School Didactic Model

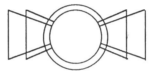

3	*Research*	*Practice*
Descriptive aspect	Conceptual and empirical research within the framework provided by the model.	Analysis of practical pedagogical work. Identifying problems requiring normative and prescriptive decisions.
Normative aspect	Development of teaching advice on the basis of content theory, psychology, philosophy and cultural-historical insights. Applied research in didactics.	Practical pedagogical activity carried out in relation to instructional planning and decisions made concerning content, goals, methods, students, context, etc.

---

prescriptive concerning methods to be used. However, it is not value-neutral. The views represented are summarized in Table 3.1. The structure of the table is as follows.

Section one describes how behind the presented descriptive school didactic model a value-dimension is to be found. At this level my personal understanding of what the model is developed for is explicated. Firstly, in the present case the motive for developing the model was to develop a conceptual language that acknowledges the complexity of the pedagogical process in institutionalized education. Secondly, the point is to support teachers in their development of their own professional activity by making use of the model in question. Thirdly, this in turn is something that could increase teachers' autonomy in relation to the collective level of decision-making which, finally, would increase the teacher's possibility of paying attention to the individual student's needs and interests.

Another possibility offered by the model is that teachers' and researchers' reflection may be compared to some extent. However, many models of professional development and reflective practice have been developed without paying enough attention to what role a theory of education could play in that process. In order to answer that question one must first have an acceptable model of the instructional process. Hopefully the present model can meet the demands made on such a model.

Observe that these values have not been explicitly built into the model even though they have functioned as the driving force in the development of the model. The reason is that an individual researcher cannot be given the right to *decide* what values should regulate education in the society, although the researcher may well participate in such a discussion. The risk involved in the present position is that the model may be used for purposes other than those for which it was developed. The advantage again is that an ideologically locked position is avoided; if the model had certain values built into it and if these values were realized, the consequence would be that there could be no more room for criticism among teachers. Or rather, criticism would have no function as the model's ideology and the content of a collective curriculum coincide.

Thus the structure of this model is valid even though the values of a given community change over time. The tension between the collective level of e.g. the curriculum and the individual teacher can in principle not be neutralized because of the model. Naturally there can exist a perfect harmony between the values or norms represented by an individual teacher and the collective level, but this then results either from the teacher's acceptance of the collective norms or from a change on the collective level which better suits an individual teacher. The school didactic model does not lose its function in either of these cases.

On the second level then the model itself is explicated. This has been done previously and will not be repeated here.

Finally on the third level I have described how both the researcher and the teacher are related to the model with respect to normativity and descriptivity. For both groups a descriptive and normative aspect can be identified. For a teacher the analytic aspect of the model means that they can reflect rationally and systematically on their practical pedagogical activity. The normative and prescriptive aspect refers to the value-laden decisions a teacher makes concerning goals, contents and working methods in relation to e.g. the subjects' needs, the curriculum, resources, personal competence, local context etc. It also includes the practice of teaching and evaluation of both achievements and process.

From the researcher's point of view again, the analytic or the descriptive aspect refers to conceptual and empirical research within the framework of the model and, additionally, to ontological reflection on whether the model does justice to the pedagogical activity in the institutionalized school or not. In fact, in a sense the very construction of this model itself may be categorized as belonging to this field.

The normative aspect of the model from the researcher's perspective concerns applied didactic research aimed at developing e.g. teaching materials or instructional methods. The second part of this study may be seen as applied didactic research; the aim being to analyse pedagogical implications of learning theories.

The Role of Didactic Theory in Teachers' Pedagogical Reflection

The fundamental reason why teachers and researchers may be compared in the sense described above is that there is a similarity with respect to how these groups are related to practice and theory. The point is that individual reflection and learning may, to a certain degree, be compared to the process of scientific research and its way of creating knowledge. This point may be clarified by using David Kolb's (1984) model of experiential learning (see also Jarvis, 1987).

According to Kolb (1984), the individual learning process may be described by a four-step model or circle starting from (a) ordinary everyday experience. The subject is then (b) reflecting on these experiences. The third step (c) is a kind of abstract generalization while the final step (d) consists of new experiences on the basis of the conceptual structure developed.

The important thing here is the third step, abstract generalization. The individual reflects on the sense in which experiences and insights are valid in new situations. However, what is not obvious in Kolb's (1984) model is the relation between the individual subject's structured experience resulting from reflection, and the previously produced body of knowledge within a culture. Among others, Bereiter (1994, p.8) has emphasized the importance of this; the subjectively reflected experience must be related to previously existing collective knowledge in a certain field if this common body of understanding is to be developed. And it is only in relation to this common body of knowledge that individual knowledge gets its profile and meaning.

The individual may turn to previous collective conceptual abstractions (knowledge) in reflecting on private experiences and organize her experiences with the help of this previous knowledge of the field. Using didactic theory in this way, teachers may on the one hand organize their pedagogical experiences, on the other evaluate to what extent the model or other models are useful in structuring their experiences of teaching (see also Chapter 8). If one considers acting as a teacher on the basis of structured reflection, one can say that the teacher uses the actual model as a lens through which new impressions are interpreted.

To my understanding the scientific research process is structurally close to the one described. It is not difficult to point out differences, but the similarities are considered more fundamental. Also, the scientist makes observations, both structured and unstructured. We talk about confirmatory and exploratory research. In other words, the scientist usually interprets observations explicitly in relation to theory, or against previous abstract conceptualizations, and organizes them accordingly. Like the researcher, the teacher may also evaluate in what respect and to what extent the model is useful in handling empirical experience or observations and what consequences different choices have (Koskenniemi, 1978, p.225).

The idea of the similarity between the teacher's and the researcher's way of working with respect to the normative and descriptive aspects gets support when comparing Kolb's (1984) model with Lahdes' (1988) model of didactics and its dimensions. Erkki Lahdes makes a distinction between the dimensions of (a) a descriptive–normative aspect of education and (b) a theory–practice aspect. Lahdes' (1988) model is presented in Fig. 3.6. While Kolb's (1984) and Jarvis' (1987) models are models of an individual's experiences, reflection and conceptualization, Lahdes' (1988) model describes a collective, cultural process of creating knowledge of the educational field. Lahdes (1988) explains that the model may be applied both to the research cycle and also in order to describe the development of the individual teacher. It is not difficult to see the structural similarity between Lahdes' and Kolb's (1984) models. One could say that Lahdes' model may be seen as a development of the general thoughts presented by Kolb for the area of education on a collective level.

Lahdes' (1988) model is more a model of the relations between theory of teaching, practical pedagogical work and research, than it is a theory of the teaching process itself. The model is thus a general model of how educational theory and practice may be related to each other.

It must also be obvious to the reader that the model presented in this study differs fundamentally from the one presented by Lahdes (1988). The model of school didactics in this study is one example of a theory of teaching in Lahdes' model. When Lahdes suggests that teaching advice

3. A MODEL OF SCHOOL DIDACTICS

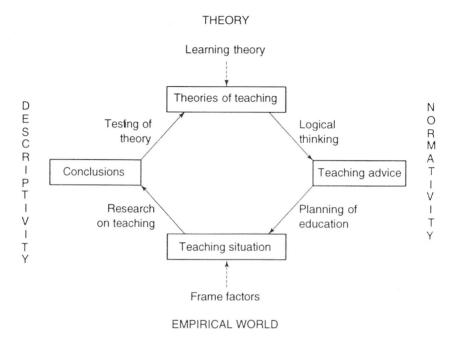

FIG. 3.6. The relation between theory of didactics and pedagogical reality according to Lahdes (1988, p. 160), my translation from Finnish.

may be reached by logical thinking with theory as the point of departure, the position of the present study is that empirical research could be included here also—educational research may deal with the development of instructional strategies. This kind of research is called applied didactic research. It is prescriptive by nature; it aims at prescriptions concerning how a teacher should teach.

The second part of this study explicitly attempts to investigate the pedagogical implications of learning theory within the frames of the descriptive model of didactics presented.

NOTES

1. It is useful to keep in mind the difference between *sociological* research on the development of professions of which the teachers' profession may be viewed as one (at least a semi-profession) and *pedagogical* studies trying to clarify what good teachers' competence consists in.
2. This model or previous versions of it have earlier been presented in Uljens (1993a,b; 1994a,c; 1995a,d,e).

120 SCHOOL DIDACTICS AND LEARNING

3. It is interesting to note how little attention has traditionally been paid to how parents understand or experience the curriculum.
4. It is important to talk about the *teacher's belief* in what the official, collective interpretation of the curriculum is. Teachers thus assume that their understanding of the situation is relevant.
5. See Terhart and Wenzel (1993, pp.12–56) for an overview of how the problem of method is understood among contemporary researchers in the field as well as in the literature in the field.
6. "In Wirklichkeit können methodische Anordnungen immer erst getroffen, Regeln erst empfohlen werden, wenn die didaktischen Fragen entschieden sind. So ist die Methode immer etwas zweites" (Weniger, 1952, p.18).
7. In reflecting on the form of representation, it is necessary to distinguish between the sign (form of representation) and what is signified (content). This is important since the form of the sign (representation) itself often has specific cultural connotations (a text, picture, graph, film etc.).
8. This discussion is continued in Chapter 8.
9. See also the existential phenomenological approach in education developed by Rauhala (1978, 1990) and Lehtovaara (1992).
10. It may be necessary to say that an attempt to capture these different dimensions of the pedagogical situation requires many different empirical research methods.
11. "Der Begriff der Schule ist hierbei im weitesten Sinne gemeint. Neben den staatlichen und privaten Bildungsanstalten sind hierbei schulähnliche Betriebe (Fahrschule, Skischule, Segelschule u.ä.) und der schulmässige Einsatz von Massenmedien (Schulfunk, Schulfilm, Schulfernsehen) eingeschlossen. Alle diese Einrichtungen praktizieren eine institutionalisierte Form des Lehrens und Lernens, also Unterricht." (Schröder, 1992, p.343)
12. "Die wichtigsten Problemfelder der Schulpädagogik sind somit:
 – die Theorie der Schule, einschliesslich schulrechtlicher und schulorganisatorischer Fragen, sowie Probleme der Gestaltung des Schullebens und der Schulhygiene,
 – die Theorie der Unterrichts, einschliesslich der Probleme des Curriculums, der Unterrichtsformen und -prinzipien, sowie der Unterrichtstechnologie und Mediendidaktik,
 – die Unterrichtspraxis unter besonderer Berücksichtigung einer lernwirksamen Unterrichtsplanung und Gestaltung, einschliesslich der Effektivitätskontrollen." (Schröder, 1992, p.311, bold-faced printing in the original not marked here)
13. cf. Lahdes (1969, 1986) and Harbo and Kroksmark (1986).
14. "Curriculum theory" refers to models or theories explaining how curriculums are constructed, i.e. why it is that we have such things as curriculums and why they look the way they do. Curriculum theory also covers how curriculums function in regulating education.
15. "1. Ein *didaktisches Modell* ist ein erziehungswissenschaftliches Theoriegebäude zur Analyse und Modellierung didaktischen Handelns in schulischen und nichtschulischen Handlungszusammenhang.
 2. Ein didaktisches Modell stellt den Anspruch, theoretisch umfassend und praktisch folgenreich die Voraussetzungen, Möglichkeiten und Grenzen des Lehrens und Lernens aufzuklären.
 3. Ein didaktisches Modell wird in seinem Theoriekern in der Regel einer wissenschaftstheoretischen Position (manchmal auch mehreren) zugeordnet." (Jank & Meyer, 1991, p.92)
16. The English translation of the questions is cited from Klafki (1995). For a German version see Klafki (1958; 1963, pp.126–153).
17. Klafki writes: "The second step of instructional planning, methods planning, can only

proceed from didactic analysis. Methods are concerned with the 'how' of teaching, more precisely with the paths the children and the contents ... can follow for a fruitful encounter between the two to be achieved. This interpretation of method planning clearly shows its dependence on didactic reflection." (1995, p.28)

18. It is evident that the concept of *Bildung* belongs to the most complex German educational concepts. This is not because a certain definition of it would be difficult to understand. Rather the complexity results from many parallel interpretations or definitions of it. Therefore it is out of the question to include a description of the varieties of this concept in the present study. Suffice it to say that this would require an analysis of the conceptual systems developed by Wilhelm von Humboldt (1767–1835), Johann Heinrich Pestalozzi (1746–1827), F. D. E Schleiermacher (1768–1834) and J. F. Herbart (1776–1841).

19. "• Dynamik (durch das Adjektiv 'wachsend'), mit dem Hinweis, dass Bildung nicht abschliessbar ist und nie ein verfestigter Endzustand sein kann,
    • Beteiligung (durch 'Teilhabe'), wobei die Teilhabe als Partizipation an den Grundeigenschaften des Seins etwas relativ Dauerhaftes und Mehr als gelegentliche Teilnahme ist,
    • kulturelle Identität (durch 'wachsende Teilhabe an der Kultur'), wobei ein Zugehörigkeitsgefühl und -bewusstsein an der Kultur gemeint ist,
    • Zielorientierung (gesetzt als 'Persönlichkeit'), gesehen in einem Reifegrad der entwickelten Individualität, wobei sich Persönlichkeit auszeichnet u.a. durch ausgewogene Entfaltung, durch lebendige Beziehung zu den Kulturwerten und durch Orientierung an Werten und durch Humanität." (Henz, 1991, pp.126ff.)

20. "Bildungstheoretische Ansätze der neueren Zeit betonen die Ausenandersetzung des Menschen mit seiner Mitwelt durch Bildung, das Ertragen von Spannungen und Wiedersprüchen und die Selbtsbestimmung der menschlichen Person." (Schröder, 1992, p.36)

21. "Mit welchem Inhalten und Gegenständen müssen sich junge Menschen auseinandersetzen, um zu einem selbsbestimmten und vernunftgeleiteten leben in Menschlichkeit, in gegenseitiger Anerkennung und Gerechtigkeit, in Freiheit, Glück and Selbsterfüllung zu kommen?" (Klafki, 1986, p.461).

22. "From among the wealth of the conceivable contents yielded by our civilization, certain contents or thematic areas have been selected as contents of education (*Bildungsinhalte*)." (Klafki, 1995, p.17)

23. Nohl's translation as cited by Klafki (1995).

24. Since this point is crucial, Weniger's view will be cited at length here. Weniger claims that the individual through meeting with different parts of a culture is able to make this content their own "property" without destroying the content as such: "Sie sind sein geistiges Eigentum geworden, wie man dann bildlich sagen darf, sie gehören zu ihm, und es ist ja die Eigentümlichkeit des Geistigen, das es so etwas gibt: ein in sich geschlossenes, selbständiges Gebilde wie eine Sonate, ein Geschichtliches Menschenleben, ein Gedicht, eine Kulturepoche ... kann ganz von einem Menschen ergriffen und besessen werden und bleibt doch, was es ist, bleibt unverbraucht und selbständig. Aber für den durch dieses Gebilde 'Gebildeten' haben ist es sein Bildungsgut geworden, er hat die in ihm verborgenen Werte als 'Bildungswerte' im Gang seiner Bildung erfahren, er besitzt sie" (Weniger, 1952, p.487).

25. "Bildung nennen wir jenes Phänomen, an dem wir—im eigenen Erleben oder im Verstehen anderer Menschen—unmittelbar der Einheit eines objektiven (materialen) und eines subjektiven (formalen) Momentes innewerden. Bildung ist Erschlossensein eines dinglichen und geistigen Wirklichkeit für einen Menschen—das ist der objektive oder materiale Aspekt; aber das heisst zugleich: Erschlossenein dieses Menschen für dieses seine Wirklichkeit—das ist der subjektive oder formale Aspekt zugleich im 'funktiona-

len' wie im 'methodischen' Sinne.... Bildung ist kategoriale Bildung in dem Doppelsinn, dass sich dem Menschen eine Wirklichkeit 'Kategorial' erschlossen hat und dass eben damit er selbst ... für diese Wirklichkeit erschlossen worden ist." (Klafki, 1963, pp.43–44)

26. "Die generelle Zielbestimmung des Unterrichts wird hier darin gesehen, den Lernenden Hilfen zur Entwicklung ihrer *Selbstbestimmungs-* und *Solidaritätsfähigkeit*, deren eines Moment Mitbestimmungsfähigkeit ist, zu geben. Selbstbestimmungs-und Solidaritätsfähigkeit schliessen, als konstitutive Momente, rationale Diskursfähigkeit, d.h. Fähigkeit zu Begründung und Reflexion, entwickelte Emotionalität und Handlungsfähigkeit, d.h. die Fähigkeit ein, auf die eigenen Beziehungen zur natürlichen und gesellschaftlichen Wirklichkeit im Sinne begründeter Zielsetzungen aktiv einzuwirken." (Klafki, 1985, p.256)

27. Klafki (1985, p.259) writes: "Primacy of goal-decisions in relation to all other decisions in teaching (Unterricht) means: both decisions about *what* in each case and in which perspective some topic is to be the theme of teaching, or rather: what emerges in the process of teaching as themes in perspective, and also decisions about methods and means of instruction, further the evaluation of the significance of the topical socio-culturally mediated 'anthropogenic' as well as institutional preconditions for instruction can only be justified on the basis of the instructional goal-setting."

28. See Blankertz (1987, p.105) for a criticism of the division between norms and facts.

29. I have argued elsewhere (Uljens, 1995e) that how to make use of didactics in teacher education is a separate problem. Whether teacher education takes place at a university or not makes a fundamental difference as to how theory of didactics can be treated. The "didactics of didactics" or "the didactics of education as a scientific discipline" within teacher education is a problem in its own right.

II SCHOOL DIDACTICS AND PEDAGOGICAL IMPLICATIONS OF LEARNING THEORY

4 Analysing Learning Theory—Its Aim and Design

INTRODUCTION

The aim of the second part of this study is to investigate the cognitivist theory of learning with respect to its pedagogical implications. This part of the study is to be conceived as a clarification of the presented pedagogical model; if pedagogical practice aims at affecting an individual's possibilities of reaching competence through the process of learning, then it is reasonable to expect that the theory of didactics recognizes the problem of learning.

In the descriptive model presented earlier, learning theory is accepted as having a prescriptive function. The idea is as follows: Firstly, teachers' knowledge of human learning (learning theory) may play a part in pedagogical practice as a teacher may reflect analytically on what it means to attain some specific competence. Then, such reflection may influence the teacher's decisions on how they organize, carry out and evaluate the TSL process. In doing so the teacher reflects analytically and acts in a prescriptive fashion; "if acquiring competence 'X' means 'Y', then one should do 'Z' in order to facilitate the reaching of that competence". Secondly, for the exact reason presented above it is important to carry out didactic research on what kind of pedagogical implications different theories of learning have.

THE SCHOOL DIDACTIC MODEL AND THEORY OF LEARNING

It was claimed that learning theory is often understood as having a prescriptive function according to the type: "if human learning is constituted in the form of 'x', then teaching must proceed in accordance with this". Models of teaching solely based upon such reasoning were criticized as being too narrow in their approach. Yet it is clear that every theory of teaching must relate to human learning in one way or another. The question then is what role learning theory has in the descriptive model developed in this study.

The general position adopted here is that we may investigate pedagogical implications emanating from learning theory within the frames of the present school didactic model. Prescriptive pedagogical propositions may thus be developed within the framework of an otherwise analytic model. By letting the presented didactic model frame the present analysis, it is obvious that the development of prescriptive principles on the basis of psychology only forms a limited part of didactic research. It also clearly shows that the prescriptive principles developed should not be mixed up with the theory of didactics.

When learning theories are investigated in order to discover the implications of a certain approach, this may be called descriptive research in didactics. Then, recommending methods and applying such recommendations will constitute prescriptive, value-bound activity.

When didactics is considered the conceptual frame for the TSL process, it means that learning is problematized to the extent that this is reasonable from a didactic point of view. In other words, we should not ask what the implications of learning theory for pedagogical practice are unless we have an idea of how pedagogical reality is constituted in the first place, and how this reality should be approached scientifically. This means that we can approach learning theory from several different perspectives within didactics. For example, we could ask whether learning theory can help us with the problem of choosing contents in education; we may also consider what view of mankind different theories represent and then decide whether this view is consistent with our educational values. Psychology of perception and cognition may also be helpful when we have to decide how the educational content is to be represented in pedagogical situations. The point of this reasoning is to show that by starting from didactic theory, by subordinating psychology to education, we use pedagogical problems to guide us in turning to other disciplines.

It is, however, important to remember that methodical or instructional advice based on psychology cannot be limited to instructional techniques or methods expected to be used by the teacher. An explication of the nature of human knowledge represented by learning theory is also relevant. The reason is simply that the teacher must be able to identify changes in an individual's competence in different areas in order to proceed with his work.

Psychological Theory and Values. It appears at first sight as if there were a fundamental difference between developing teaching methods on the basis of ethical values and on that of psychological theory; advice developed on the basis of learning theory seems to be more value-neutral than that developed on the basis of ethical norms. However, one should not forget that learning theories are also ideological in many respects (Sampson, 1981). If we emphasize the values lying behind psychological theory, then the relation between psychological theory and teaching methods is the same as between normative philosophy and methods. The fundamental difference is, however, that psychological theory is developed as empirical science, which gives it an additional dimension compared with pure normative, ethically based propositions.

Pedagogical Decisions and Learning

From the perspective of practical pedagogical activity, the role of learning is that a teacher's understanding of learning and the results of learning may be seen as an aspect of their pedagogical reflection. This understanding is assumed to be important to the teacher's practical activity.

More specifically we can say that in planning the pedagogical process in advance, in carrying it out as well as in reflecting on it afterwards, teachers make prescriptive and normative decisions. Some of these decisions depend on the teacher's understanding of learning. This means that conclusions based on analytical reflection on the nature of human learning in some specific domain of knowledge may be used in a prescriptive sense when teaching.

The impact of teachers' knowledge of learning on their teaching is not, however, self-evident. Bannister (1982) argues that it is difficult to see a difference in teaching methods used in an average psychology department compared with other university departments (like those of history, geography, biology etc.). This interpretation is widely supported (see Desforges, 1985, for an overview). Thus, simple knowledge about human learning does not make an individual a good teacher. Nor is it likely that only conceptual insights into pedagogically prescriptive principles worked out on the basis of learning theory will make anybody an excellent teacher. How this kind of knowledge develops among student teachers during pre-service teacher education as well as during a teacher's professional career is a problem of its own. Similarly the question of how to arrange successful teacher education is a problem apart (i.e. the didactics of didactics) and will not be dealt with in this study.

128   SCHOOL DIDACTICS AND LEARNING

A specific view of learning is always related to parallel decisions concerning other factors. In planning a specific pedagogical operation, a teacher pays attention simultaneously to a large number of questions (the curriculum, individuals, resources, personal competence, context etc.). A single instructional principle developed on the basis of learning theory is much more limited; it constitutes only one of the many questions a teacher must acknowledge in their planning. It should also be observed that each and every learning theory admits of many different types of teacher activities and working methods. It may even be the case that very few—or no—teaching activities are typical of some specific learning theory. Therefore it is relevant to look at how the different pedagogical decisions a teacher must make are related to different theories of learning. In other words we may ask: "How are pedagogical decisions concerning intentions, contents, methods and media in the pedagogical process related to learning theory?"

Learning theory is not to the fore in the descriptive model developed. The reason for this "hidden" role of learning theory is that teaching as a phenomenon is not logically dependent on learning; a learner does not necessarily have to reach a certain insight in order to say that teaching has occurred. It was also concluded in Chapter 2 that the individual learner's study activity is not always successful in influencing the learning process so that desired results will be reached.

Still, if there were not such a phenomenon as learning, both teaching and studying would be quite meaningless. Only in this respect are teaching and studying dependent on learning; or rather, teaching and studying are meaningful activities because of this human capacity to change.

The next question is how learning should be approached from a pedagogical perspective. The point of departure is that as teaching is aiming at supporting the studying–learning process and since it is necessary to evaluate the results of the TSL process, the process and the result of learning are identified as the two fundamental aspects of learning. It is also hard to imagine a theory of learning that would not be explicit with regard to these two questions.

The question is thus how the process and the result of learning are related to the pedagogical decisions a teacher must make. The scheme presented below relates the process and the result of learning to pedagogical questions requiring decisions by the teacher (i.e. concerning goals, theme, method, media) in planning, carrying out and evaluating the teaching (Fig. 4.1).

In short, the scheme suggests the following. First, it indicates that the method of teaching is closely connected with the learning process. The motive is that even though learning always has a content, intentional teaching tries to govern the learner's study process, through which an

4. ANALYSING LEARNING THEORY   129

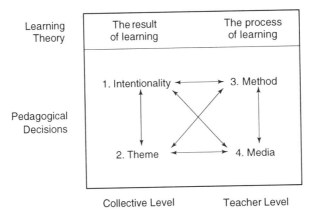

FIG. 4.1. The interdependent relation between pedagogical decisions concerning intentions, theme, method, and media, in relation to the learning process and learning result and in relation to decisions made on the collective level and the teacher level.

individual's understanding of the content changes. Teaching methods as such can never guarantee that a result will be reached, though teaching intends to influence the studying–learning process.

Second, the results of learning are often evaluated by measuring students' achievements (a) in learning in some field of knowledge and (b) in relation to certain goals. In Fig. 4.1 this is indicated by placing educational intention and theme (content) close to the result of learning (on the left side of the figure).

It must, however, be said clearly that questions concerning the process of learning may also be related to the educational intentions and the theme. For example, ethical values may tell us not to use methods of indoctrination in teaching. Second, the learning process may differ in learning different types of items. Further, the result of learning may also be discussed in relation to the methods and media used (the evaluative process may be seen as belonging to the methods of teaching).

Finally, the figure shows that the pedagogical intentions and content dealt with are primarily decided upon a collective level. The methods and media of the teaching process, on the other hand, are traditionally controlled by the individual teacher. But again, the teacher also makes continuous decisions concerning the choice of content and goal. Perhaps one could say that while the collective level is ultimately responsible for the *Bildungsinhalt* (the content of education), the individual teacher is ultimately responsible for seeking the relevant *Bildungsgehalt* (the educative aspect of the content). In the same sense the collective level interferes with the teaching methods used. Legislation, for example, regulates the teacher's freedom in this respect.

I have tried to show that the process and result of learning can be related to the fundamental pedagogical problems requiring decisions by the teacher. Hopefully the model above has not oversimplified the relations.

The primary focus of this study is on questions concerning the *content* and *method* of teaching in relation to theories about the process and result of learning. Focusing on method and content also means that the questions of educational objectives are not analysed here. Analysing pedagogical objectives or intentions in relation to psychological theory could mean, for example, focusing attention on the ideological dimension of psychological theory. A second restriction is that no specific attention is paid to the question of media.

We are now ready to take a second step in the development of the design of the empirical study.

EPISTEMOLOGICAL AND ONTOLOGICAL INQUIRIES AS THE INSTRUMENTS OF ANALYSIS

As we have seen, we may reflect on learning theory both in terms of the process and the result of learning if we are interested in pedagogical implications of learning psychology. Both questions may have pedagogical implications with respect to decisions concerning content and method.

These two questions concerning learning may now be answered by investigating how a theory of learning explains (a) what is meant by representing, possessing or exhibiting some kind of competence, knowledge, insight or skill (the result of learning) and (b) how changes in human competence should be described (the process of learning).

These two questions may also be expressed in terms of problems within the philosophy of mind. Two questions are relevant in this respect. They are concerned with epistemological and ontological problems (Table 4.1).

The Epistemological Problem

The term epistemological problem refers in this study to how the relation between the content of awareness and external reality is explained. This problem is sometimes identified with the question dealing with the experience of the existence of outer reality. However, it should not be confused with the metaphysical question concerning the nature of

TABLE 4.1
Summary of the Mind–World Relation and Mind–Brain Relation

Problem	Ontological problem	Epistemological problem
Relation	Mind–Brain	Mind–World
	The content of awareness and its relation to physiology	The content of awareness and its relation to outer reality
Question	"What language is suitable in describing conceptual knowledge?"	"What is the relation between conceptual knowledge and 'outer reality'?"

external reality as such, independently of human experience of it. In this study the epistemological problem refers to what an individual is aware of when he is said to have conceptual knowledge of something, and how the relation between the individual and the world changes during learning. Awareness refers in this study to the phenomenological dimension of the individual's mental life, i.e. what we as individuals claim to conceive as the content of our consciousness and to which we have access by reflecting on our experiences, in short our phenomenal experience. However, instead of talking about the awareness–world problem or of the consciousness–world problem, the frequently used expression mind–world problem is chosen here.

Traditionally two alternatives have been recognized: reality as such or reality as perceived (see Uljens, 1994b, pp.33–48). This first problem is thus concerned with how the content of an individual's awareness refers to the reality outside the awareness. We can also ask how outer reality is perceived by an individual or how we explain the arousal of different kinds of contents of the awareness. Because of this the epistemological problem may be called the mind–world problem. This problem is most extensively debated in the history of philosophy. Traditionally it is connected both to intentionality and epistemology. One of the main questions has been whether a subject is aware of external reality as such or only aware of the content of his own awareness. Related problems are how one can decide whether an understanding of something is true or false, i.e. the classical epistemological problem, and how the relation between the individual and the world should be explained when an individual's conception of the world changes.

The Ontological Problem

The ontological problem of awareness refers, in this study, to how we should describe the content of awareness, i.e. in what terms we should express ourselves with regard to the content of mind. Regardless of what we assert about what an individual is aware of—perceived reality or external reality—we have to decide how we are going to describe human awareness with respect to (a) the content of human awareness and (b) changes in this awareness.

In the philosophy of mind there are many subquestions within this field (qualia, unconsciousness, etc.). In the present context we actualize only one question, namely the question of how conceptual knowledge should be described. The ontological question concerning how we should describe the content of mind is also identified as the methodological problem or the mind–body problem in the literature. Here we use the expression ontological mind–brain problem. This principally concerns whether one should talk about the content of the human awareness on a phenomenological (experiential), a representational–computational, or a physiological–neurological level.

In dealing with the ontological problem, a distinction can be made between different types of dualistic explanations (substance dualism, emergent dualism, interactionist property dualism) and monistic explanations (idealism, different versions of materialism). Dualistic conceptions say that awareness must be considered as an entity which cannot be reduced to physiological processes of the brain or be explained by some other kind of physical system. Materialistic conceptions are reductionist in this sense (Uljens, 1994b, pp.49–69).

The relation between these two problems is as described in Table 4.1.

Still another way of expressing the relations between the ontological mind–brain and the epistemological mind–world problems is shown in Fig. 4.2.

Figure 4.2 indicates three relations, of which two reflect the problems

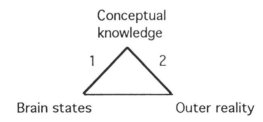

FIG. 4.2. The ontological mind–brain problem (1) and the epistemological mind–world problem (2).

described in the present study; (1) the ontological mind–brain problem and (2) the epistemological mind–world problem. The relation between brain states and outer reality is not the explicit object of our analysis but will be dealt with to the extent that it appears relevant. Both external reality and the brain are often thought of as existing in terms of matter. This is the reason why we may find dualistic and monistic explanations of both problems.

Philosophy of Mind and Learning

We have previously related the process and the result of learning to the pedagogical level of reflection. Now I relate the process and the result of learning to the epistemological and ontological problems discussed above.

Four relations between learning theory and the philosophy of mind are considered central. These relations (A–D) are clarified in Fig. 4.3. It shows how the chosen problems in the philosophy of mind are thought to be related to the process and result of learning.

Understanding the Process and the Result of Learning in Terms of the Epistemological Problem

The psychological question of learning is connected with the epistemological question of what it is to know something. If knowing is to be conscious of something in a specific way, and learning is about changes in this consciousness of something, then there is a clear connection between learning and epistemology (Bechtel, 1988, p.2; Goldman, 1990, p.30; Uljens, 1992a, pp.103 ff.). One could assume that every theory of

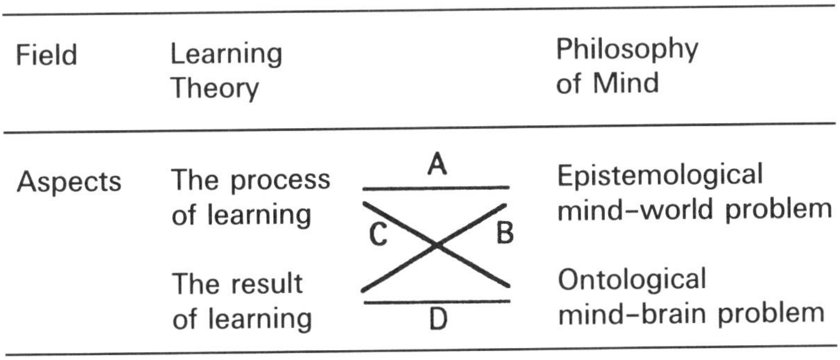

Field	Learning Theory		Philosophy of Mind
Aspects	The process of learning	A C✕B	Epistemological mind–world problem
	The result of learning	D	Ontological mind–brain problem

FIG. 4.3. The process and the result of learning related to the epistemological and ontological problems.

learning implicitly or explicitly starts from a specification of what knowing is, so as to make it possible to talk about what happens when changes occur in this knowing. This is not to say that the epistemological problem is to be made dependent on the psychological problem of reaching knowledge. The reason is simple—a student can acquire false knowledge after having been engaged in a reflective learning process. The context of discovery should thus not be mixed up with the context of justifying knowledge claims (Reichenbach, 1938). Yet a theory of learning cannot ignore the nature of the knowledge reached. In this respect I agree with Taba (1966, p.36) when she claims that "while processes of thought are psychological and hence subjected to psychological analysis, the product and content of thought must be assessed by logical criteria and evaluated by the rules of logic."

Since it seems useful to discuss learning based on what it is to know something, we have moved into the area of the philosophy of mind. We can call the field discussed above epistemological, i.e. concerned with how one should explain what it means when a person is said to be aware of something.

The Process of Learning in Terms of the Epistemological Problem

This first aspect of the epistemological problem concerns how the relation between an individual's psychological reality and the world changes during the process of learning. The process of learning is thought to result in knowledge about something in the world, or, differently expressed, in a qualitative shift in understanding something. This aspect of learning may be dealt with from an epistemological perspective.

The Result of Learning in Terms of the Epistemological Problem

When an individual has reached knowledge of something, precisely what is it that they are aware of? Is it something in external reality or something which is embraced in awareness? When we say that we possess knowledge of something, what is this something? Traditionally, various idealist or realist answers are given to this question.

Pedagogical Relevance

From a pedagogical perspective the two problems (above) are crucial, as the aim of pedagogical activity is to support the development of the learner's understanding of the surrounding reality or competence to act in it. More specifically the question is how the teacher should structure a specific content for pedagogical purposes in order to support the individual's learning. Also, when students' knowledge or insights are being evaluated, the relation between the logical structure of the content is often compared with how the content is psychologically structured by the individual.

Understanding the Process and Result of Learning in Terms of the Ontological Problem

When we want to talk about a change in human understanding, i.e. the learning process, we must be able to describe the content of awareness, assuming that learning has something do do with the change in this awareness. The ontological problem within the philosophy of mind offers us an approach to discussing how we should describe the content of awareness and changes in this awareness.

When considering how this problem has been answered in the history of philosophy, we cannot avoid meeting the mind–body problem (or as it is called here the mind–brain problem). It has been asked whether it is possible for mental processes and states of awareness to be expressed, for example, in neurological terms or whether a phenomenological terminology should be used (see Uljens, 1994b).

The ontological mind–brain problem is therefore considered as an instrument in dealing with how the content of awareness should be described. This problem is a fundamental one to be answered by every theory of learning.

The Process of Learning as an Ontological Problem

Assuming that learning is related to a change in an individual's awareness (whatever a subject is or may be aware of), the question is how we should describe that change.

The Result of Learning as an Ontological Problem

The final question is: What language should be used to express what a person is aware of when that person is said to know something or to be aware of something? This is naturally related to the previous problem concerning how we should describe a change in this awareness.

Pedagogical Relevance

The language in which we discuss a mental state is considered pedagogically relevant since this language gives us the instrument for describing changes in human understanding. When we are able to describe changes, we are also ready to discuss how it is possible, by pedagogical means, to support and evaluate changes. By such a language we are also able to evaluate to what extent, or in what respects, individuals have reached an intended goal or the intended knowledge.

Finally, as teaching is intended to support learning, and learning is seen as something that the individual is able to influence by studying, it would be interesting to know whether a teacher really *can* influence the individual's learning processes as such, i.e. not only to support or affect study activities.

The Design of the Study

In a condensed form the two problems of this part of the study can be expressed in terms of the following questions:

1. What position does the cognitivist approach to learning represent with respect to the epistemological mind–world problem and the ontological mind–brain problem?
2. What are the pedagogical implications of cognitivist learning theory like, in the light of an epistemological and ontological analysis?

In the procedure described above we have used a didactic model as a general frame of reference in order to approach and investigate learning theory.

In the descriptive model developed, the problem of learning is subordinated to the pedagogical decisions that have to be made in planning, carrying out and evaluating the pedagogical process. In other words, the extent to which the theory of learning plays a role in the pedagogical process is spelled out by the didactic theory. The school didactic model is thus used as a research model in the second part of the present study.

By using the traditional didactic triangle we may express the focus of this part of the study as shown in Fig. 4.4.

Firstly, the epistemological problem regarding the process and result of learning may be seen in terms of how the relation between the individual student and the content is specified (1). Secondly, the ontological question concerns how the process and the result of learning should be described on the individual level (2). Thirdly, the second part of the empirical analysis is focused on the pedagogical implications related to the previous two problems (3a, 3b).

The epistemological mind–world problem and the ontological mind–brain problems are displayed in Fig. 4.5 in relation to learning theory and pedagogical decisions.

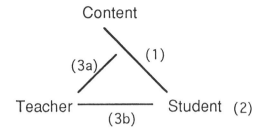

FIG. 4.4. The traditional didactic triangle indicating the investigated relations in the study. (1) The epistemological problem in terms of how the relation between the individual and the content is specified with respect to the process and result of learning, (2) the ontological problem indicating how the process and result should be described on the individual level and, (3a) and (3b) the pedagogical implications related to the previous specifications.

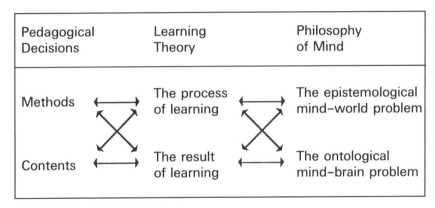

FIG. 4.5. The overall design for the analysis of pedagogical implications of learning theory based on an analysis of learning on the level of the philosophy of mind.

Starting from the descriptive model, methods and content were previously considered two important aspects in understanding the pedagogical process. Like many other pedagogical questions, these two are also related to the process and the result of learning in different ways.

The analysis of how learning is understood within cognitivism required instruments that were offered by the philosophy of mind. The motive for choosing that level of analysis was that every learning theory specifies, explicitly or implicitly, what an individual is aware of in having conceptual knowledge and also how this awareness should be described.

Using Popper's terminology, the attention of this study is first focused on World 2, i.e. how the psychological reality should be described (the ontological mind–world problem), and further how this reality is to be understood with respect to World 1 objects, in this case brain physiological processes. Second, we turn to the relation between World 2 and World 3, i.e. how the psychological reality is related to the logical structure of some subject matter within an instructional context. Observe that as these World 3 objects (cultural products) are manifested in World 1 objects (physical things), the epistemological mind–world problem similarly concerns the relation between World 2 and World 1 objects.

Having defined how cognitivism may be characterized with respect to the epistemological and ontological problems (Chapter 6), we are ready to confront the pedagogical implications of cognitivist learning theory (Chapter 7). In Chapter 7 we try to utilize the results from Chapter 6 in identifying pedagogical implications of cognitivism.

The design of this study allows us to approach the problem of learning from a didactic perspective as the process and the result of learning have been motivated by the pedagogical decisions a teacher makes. Having analysed learning theory on the level of the philosophy of mind we move back to the level of prescriptive pedagogical reflection. Here we indicate how previously presented pedagogical implications can be organized and discussed in terms of the analysis carried out.

An important dimension of the analysis is how the chosen instruments of analysis function in organizing pedagogical implications of learning theory within a didactic frame of reference.

5 The Object of Analysis—Cognitivist Learning Theory

INTRODUCTION

The aim of this chapter is to present the approach to research on human learning that will be investigated with respect to its pedagogical implications, namely cognitivism. Why, then, has this approach been chosen from among the range of existing approaches including ecological psychology, gibsonianism and constructivism, phenomenography and cultural–historical theory? The factors directing the choice of approach have been the following.

First, cognitivism is a well-established school of thought within research on learning and related issues. Various psychological problems have been investigated from several perspectives; there is research on language development, problem solving, attention, deductive thinking, memory, decision making, perception and, more recently, learning etc.

Second, cognitivism is a contemporary approach, framing a huge amount of empirical research.

Third, there has been empirical research both on learning and instruction within the cognitivist paradigm.

However, all these criteria hold true for other approaches which have been mentioned; any one of them could have been chosen instead of cognitivism. The ultimate reason why cognitivism was chosen is that it represents mainstream research on learning today. It is a widely accepted view of human cognition and, as has been said, is used internationally as a framework for a great deal of empirical research. Even though the approach is severely criticized, it is well-known and widely accepted. In relating the theory of didactics to learning, it was considered wise to analyse a widely recognized approach. In addition, as the adopted instruments of analysis are not usual in educational psychology, it is reasonable that the object of analysis should be familiar.

It should clearly be stated that even though the object of analysis of this part of the study is cognitivist theory of learning, this does not mean that the theory as such is supported by me personally. In fact I disagree with most of the fundamental assumptions of cognitivist learning theory. Therefore this school of thought serves only as an object of analysis in this study. As the main idea of this book is to explicate the relation between theory of didactics and learning this choice was considered reasonable, although I am perfectly aware that some readers may classify me as an outdated representative of cognitivist learning theory. I should say that I have dealt with contextual issues of cognition and learning in other publications (e.g. Uljens & Myrskog, 1994; Mertaniemi & Uljens, 1994).

THE COGNITIVIST APPROACH

The general framework dominating contemporary research within cognitive psychology is the information-processing framework. The framework is typically accepted by the cognitivist view of human mental life (Winne, 1987, p.499). According to Eysenck and Keane (1991, p.9) this framework may be presented as follows:

- People are viewed as autonomous, intentional beings who interact with the external world;
- The mind through which they interact with the world is a general-purpose, symbol processing system;
- Symbols are acted on by various processes which manipulate and transform them into other symbols which ultimately relate to things in the external world;
- The aim of psychological research is to specify the symbolic processes and representations which underlie performance on all cognitive tasks;
- Cognitive processes take time, so that predictions about reaction times can be made if one assumes that certain processes occur in sequence and/or have some specifiable complexity;
- The mind is a limited-capacity processor having both structural and resource limitations;
- This symbol system depends on a neurological substrate, but is not wholly constrained by it.

Cognitivism can thus be characterized by the fact that thinking in terms of describable processes is taken to be the very model for the most important forms of mental life. Intelligent behaviour is also explained in terms of cognitive processes (Haugeland, 1978, 1985; Hautamäki, 1988). Many cognitivist assumptions are accepted by contemporary cognitive science. This is evident from Cummins' (1989, p.19) statement: "Cognitive science is founded on the empirical assumption that cognition . . . is a natural and relatively autonomous domain of inquiry". This "makes it possible for cognitive science to ignore . . . such mental phenomena as moods, emotions, sensations, and . . . consciousness" (ibid. p.19). In this respect cognitivism is identical with mentalism.

Sometimes this internal cognitive system is thought to function in a manner very similar to a person who is analysing, computing or making inferences. In cognitivism such a system is supposed to exist within the individual. In Tolman's words one could say that cognitivism like mentalistic thinking, "infers purpose from behaviour" (see Tolman, 1920, 1948). It is thought that observed intelligent behaviour is generated by a rather autonomous, hidden system.

Suppes, Pavel, and Falmagne (1994) summarized the features of the cognitivist approach by following three tenets:

1. Brains, as well as digital computers, are physical symbol systems. The symbols must be realized physically; there cannot be a purely mental disembodied concept of symbol.
2. There is a formal or combinatorial syntax and semantics for mental representations. The formality of these representations is what distinguishes symbol systems in their structure from, for example, the usually incomplete descriptions of atomic or neural structures as such. The syntax and semantics of mental representations are implied to be much closer in principle to the formal systems of mathematical logic than to the structural descriptions of physiology or chemistry.
3. The formal syntax of mental representations is manipulated, as in the case of formal mathematical systems, by explicit syntactic rules.

Cognitivism is connected with folk-psychology, primarily because both want to explain what normal human rationality is. Cognitivism, however, wants to substitute scientific psychology for human rationality. In cognitivist psychology it is argued that human rationality should be explained in terms of an individual's thought processes. Further, it is argued that folk-psychology uses fuzzy concepts and assumptions, which should be replaced with a stricter approach. Finally, cognitivist theory is often identified with representational theories of mind, i.e. cognition "must be described in terms of symbols, schemas, images, ideas, and other forms of mental representation" (Gardner, 1987, p.39).

From Behaviourism to Cognitive Science

In order to describe how the cognitivist approach is delimited in this study, a short historical overview is presented. Furthermore, as cognitivist assumptions are widely accepted in cognitive science, cognitivism will be related to cognitive science. Finally, the relation between cognitivism and computationalism is clarified.

In connection with the transition to the 60s, psychological research in the west left the behaviouristic paradigm (Watson, 1929). It is thus during the last 35 years that the fundamental positions of cognitive science have developed. However, it has become popular to say that cognitive science has a recent past but a long history. Indeed there are several different influences from which cognitive science originates. In order to understand why cognitive science has taken the direction it represents today, it is useful to take a look at the state of western psychological research at the end of the 50s.

With the growing problems of denying the usefulness of an intentional model for explaining human behaviour as a complement to the behaviouristic theory, three paths or possibilities seem to have been attractive at the end of the 50s (cf. Leahey, 1987). First, inner processes or purposeful behaviour could be explained by cognitive maps in accordance with Tolman's (1948) proposal. The risk of choosing this model lay in accepti the existence of a small homunculus. This would have meant that purposeful behaviour had been the result of the decisions of "a small inner man". Since Tolman's model implied that there must be somebody who read a subject's mental map of reality one may agree when Leahey (1987) writes that "there really was a Ghost in Tolman's machine" (p.398).

A second possibility was to continue to explain behaviour from a mechanistic Hullian model of explanation (Hull, 1943, 1952) or to proceed with Skinner towards a more radical version of behaviourism (Skinner, 1938, 1957). Both these alternatives would have led to a denial of the intentionality problem.

A third alternative was to accept purposiveness as a fundamental human feature beyond which we cannot or at least need not go. Primarily this was Wittgenstein's (1953) position. The problem with this alternative was that one would have been forced to abandon psychology as a science. Psychology would have been excluded from the scientific community since the accepted norms of science were those of logical positivism.

However, it was Hullian mechanistic behaviourism that remained as the dominating perspective throughout the 50s. Tolman's ideas did, however, co-exist as a basis for the growing interest in the cognitive alternative.

Especially after the introduction of the mediating behaviourist model, it became easier to accept the cognitive thoughts from a behaviourist perspective. The mediating behaviourist model (S–{r–s}–R) became well-known. Osgood wrote in 1956 that "The great advantage of this solution is that, since each stage is an S–R-response, we can simply transfer all the conceptual machinery of single-stage S–R psychology into this new model without any new postulation". But, as Leahey (1987, p.393) points out, no conceptual language other than the behaviouristic was known at that time. Noam Chomsky was the one who radically reacted against Skinner's verbal behaviour (Chomsky, 1959). Nonetheless, this was done from a nativist perspective, which makes Chomsky's reaction different from the cognitivist view that was developing.

It may also be illuminating to pay attention to Hull's mechanistic behaviourism in connection with Tolman's intentional behaviourism in trying to understand contemporary cognitivism. Hull's programme was to explain behaviour from a mechanistic perspective. Behaviour was described in logical–mathematical equations whereby a cognitive dimension was wholly denied. Tolman, who also denied a mentalistic view of mind, nevertheless maintained that intention and cognition were necessary concepts. However, even at an early stage he exhibited a more mentalistic view of mind. For example, Tolman wrote in 1920 that "thoughts can be conceived from an objective point of view consisting in internal presentations to the organism [of stimuli not present]". These ideas were later elaborated in more detail in connection with his experiments with rats (Tolman, 1948), but by 1926 he had already developed the main ideas for his theory of cognitive maps. The point for anyone interested in the background influences on cognitivism is the combination of Tolman's mental map and Hull's logical–mathematical equations. It appears that both of these approaches have survived in contemporary cognitivism as the interest has been to express mental activities in terms of symbolic representations and rules.

There are also several other influences which have affected the development of research on intelligent behaviour to become what it is today within cognitive science. In the following text some of these influences will be discussed.

First one may acknowledge the impact of the development of the principles of formal logic. It is useful to remember that one of the great developments in 20th century philosophy has been a keen interest in logic, e.g. Frege, Russell, Whitehead and Wittgenstein. In a way this philosophical debate has also worked as a hotbed and ontological basis for the structural and syntactical interest within cognitivist theory. As Genesereth and Nilsson (1987) remind us, formal logic has attained an almost paradigmatic position both within cognitive science and artificial intelligence. A fundamental reason why logic obtained such a central position within cognitive science is that logic advanced the possibilities of handling declarative knowledge—an important type of knowledge.

Second, the theory of information or theories of communication systems developed by Shannon and Weaver (1949) and Broadbent (1958) together with Turing's (1950) work with intelligent machines has clearly inspired the development of cognitivist theory although the so-called Turing-machines were developed in accordance with behavioural simulation of intelligent systems. With the growing interest in intentionality problems within psychology and the development of computers in the 50s, the emphasis shifted towards a discussion of *functional* simulation of cognitive behaviour. It was now thought that simulations were models of intelligent systems only if they realized operations in order to reach functions in the same manner as the system simulated did.

A third fundamental background concept of cognitive science is the schema-concept introduced by Kant. The mental categories that Kant proposed constituted an important break compared with the associative theory that had been developed since Aristotle. In cognitive science the schema-concept has been considered useful since cognition is seen as a symbol-processing system that both regulates attention and the receiving of information and also includes the syntax according to which information is processed. However, during the 20th century the schema-concept has been applied in several ways (cf. Bartlett, 1932; Neisser, 1976; Piaget, 1953; Selz, 1924), which makes it impossible to present a precise definition of it (Eckblad, 1981). Nevertheless, a most influential single conceptualization of the schema-concept with respect to cognitive science was the one presented by Bartlett (1932) in his criticism of Ebbinghaus's approach. For Bartlett the schema was primarily a structure of organized knowledge which affected what individuals recalled when reading texts. Bartlett's argument about "effort after meaning" pointed out that "knowledge of the world is interpreted through schemata based on past experience".

However, in different cognitive theories the functional status of the inner system varies. For example Ulric Neisser's and Jean Piaget's schemes are not as dominating as a scheme in more radical cognitivism. Neisser and Piaget do not presuppose an autonomous existence of either schemes or constructs. However their schemes are not passive. Both Piaget's and Neisser's schemes direct the attention exhibited by the person towards the world. For Piaget an object gets its meaning when it is assimilated in the scheme, or system of schemes, but the difference to cognitivism is that the assimilation process "is not assumed to involve hypothesis testing, analysis, inferences or any kind of cognitive operations" (Lundh, 1983, p.14). Thus Piaget does not specify operations by which information is assimilated into the scheme, which is one of the major goals in information processing psychology. In spite of these differences the main point here is the transition from an associative to a schema-theoretical model of explanation (see Leiser & Giliéron, 1990 for a discussion of the relation between cognitivism and Piagetian psychology).

A fourth important background factor for the development of the cognitive science approach has been the development of computers. The expectations exhibited in the AI literature in the 60s reflected much hope concerning the solution of the nature of human cognition. The dominating contemporary views in cognitive science were also developed when the classical von Neumann architecture was the paradigm of designing computers. This architecture correlates well with the idea of symbols and rule systems as the basis of human mental life where cognition (thinking) is seen as the application of formal rules on syntactically structured internal representations. Even though the more recent development of parallel distributed processing models breaks with the serial processing of the earlier architecture, the most important assumption remains, namely that computational processing of information simulates human cognition. In fact the change in interest towards connectionism only supports this interpretation. However, one cannot say that the cognitivist or computational view of the mind has developed after the development of the computer. Fodor (1981, p.140) reminds us that the "computer metaphor predates the computer by about three hundred years". Nevertheless, computers have supported theory development in "non-physicalist" terms.

A fifth factor that has had a general influence on research in cognitive science is the renewed interest in the philosophy of mind during the last few decades. During the same period philosophers have also been more interested in developing conceptions of the human mind that are consistent with empirical research on cognition.

A sixth influence is the research carried out by neuropsychologists. The approaches that attempt to explain different aspects of human cognition from a physiological perspective have increased dramatically in the last decade (cf. Churchland, 1986).

Cognitivism and Cognitive Science

In this study I have had to make decisions concerning the delimitation of the cognitivist approach. This is a complex task because the research is so diverse. On the other hand it is not difficult since the cognitivist approach is quite easily recognized thanks to central works representing it. The principle guiding the choice of particular pieces of research has been that they must be accepted by the scientific community they represent as research items where fundamental ideas are explicated.

Secondly, we have the problem of what directions within the cognitivist approach should be focused on. In order to indicate how cognitivism is delimited, its relation to cognitive science and computationalism is specified.

Cognitive science is taken to be a recent concept referring to efforts to coordinate research on different aspects of cognition within different disciplines. Hunt (1989, p.603) writes:

> Cognitive science is an attempt to unify views of thought developed by studies in psychology, linguistics, anthropology, philosophy, computer science and the neurosciences.

We have noticed that research today in the area generally called cognitive science is characterized by a multitude of theoretical approaches and that it has been difficult to relate theories to each other.[1] In order to handle this problem, cognitive scientists have used concepts like framework (approach, meta-theory, paradigm), theory, model and cognitive architecture. The concept closest to the level of analysis adopted in this study is that of framework (Eysenck & Keane, 1991, p.31):

> A framework is a general set of ideas which is drawn upon by theorists within a particular discipline . . . The important thing about frameworks is that they should be regarded as useful or not useful rather than correct or incorrect. The reason for this is that they consist of high-level assumptions which cannot be tested directly at an experimental level.

It has also been suggested that cognitive science is not just a perspective on cognition, but a new discipline (Norman, 1980; Pylyshyn, 1984). As a concept, cognitive science would thus refer to a research object, human cognition, not to a specific kind of theory of its object, cognitivism. Whether cognitive science should be regarded as a perspective or a new discipline is of a certain importance because of its consequences for the present study. If various traditional disciplines preceding cognitive science are able to answer the questions posed by cognitive science, it cannot be established as a discipline. On the other hand, if a multi-disciplinary approach like cognitive science is necessary for answering basic questions concerning cognition, then at least that area of existing disciplines dealing with cognition has to be separated from the traditional disciplines.

The most obvious feature of cognitive science is its cognitivist stance. Thus cognitivism will be considered as one of the features distinguishing cognitive science from other approaches. Cognitivism means that *thinking* (cognition) is taken as the very model for most kinds of human mental life (cf. e.g. Haugeland, 1978).

How does cognitive science then relate to cognitive psychology? They both specify a common object of research—cognition. The difference is, however, that while cognitive psychology is psychological theory, cognitive science adopts an interdisciplinary approach to research on cognition.

A division of labour has been suggested between experimental cognitive psychologists, cognitive scientists and cognitive neuropsychologists (Eysenck & Keane, 1991, p.10). In these researchers' view cognitive psychology comprises the traditional experimentally oriented research but without computational modelling. Computational modelling of mental processes is again the main feature of cognitive science. Finally, cognitive neuropsychology is traditionally focused on cognitive impairment with a view to developing knowledge of human cognition.

Within all of these research approaches the object of research has been human cognition. However, since the concept of cognitive science has been established recently and this direction is of specific interest in this study, there is reason to look at how this concept has been defined. Often it is defined as the interdisciplinary study of acquisition and use of knowledge including several disciplines like artificial intelligence, psychology, linguistics, philosophy, anthropology, neuroscience and education.

It is also true of information processing psychology that it refers to a field of interrelated theories McShane, 1991, p.10):

> At present, information processing is an approach taken by different theorists who derive their theoretical constructs from a common loosely related framework. It is possible, of course, to construct theories within the information processing framework but it would be a mistake to assume that there is a single grand theory of information processing.

It is often stated that one of the fundamental aspects of cognitive psychology is that it tries "to specify the internal processing involved in perception, language, memory and thought". We may thus conclude that cognitive psychology as information processing psychology may be seen as a fundamental part of cognitive science.

Computationalism as a Cognitivist Approach

According to the computational conception of mind, mentality is seen as a composite of processes that are computational. According to this view the mind can at some level be described as a purely computational device, in other words as "a symbol manipulating engine that operates only on syntactic features of inputs and its own internal representation" (Cole, 1990, p.3). This means that computations are performed on the basis of purely formal or physical properties of the states of the system. The subproperties do not have any semantic or pragmatic properties and nothing which directly corresponds to beliefs, knowledge or other folk-psychological explanations.

This view of the mind has also been called the computer metaphor because of the importance of the electronic computer in explaining human cognition within cognitive science. It is difficult to overestimate the role of the computer in cognitive science since it is claimed that ". . . it is important to all understanding of the human mind" (Gardner, 1987, pp.6, 38). The computer has two main functions within cognitive science. The first reveals its core idea, which is that the computer serves as a model of human thought. It is considered that it is ". . . the most viable model of how the human mind functions" (Gardner, 1987, p.38) and that it ". . . serves a theoretical and philosophical role". The concept of the computer itself serves as a "theoretical model for cognitive science" (Cole, 1990, p.2). The second function the computer has is as a tool by which empirical data are analysed and also, more importantly, as a means of simulating cognitive processes. For this reason the representations mentioned above must be expressed in an internal language which is more like a computer language than natural language, since it has to contain "definitions for well formed structures and operations upon them" (Hunt, 1989, p.604). Fodor (1975) has called this internal language mentalese. Information processing theories thus answer two questions: what kind of language mentalese is and what sort of operations manipulate these data-structures.

When we talk about the computer metaphor it must be remembered that some researchers use the computer precisely as a metaphor. Neisser, (1976) for example, argued that though programmes have very much in common with cognition, one should stay at the level of metaphor. Others, like Pylyshyn (1984), see the similarity more literally.

It has also been suggested that this area of research, which is concerned with trying to express human cognition in terms of abstract models, could be called cognitive modelling. This view is "based on the conception of the human brain as a physical symbol system consisting of a representation system and the processes which manipulate it" (Aitkenhead & Slack, 1987, p.ix). This modelling approach has developed within two areas, cognitive psychology and artificial intelligence.

Within cognitive psychology modelling means formulation of information processing models. These are evaluated against experimental data. Within computationalism cognitive modelling means building computer-based models of cognition. This approach to conceiving computationalism conceives of it as a technology, not a psychology. The aim here is to develop artificial systems that can achieve intelligent behaviour. However it is important to notice that one can also view computationalism from another perspective, that is, as an attempt to develop a theory about human intelligence, i.e. to see computationalism as a psychology. The aim is then to explain human behaviour as such as in cognitive psychology. The generally accepted simulative goal has been evident since its very beginning at the end of the 50s. Newell, Shaw and Simon wrote in an early paper called *Elements of a theory of problem solving* (1958):

> The heart of [our] approach is describing the behavior of the system by a well specified program, defined in terms of elementary information processes ... Once the program has been specified, we proceed exactly as we do with traditional mathemathical systems. We attempt to deduce general properties of the system from the program (the equations); we compare the behavior predicted from the program (from the equations) with actual behavior observed ... [and] we modify the program when modification is required to fit the facts.

This view was developed in a later publication (Newell & Simon, 1972). The aim has been to develop computer simulations of such steps as human beings take in the course of solving problems. The methods to achieve this aim are of course different within the two traditions. It is this common modelling interest of cognitive psychology and AI which has also been called cognitive science.

This way of carrying out empirical research within cognitive science has, according to Winograd (1980, p.226), followed the pattern described below. What is simulated is human cognition:

1. The scientist observes some recurrent pattern of interaction of an organism;
2. He or she devises some formal representation (for example, a set of generative rules or a "schema") that characterizes the regularities;
3. The organism is assumed to "have" the representation, in order to be able to exhibit the regularities;
4. (Depending on the particular subfield). The scientist looks for experiments that will demonstrate the presence of the representation, or designs a computer program using it to see whether the behaviour can be generated by the program.

A final point in specifying the computationalist approach or cognitive science is the de-emphasizing of the influence of emotions, cultural and historical factors (Gardner, 1987, p.6). Further, the background or present context in which particular cognitive processes take place is not taken into account when these processes are explained. I have pointed out that it is argued that de-emphasizing the context, historical or social, present or past, is only a methodological issue. Accordingly, representatives of the approach claim that they do not deny the possible importance or influence which these surrounding factors may have on cognitive activities, but they are rather regarded as undeniably disturbing elements. It is concluded that "... an inclusion of them at this point would complicate the cognitive science endeavour" (Gardner, 1987, p.6). What appears here is a view that it is possible to study human cognition as such without regarding the context in which this activity occurs.

Theories on Different Levels

A final way of structuring the field is to focus on the variation of how different subparts within cognitive psychology define their field.

Sometimes a division between the following levels is suggested:

1. Intentional psychology focuses upon how an individual deals with his or her environment (phenomenology, representational theories);
2. Sign-level psychology seeks to develop internal processing models of cognition (computationalism, functionalism);
3. Physical-level psychology tries to explain mental events in purely physicalist or neuroscientific terms (eliminative materialism, type-identity theory, physical theories, connectionism).

It has been suggested that in certain respects the different psychological approaches do not compete. Pylyshyn (1984) again argues that it is possible to identify three levels of psychological theory within cognitive science which all represent a computational view of mind. They are:

(a) Representational theories;
(b) Information-processing theories; and
(c) Physical theories.

Representational theories express how the external world is captured by mental models.[2] Information-processing theories deal with the human mental language (mentalese, cf. Fodor, 1975), trying to define it. Physical theories would explain this inner language in terms of brain processes. Fodor (1975) has argued that information-processing theories must intervene between physical and representational theories because the representation must be handled by some general language.

The differences between the ways of structuring the field are thus not overwhelming and it seems that the cognitive science approach supports these structures with minor variations (Bechtel, 1988, pp.54–78).

Cognitivism and the Level of Analysis in this Study

The two problems discussed, i.e. the ontological and the epistemological, have been emphasized in various ways within cognitive science. Within representationalist theory the epistemological problem is easily identified (i.e. how the relation between the content of mind and the external world is specified). But the ontological problem is also discussed clearly; a representational level of description is defended against e.g. eliminative materialism. Within computational and connectionist theory again, the ontological problem, i.e. how we should describe the content of awareness, is primarily dealt with.

It is hoped that the previous discussion has shown how difficult it has been to construct an object of analysis in this study that could be kept clearly distinct from other approaches. Although there are differences among different directions of the cognitivist school of thought, it is considered possible to deal with these directions as representing one and the same framework. The main interest concerns how the cognitive paradigm in general and the cognitivist information-processing approach in particular, as well as what is called representational theories, explain conceptual learning. Thus, the study does not include computational learning theory or connectionist theories (see Anthony & Biggs, 1992; Kivinen, 1992). Instead, attention is paid to approaches of cognition which view learning as conceptual change and share the view of the individual as receiving and manipulating information.

COGNITIVISM AND THE THEORY OF LEARNING

The cognitive theory of learning in general has for the last three decades focused on acquisition of knowledge structures rather than behaviour. Behaviour has been seen as something resulting from what a subject has learned, i.e. behaviour as such is not learned. During the same period attention has shifted from investigating changes in the environment which would provide for appropriate responses to focusing on changes within the learner as well as on the learner's activity. Nonetheless cognitive psychology makes use of behavioural data, but these data are used to deduce mental processes or structures that are thought to result in behaviour.

It is not very easy to describe how learning is conceived of within cognitive psychological research. This is partly due to the problem of how the field should be limited, as we noted in the previous chapter. Another reason is that there does not seem to exist any elaborate and generally accepted theory of learning within cognitive psychology and cognitive science. This is the conclusion several leading researchers in the field e.g. Fodor (1980, p.149), Bereiter (1985, p.201) and Ohlsson (Sandberg & Barnard, 1991, p.139) have arrived at:

> There literally isn't such a thing as the notion of learning a conceptual system richer than the one that one already has; we simply have no idea of what it would be like to get from a conceptually impoverished to a conceptually richer system by anything like a process of learning.

> It seems to be generally agreed that there is no adequate theory of learning—that is, no adequate theory to explain how new organizations of concepts and how new more complex cognitive procedures are acquired.

> There is a widespread belief that . . . we have many theories of learning. If you put some reasonable constraints on what you are willing to call a theory of learning that is not true at all.

One reason for this situation is that cognitivist psychology has developed models describing performance of tasks rather than learning (Glaser & Bassok, 1989, p.634):

> Over the past quarter of a century, cognitive research has focused primarily on the analysis of competence. Studies of memory, language, and problem solving have examined the nature of performance and the outcomes of learning and development . . . The least developed component of instructional theory is explication of the process of learning—a contrast indeed to behavioral psychology, where learning was of major concern . . . [T]he study of the transition processes that a theory of learning must account for has been a depressed endeavor until recent years.

Simon (1979, p.981) has defended the situation by claiming that it is natural to first explain what it is to have knowledge before we try to explain how this knowledge is reached. Norman's (1987, pp.328–329) position is similar:

> Today the study of learning is not considered a central part of either psychology or artificial intelligence. Why? Perhaps the understanding of learning requires knowing about problems or representation, of input (perception), of output (performance), and of thought and inference.

In principle this is the same argument that was presented by Alain Newell and Herbert Simon in 1972; it is difficult to understand what learning is about without having an idea of the knowledge states between which a transition is supposed to occur. The performance system must be known.

Yet Norman (1987) admits that one reason why "so little is known about learning" is in part due to "lack of trying". There is an ongoing change in interest in favour of learning theory in contemporary cognitivism (see e.g. Glaser, 1990).

However it is interesting to note that even though learning has not been of prime interest in cognitive psychology for the last few decades, many researchers are very explicit on what an adequate theory of learning *should* explain. To them, the main goal of learning theory seems to be to explain what it means for an individual to "get from a conceptually impoverished situation to a conceptually richer system" (Fodor, 1980) and "how new organizations of concepts and how new more complex cognitive procedures are acquired" (Bereiter, 1985). What learning theory thus should explain is the changes of the conceptual system and cognitive procedures. Stellan Ohlsson (in Sandberg & Barnard, 1991, p.139) also has a clear view of what a learning theory should be about:

> To me a learning theory should be saying: here are the mechanisms that are responsible for any kind of cognitive change, here are the conditions under which these are triggered. Here are the knowledge structures that they operate on and here is how they would change these knowledge structures under such and such circumstances.

Attention with regard to research on learning within cognitive psychology for the last decades has, to the extent it has existed, been very much focused on cognitive, conceptual learning. Shuell (1986, pp.415–418) has summarized features characterizing contemporary cognitive learning research. He distinguishes five features concerning the impact of cognitive psychology on learning theory:

a) A view of learning as an active, constructive process
b) The presence of higher-level processes in learning
c) The cumulative nature of learning and the corresponding role played by prior knowledge
d) Concern for the way knowledge is represented and organized in the memory
e) Concern for analysing learning tasks and performance in terms of cognitive processes that are involved.

The dominant contemporary cognitive approach to learning research conceives of learning as an "active, constructive and goal-oriented process that is dependent upon the mental activities of the learner" (Shuell, 1986, p.415). It is evident that learning is seen as dependent on some mechanisms *within* an individual subject. Shuell (1986) concludes that cognitive learning "focuses on the way in which people acquire new knowledge and skills and the way in which existing knowledge and skills are modified". He further argues that almost all conceptions of learning involve the following three criteria: (a) a change in an individual's behaviour or ability to do something, (b) a stipulation that this change must result from some sort of practice or experience and (c) a stipulation that the change is an enduring one (p.412).

In Shuell's summary the question of *what* is changing in learning is defined in the first paragraph (a): it is the "individual's behaviour or ability to do something". The second feature again refers to the conditions under which this change may occur; it excludes changes on the basis of how these changes come about. Changes in (a) caused by, for example, maturing are not counted as learning.

It is also evident that thinking is stressed in this view of learning; the "active, constructive and goal-oriented" processes are discussed in terms of "mental activities". The following features are regarded as typical of this research (Shuell, 1986):

a) The role of meta-cognitive processes such as planning and setting goals and subgoals . . .
b) The active selection of stimuli . . .
c) The attempt by learners to organize the material they are learning, even when no obvious basis of organization is present in the materials being learned . . . [and]
d) The generation of appropriate responses and the use of various learning strategies.

In several respects the general characteristics of the cognitivist approach are also reflected in an article by Robert Glaser from 1987. He claims that learning is seen as "conceptual shifts from surface-level problem representations to deep structure representations" (p.397). In these conceptual shifts, information is restructured. Learning is thus a restructuring activity which is accompanied by "an accumulation of new facts, rules and procedures" which also involve "acquiring different relations among concepts" (ibid.). The result of learning is that the individual gets a "large collection of knowledge structures that enable representation of relationships in a problem" (ibid., p.398). Further, in learning "humans . . . build up an extremely large store of structured knowledge" (ibid., p.400). In studying learning one must therefore analyse "the processes by which learners integrate and organize information" and "how cognitive structures are modified and combined" and further how students "learn . . . to construct interpretations of situations that occur in the course of learning" (ibid., p.398). If we follow Robert Glaser, we must, in order to understand what learning means more precisely within the information processing approach, look at how new facts are accumulated, what it means to build up a large store of knowledge, and how learners process information. We can see that learners' activities are emphasized strongly. Learning is thus in the hands of the learner. Gunstone and Northfield (1994, p.545) have expressed this position clearly:

> It is the pupil or student teacher who must first *recognize* his/her relevant ideas and beliefs, then *evaluate* these ideas and beliefs in terms of what is to be learned and how this learning is intended to occur, and then *decide* whether or not to *reconstruct* their ideas and beliefs.

Metacognition. The view that learning is highly cognitive and occurs within the individual is also evident from the interest that has developed in meta–cognitive activities, i.e. in higher-level processes in learning. This interest is primarily focused on individual regulation, planning, predicting and monitoring one's own learning process.[3] The question is here how an individual organizes their activities in connection with the goal that an individual has in the learning process (cf. e.g. Brown, 1978; Flavell, 1979). Another aspect of this interest is concerned with what an individual does know about the field that they are trying to enter into by learning. We will return to this second question in relation to the question of the role of prior knowledge.

Sternberg's (1987) theory exemplifies this metacognitive interest very well. He differentiates between nine executive processes or metacomponents that regulate learning activity. The metacomponents are: "higher order or executive processes used to plan what one is going to do, to monitor it while being done and evaluate it after it is done". These metacomponents then regulate three so-called lower-level performance processes. The lower-level knowledge-acquisition components are: selective encoding of information (i.e. paying attention only to relevant information and neglecting what is irrelevant), selective combination (i.e. integrating disparate pieces of new information in a meaningful way) and finally selective comparison (i.e. relating this previously encoded information to old, stored information in the memory).

Gagné and Briggs' (1979) position clearly exemplifies the emphasis laid on cognitive processes explaining learning. They distinguish between the following kinds of processes "presumed to occur during any kind of learning" (p.154):

1. *Attention*—determines the extent and nature of reception of incoming stimulation;

2. *Selective perception*—transforms this stimulation into the form of object features, for storage in short-term memory;
3. *Rehearsal*—maintains and renews the items stored in short-term memory;
4. *Semantic encoding*—the process which prepares information for long-term storage;
5. *Retrieval*, including search—returns stored information to the working memory, or to response generator mechanism;
6. *Response organization*—selects and organizes performance;
7. *Feedback*—an external event which sets in motion the process of *reinforcement*;
8. *Executive control processes*—select and activate cognitive strategies; these modify any or all of the previously listed processes.

Brief Overview of Cognitivist Approaches to Learning

We should now look at the theories that have been current for the last thirty years. This discussion gives the general characteristics of some theories while others are dealt with in more detail.

We may begin by acknowledging the work done by Jerome Bruner (1960, 1966). In the present context he is recognized as one of the important background figures of cognitive learning theory by drawing attention to, and developing the view of, the learner as an active, selective and organizing individual. Like most other western psychologists in the 50s, he was inspired by information theory and the development of computers, which clearly affected his theories of learning at that time. Learning was discussed in terms of discovery, invention and "going beyond the information given" (Bruner, 1960). Later, in the 70s and 80s, he emphasized language much more as a cultural phenomenon and stressed that learning in some respects was to be conceived as social by nature. Negotiating and sharing in relation to cultural contexts were frequently occurring concepts. In this view learning is not seen solely as a receptive individual function through which the individual receives information or knowledge about the surrounding world. To learn, according to Bruner and Haste (1987), is also to participate in the construction of the social world and to take part in the creation of a common culture.

Another early cognitive theory of learning was Ausubel's (1963) model of meaningful verbal learning. It relies heavily on the schema-concept. The cognitive structure in Ausubel's theory consisted as a model organizing perceived information; in learning, information was subsumed in an existing cognitive structure. Another aspect stressed in Ausubel's theory was that of conceiving learning as a result of the individual facing information that differed, or was distinguishable from, existing individual cognitive structures. Ausubel stresses the relation between the logical structure of information and the individual's psychological organization of the world. For Ausubel, as for Bruner, the common concepts in language form the fundamental basis required for successful learning. Language and concepts are therefore required in building the cognitive bridge between psychological and logical reality (Ausubel, Novak, & Hanesian, 1978).

A third earlier theory is Wittrock's (1974) theory of generative learning. The notions of rule and inference were central to the generative model. Learning was conceived of as generating (constructing) connections between pieces of information in the long-term memory by trying to discover underlying relationships and rules pertaining to the information. Thus learning occurs through suggesting connections between potential or possible relationships and then testing these assumptions.

Most approaches to learning view the concept of de-contextualization or generalization as central to their theory; knowledge that is originally acquired in a specific context must become more abstract so that it may be used in other situations. Today, when learning is largely understood as contextual in nature, it is important to note that the demand concerning the transfer of competence from one context to another has not disappeared (Singley & Anderson, 1989). The question of how competence, skills and knowledge are de-contextualized in order to be more generally applied is still an urgent one for all theories of learning, but is not well understood. Even though the process of de-contextualization or generalization of knowledge is taken to refer to extending its range of application to other situations, it is not always specified what this generalization process contains or how it is realized. On the other hand, one might expect contextual theories on cognition to be better suited than others for dealing with the relation between context and competence.

How are the learning processes then defined? Previously we looked at Sternberg's (1987) theory, in which metacognitive activities are stressed. In Norman's (1982) and Rumelhart and Norman's (1987) schema-based theory these metacognitive activities are combined with the idea of long-term memory. They suggest three kinds of learning:

- Accretion—i.e. encoding new information in existing schemata;
- Restructuring—i.e. creation of new schemata;
- Tuning—i.e. the modification of a schema as a result of using it in different situations.

Accretion means that new information is interpreted in terms of an already existing schema. After this the actual piece of information is added to the long-term memory without changes in its structure. Shuell (1986, p.421) has compared this process to memorization. Restructuring again refers to a change in knowledge in terms of a changed structure. New structures are constructed in interpreting both old and new information. However, for restructuring to occur, there is no need for new information; this process may just change the relations between existing pieces of information to form new patterns. Tuning has been characterized as a series of accretions (or accommodations), (Hergenhahn & Olson, 1993, p.366). Norman (1982, p.81) writes:

> Tuning is the fine adjustment of knowledge to a task. The proper schemas exist and appropriate knowledge is within them. But they are inefficient for the purpose, either because they are too general or because they are mismatched to the particular use that is required of them, so the knowledge must be tuned, continually adjusted to the task.

Brown and Van Lehn (1980), who have developed their theory primarily within arithmetical learning, claim that learning occurs at impasses. They claim that when an individual reaches a certain situation which cannot be handled by existing procedures, then they must invoke new procedures in order to deal with the problem, must invent repairs or patches. The heart of this theory is that a student is thought to use general-purpose problem-solving heuristics to guide repairs. However, what is counted as general heuristics and domain-specific strategies depends on the problem at hand.

Another theory that is clearly an information-processing theory is John Anderson's "Adaptive Control of Thought" (ACT), (Anderson, 1983). This theory to a large extent makes use of semantic networks to represent declarative knowledge and production rules to represent procedural knowledge. His three-stage model of procedural learning involves the following steps: first a subject interprets and solves a problem by using existing declarative knowledge, secondly, in a knowledge compilation stage, declarative knowledge is converted into procedural knowledge. The third step or phase involves tuning. In the tuning stage, procedural knowledge is refined by generalization, discrimination and strengthening. These are processes where production rules become broader or narrower in applicability or whereby some rules are strengthened or weakened.

Anderson's theory makes use of both the idea of semantic networks and productions (If . . . Then rules). According to the semantic (declarative, associative) theory of network, concepts are represented by nodes (pieces of information). These are linked to each other on associative principles, i.e. because the concepts are similar, because they occur together or because they are in contrast or opposition to each other. On the basis of these associative principles, combinations of concepts form networks. It should be noticed that this view has very long traditions especially in British empiricist philosophy. If knowledge is seen in terms of associations between concepts, what then is learning? In traditional semantic network theory it is thought that concepts (or nodes) are connected with each other with various strength in relation to their similarities, i.e. similar concepts are connected with each other more firmly than more distant concepts, e.g. "a dog and a cat node may be connected by a link with an activation of 0.5 whereas a dog and a pencil may be connected by a link with a strength of 0.1" (Eysenck & Keane, 1991, p.17). Thus, "in learning that two concepts are similar, the activation of a link between them may be increased" (ibid.). In Anderson's ACT this way of reasoning about learning is combined with productions. In principle the point is that a production system operates by matching the information stored in the working memory with If-parts of the If–Then rules in the long-term memory. Suitable consequences (i.e. then-parts) are executed. If there are many If-parts that match the information, then new rules (conflict-resolution rules) select the rule that best fits the information as discussed in Anderson (1982, pp.249–250):

> One of the fundamental assumptions of cognitive learning theory is that new knowledge is in large part "constructed" by the learner. Learners do not simply add new information to their store of knowledge. Instead, they must connect the new information to already established knowledge structures and construct new relationships among those structures. This process of building new relationships is essential to learning.

An important difference from many other cognitivist theories lies in the assumption that only this process is involved in all types of learning. It is thus a content-neutral theory of learning. In Anderson's theory, learning is seen as a constructive process.

Laird, Newell, and Rosenbloom (1987) have, in one sense, developed Anderson's ACT in their so-called SOAR, a problem-solving system making use of production rules. Like Brown and Van Lehn's (1980) approach, it works on impasses in problem solving. Encountering a too difficult problem, subgoals are set up; if a solution is successful, it is stored as an operator that will possibly be used in the future. In this sense SOAR falls between ACT and impasse-learning theory. From a theoretical perspective, chunking is a crucial concept in SOAR architecture. By chunking, those representations and procedures which occur together can be accessed together. Chunking of information makes it possible to overcome resource limitations of the information processing system.

Learning as Restructuring

Summarizing, we may say that the concept of restructuring seems to be crucial to understanding the contemporary cognitive theory of learning. One acknowledged problem with regard to restructuring is the difference between global and domain-specific restructuring. Usually Piaget's stage theory is referred to as an example of global restructuring. The motive is that "restructuring requires a change in the structures that determine the nature of the representational format available to the child" (Vosniadou & Brewer, 1987, p.52). It is thought that all knowledge acquisition is constrained by the different stages that the child represents (see Carey, 1985).

Criticism of the global restructuring theory has been growing for the last few decades. Increasingly restructuring is viewed as a change in a subject's knowledge rather than as a change in a subject's logical capability (Novak, 1977).

Within domain-specific restructuring, two kinds of restructuring have been distinguished: weak and radical restructuring. In weak restructuring it is thought that the relations between central concepts of a domain change. According to radical restructuring, not only the relations between concepts but the core concepts themselves change. In Carey's (1985, p.5) words the difference between weak and radical restructuring is the following:

> [In weak restructuring] new relations among concepts are represented, and new schemata come into being that allow the solution of new problems and change the solutions to old problems. The second, stronger sense includes not only these kinds of change but also changes in the individual core concepts of the successive system.

Carey (1985, p.6) exemplifies weak restructuring by novices gaining expertise in chess; novices and experts share "individual core concepts" (about pieces, moves, rules, goal). Then, becoming an expert in chess does not mean that an alternative theory of chess is developed. Rather, the individual moves within the same theory of chess but becomes more skilful within the given frame of reference.

An example of what is meant by radical restructuring or reaching an understanding that is more complex than an earlier one is presented in Vosniadou and Brewer's (1987) study (see also Vosniadou, 1994). They have investigated children's acquisition of knowledge in astronomy— more precisely children's understanding of relations between the earth, sun and moon. Their problem was whether a change in the children's cosmological understanding might be seen as an example of radical restructuring. In other words, are we talking about radical restructuring if a child's cosmology changes "from a theory based on a flat stationary earth and animistic accounts of the motion of the sun and the moon to a theory based on a spherical rotating earth" (p.59)? In order to reach a decision concerning whether a conceptual change (change of a schema) is called radical restructuring or not, three criteria were chosen. These were changes in a schema's individual concepts, changes in a schema's structure and finally, changes in the domain of the phenomenon it explains.

Their conclusion is positive with respect to all three criteria; the change from a geocentric to a heliocentric scheme is considered a good example of radical restructuring (Vosniadou & Brewer, 1987, p.59). First, the core concepts have changed:

> The concept of an animistic sun that sleeps at night is radically different from the concept of the sun as an ordinary star in a spiral galaxy. Similarly the shift from the view that the earth is a stationary flat object to the view that the earth is spherical and moving through space involves a change in individuals' concepts.

Second, the relations between the concepts have changed (ibid., p.59):

> The earth must shift from its position at the center of the universe. The day/night cycle comes to be conceptualized in terms of the relationship of the earth and the sun. The light from the moon comes to be conceptualized in terms of the relationship of the moon to the earth and sun.

Third, the last criterion, i.e. that the new schema must differ from the initial one with respect to the domain of the phenomena it explains, is also met (ibid., p.60):

> The child's later view incorporates only certain concepts included in the original schema (sun, moon, stars, but not clouds). At the same time the new schema uses the constructs of solar objects, light, and shadow to provide an explanation of seemingly different observable phenomena (the day/night cycle, the seasons, the phases of the moon).

Pintrich, Marx, and Boyle (1993) summarize the conceptual change model of learning by stating: "This standard individual conceptual change model assumes that ontogenetic change in an individual's learning is analogous to the nature of change in scientific paradigms that is proposed by philosophers of science" (see also Strike & Posner, 1992).

Vosniadou and Brewer's (1987) position thus supports Carey's (1985) idea that the difference between these two types of restructuring is clarified by comparing this relation to the distinction between ordinary changes in scientific theories (weak restructuring) and changes in paradigms in the history of science (radical restructuring). In periods of normal science, accepted theories are refined and change to a limited extent whereas paradigm shifts consist of solving problems arising from observations that do not fit an existing theory; "occasionally, when the child is faced with major anomalies that existing conceptual structures cannot account for, a new paradigm is required, giving rise to radical restructuring" (Vosniadou & Brewer, 1987, p.55).

The difference between weak and radical restructuring is connected with the question of prior knowledge in learning. The role of prior knowledge has been on the agenda within cognitivism since the beginning of the 70s, i.e. as long as schema-theories have been developed seriously within cognitivism. Schema theory "stresses that the organized, structured and abstract bodies of information (known as schemata) that a learner brings in learning new material determine how the task is interpreted and what the learner will understand and acquire from studying the task" (Shuell, 1986, p.417; see also Siegler & Richards, 1982).

Posner, Strike, Hewson, and Gertzog (1982, p.223) are also representatives of the view of learning as conceptual change. Radical conceptual change, or radical restructuring, is typically described in terms of accommodation. However, a radical change may develop gradually:

> Accommodation, particularly for the novice, is best thought of as a gradual adjustment in one's conception, each new adjustment laying the ground work for further adjustments but where the end result is a substantial reorganization of change in one's central concepts ... [Accommodation] rarely seems characterized by either a flash or insight, in which old ideas fall away to be replaced by new visions or as a steady logical progression from one commitment to another. Rather, it involves much tumbling about, many false starts and mistakes, and frequent reversals of direction.

It appears that the view of gradual development in schema learning is increasingly supported in the literature. While it was earlier commonly assumed that an individual either had or had not acquired a schema, Sweller (1994, p.297) instead asserts that schemas change stepwise:

> Schemas tend to be discussed as though schema acquisition results in dichotomous states: a person either has or has not acquired schemas. In fact, few intellectual skills are acquired in this manner.

The same is true for the controlling processes, Sweller (1994) argues; they are seen as either automatic or conscious. Sweller's (1994, p.298) point is that as an individual's knowledge of a certain domain increases, "the need to devote attention to the required processes is reduced."

When acknowledging the role of prior knowledge, we must also pay attention to the interest during the last decade in the role of domain-specific knowledge. It has been claimed that experts and novices solve problems in very different ways (Chi, Glaser, & Rees, 1982). As a result of this interest in, for example, Anderson's ACT and Sternberg's metacomponents, there is a contemporary controversy concerning the importance of domain-specific and domain-independent learning strategies (Rumelhart, 1981). It seems that both camps are right but to a limited extent. Advocates of general cognitive skills seem to overlook how central specific content knowledge is, while advocates of domain-specific strategies have overlooked the value of more general strategies (Perkins & Salomon, 1989). Recently a more moderate understanding has emerged. For example, Ashman and Conway (1993a, p.74) argue for an approach "based upon the premise that both content-specific and content-general knowledge and skills are important for learning and problem-solving."

Now, returning to the differences between radical and weak restructuring, it seems that representatives of this approach are capable of pointing out how prior knowledge affects the learning process in the case of weak restructuring (e.g. Bransford, 1979) while the question of how one should deal with the question of prior knowledge in relation to radical restructuring is far from clear. In the case of weak restructuring, it is clear that "[e]xisting conceptual structures cannot be enriched unless they are first identified" (Vosniadou & Brewer, 1987, p.56). And while weak restructuring or assimilation does not include a change of the schema, the very same schema, used to identify information, assimilates this information. However, in radical restructuring, identification of the conceptual structure is a problem; it is not possible to first identify and then enrich a specific structure, since learning in radical restructuring consists in a change in the very structure itself. It is not only a question of enriching an existing structure. However, it is frankly admitted that there is no generally accepted view of "what role prior knowledge plays in radical restructuring" (Vosniadou & Brewer, 1987, p.54). As a consequence, one lacks understanding of how one arrives at a conceptually more developed conceptualization (Bereiter, 1985). Similarly Carey (1985, p.200) clearly states that she is not able to explain the mechanism leading from one conceptual state to another. She puts her hope in nativism:

> My guess is that the "initial state" of human children can be described by saying that they are innately endowed with two theoretical systems: a naive physics and a naive psychology.

The Learning Paradox

The problem of the role of prior knowledge in radical restructuring has also been discussed in terms of a so-called learning paradox. It "involves the need to explain how the learner can acquire a new cognitive structure without already having an existing cognitive structure more advanced or complex than the one being acquired" (Shuell, 1986, p.415). This is originally the problem pointed out by Plato in the *Meno*. If we know what we try to learn there is no reason to learn because we already know it; on the other hand, if we do not know what we try to learn we will never be able to decide whether we have been successful or not (Plato, 1956).

However, observe that this paradox makes sense only in talking about reaching a competence that I call invention (i.e. transcending the known). In the case of known knowledge (i.e. "I know that you know how to do something, though I myself don't know how to do it") the case is different; certainly it is possible to identify knowledge or competence that one would like to reach. And identifying this does not mean that one has reached it. The paradox ceases to be a problem; in the case of identifiable competence we have a pretty clear idea of what is counted successful.

It must be carefully noticed that there is no paradox in a great part of ordinary, everyday learning. In most learning situations in everyday life we only apply earlier knowledge in new situations. For example when driving a car we never have driven before we often say that we have learned to master it. Yet it would often be more appropriate to say that we have got used to the new car, i.e. we possessed the ability to drive a car and to drive just another individual car is not to learn to drive, rather we apply or make use of previous knowledge, skills and experiences. The paradox appears instead when "learners must grasp concepts or procedures more complex than those they already have available for application" (Bereiter, 1985, p.202).

The paradox has been debated and solutions proposed during the last two decades (Bereiter, 1985; Glaser, 1987; Shuell, 1986; Vosniadou & Brewer, 1987). The most lively debate was that which developed between constructivists led by Piaget and nativists led by Chomsky (Piatelli-Palmarani, 1980). This distinction is still valid today; constructivism has its advocates (von Glasersfeld, 1987). Nativists may get support from more recent neuropsychological research (e.g. Churchland, 1986). According to earlier nativists like Chomsky (1965), the only way of explaining the learning paradox is to accept that some cognitive structures are innate and later instantiated through experience.

Conclusion

As we noticed earlier, the field of cognitive science is large and involves several theories of learning. Because of this there is no reason to reflect on every theory in detail. A preliminary understanding of what learning is about in cognitivist theory or the information-processing approach has now been reached. It is now time to turn to a more detailed analysis of the assumptions behind the view of learning discussed in this chapter.

NOTES

1. Eysenck & Keane, 1991, p.31: "One of the problems with cognitive psychology is that there has been a proliferation of theories, but it is not clear how these theories relate to each other."
2. The notion of mental model is used here in a general way, i.e. no specific theory of "mental models" is referred to.
3. On the relation between metacognition and self-regulation, see e.g. Zimmerman, 1990.

6 Cognitivism—Causal Theory of Perception, Representational Epistemology and Ontological Dualism

This chapter aims at a clarification of how the process and result of learning is conceived of within cognitivism, with respect to the epistemological mind–world problem and the ontological mind–brain problem.

When cognitivist learning theory is discussed, I will refer to information processing theories and representational theories.

As the cognitivist approach to research on learning and cognition is wide and varies to some degree, not all conclusions are equally valid for every theory previously discussed. On the other hand, the similarities between the approaches are considered large enough to allow a meaningful discussion of the pedagogical implications of this school of thought in Chapter 7.

THE EPISTEMOLOGICAL MIND–WORLD PROBLEM

In Chapter 4 the design of the second part of this study was described. The process and result of learning were chosen as the perspectives illuminating learning, while the epistemological and the ontological questions were chosen as the instruments of analysis.

The process of learning in terms of the epistemological problem was described as follows. In order to say how an individual's understanding of the world changes, we must say something about how the individual comes to know the world in the first place. This aspect of the epistemological problem involves the question of how the relation between individuals and the world changes during the process of learning.

The result of learning in terms of the epistemological problem was described in the following way. When an individual has reached knowledge of something or knows something, precisely what is it that they are aware of? Can it be something in external reality, or is it something which is embraced in consciousness?

THE PROCESS OF LEARNING

Learning as Receiving and Manipulating Information

Propositional theories of representation take a widespread approach to describing mental states and changes in them within cognitivism. Currently we may identify different directions accepting a propositional view of representations. Such theories are (a) general schema-theories (e.g. Minsky, 1975; Rumelhart & Ortony, 1976; Schank & Abelson, 1977); (b) general problem-solving theories (Newell & Simon, 1972; Sacerdoti, 1977); (c) general production systems (Anderson, 1983) and (d) general inference systems (McDermott & Doyle, 1980).

It is common to all approaches that reality is supposed to be represented in terms of some kind of symbols and that these symbols are manipulated by some set of rules in the cognitive system. Thus human cognition is viewed in terms of a symbol-manipulating system. As previously noted, this view consists primarily of two components. First, there is the idea of primitive symbols referring to something in the outer reality and, second, there are primitive operations that manipulate these symbols according to some rule system (syntax).

Information

The heart of this approach consists of how information is treated by the individual. In order to answer how information is treated, we may differentiate between three aspects of the information-processing system. A system that processes information must receive information, it must store that information and it must be able to find and change or manipulate that information.

Receiving information is dealt with in the psychology of perception and attention, and storage is dealt with in relation to human memory, while the change of information is discussed in terms of cognition or learning.

When we discuss the receiving of information, there is reason to emphasize the difference between perception and cognition. This difference is established by the fact that it is possible to perceive something without recognizing what is perceived. Thus, even though a physical object is causally responsible for a perceptual state, cognition is seen as the processing of these perceptions (Sterelny, 1991, p.35).

McShane (1991, p.95) has summarized the dominant view of information held:

> Information begins as a stimulus in the environment that is detected by the organism's perceptual receptors and is then processed by the cognitive system ... Certain features of the stimulus will receive attention and be retained ... In some cases the final information encoded and stored by the cognitive system may be quite unlike the environmental stimulus that acted as input to the cognitive system. Nevertheless, there is a lawful relation of representation between what is encoded and the stimulus that initiated the encoding; the information encoded is a representation of the stimulus input.

The view of transmission of information that lies behind this way of thinking was originally worked out by Shannon and Weaver (1949) and Broadbent (1958). According to this view it is assumed that information exists in the world around the individual. It may be quantified, transmitted, stored and manipulated (see e.g. Neisser 1976, p.57). According to Shannon and Weaver, information is transferred from one system to another if a state in system B is dependent on system A in the sense that one can find out something about A by studying system B. If enough information is transferred to system B, then specific features of A may be studied by investigating B. Thus it is thought that the representation not only directs perception but also stores information of past events. Ideas such as coding information, the distinction between serial and parallel processing, and the idea of limited-channel capacity stem from Shannon and Weaver's (1949) theory and were later introduced into cognitive psychology.

Another important background figure with respect to the view of information is the cyberneticist Norbert Wiener (1894–1964). His theory of information concludes that information can be thought of in one sense as completely divorced from subject matter, as simply a decision between equally plausible alternatives. Among psychologists this has led to a consideration of cognition (cognitive processes) apart from any particular embodiment. Consequently, attempts have been made to describe the mechanisms underlying the processing of any kind of information. There seems, however, to be a growing distrust of the idea that problem-solving strategies and skills are what should be learned (Siegler & Richards, 1982, p.930). Nevertheless, since cognition is seen as manipulating information in symbolic form, it must be possible to code all reality in symbolic form.

The fundamental idea in learning is that the individual constructs an internal representation out of the perceptual data received by the sensory system. The process of learning thus results in a mental structure. Learning changes usually refer to one of two things, either to the fact that more information is received from the environment and incorporated into an existing mental structure resulting in a more refined mental representation, or to the fact that a mental representation undergoes a radical change itself because of its inability to incorporate received information into an existing scheme. Often some version of the Piagetian concept of equilibration is made use of in explaining why radical shifts occur, as we saw in the previous chapter.

All these questions will be discussed in more detail in later chapters. The main thing here is that the epistemological mind–world problem concerning the process of learning reveals that a causal theory of perception is accepted by the information processing approach. According to the causal theory of perception, some of our experiences stem directly from outer reality (Locke). The position is also close to representational realism according to which, even though at least some of our sense experiences stem from an outer reality, we cannot have certain knowledge of this reality since we do not have access to reality as such, only to our sensory experiences of it. Consequently it is not possible for us to compare these sense impressions with reality itself. Therefore, accepting a causal theory of perception would guarantee that our knowledge is of the real world.

THE RESULT OF LEARNING

The problem of how a symbol structure reflects external reality is a fundamental feature of cognitive science in general and in particular within representational theories of cognition. In the words of Miller (1987, p.9): "I take the problem of characterizing the interactions between these two levels—between the real world and the world of words—to be the central problem in the study of human cognition" .

Miller (1987) very clearly distinguishes between perceptual presentation and symbolic representation. Perceptual presentation refers to "the way the real world presents itself to us or, more precisely, to the awareness we have at any moment of this real world we have constructed" (p. 9). Symbolic representations are again based on those cognitive categories that are created through perceptual presentation and upon historical, traditional conceptions in our culture. However, Miller claims that it is not possible to regard symbolic representation "as a simple one-to-one mapping onto presentations at the perceptual level" (ibid.). If this were the case, "cognitive theory would be simpler than it is" (ibid.). Cognitive schemata are considered to direct an individual's attention and perception. This means that a distinction is made between a presented world and a represented world.

Rumelhart and Norman (1987, p.17) have pointed out what they conceive as a fundamental point of departure in order to understand how information is represented in the memory of an individual. Their view is similar to Palmer's (1978). According to them the following is assumed by representational theories:

1. An environment in which there are objects and events;
2. A brain which attains certain states dependent on its current states and the sensory information that impinges on it;
3. Our phenomenal experience, which is assumed to be a function of our brain state;
4. A model or theory of the environment, the brain states, and experience.

Rumelhart and Norman (1987) pay attention to what a model is a model *of*. This means that the object that is represented may vary; the represented object can be the environment or it can be the brain states of an individual. In the former case the individual has a representation of his or her environment. In the latter case the researcher has a theoretical model of the subject's mental states. This means that a theory of cognition can be seen as a representation of representations.

Rumelhart and Norman (1987) make a clear distinction between real reality, states in the brain and phenomenal experience. They claim that it is possible to distinguish between different represented and representing worlds (Fig. 6.1).

These distinctions have several consequences. Firstly, the research object that one tries to develop a theory about will be brain states (2). Secondly, the experiential level, i.e. phenomenal experiences (3), is a function of brain states. This means that the experiential level is not a direct representation of objects in external reality. This is indicated in Figure 6.1 by the fact that there is no arrow between environment and phenomenal experience. It is always brain states that interfere between experience and reality (Rumelhart & Norman, 1987, p.17):

FIG. 6.1. The relations between environment, brain states and experience according to Rumelhart and Norman (1987, p.18).

172 SCHOOL DIDACTICS AND LEARNING

> [W]ithin the brain there exist brain states that are the representation of the environment. The environment is the represented world, the brain states are the representing world. Our theories of representation are in actuality representations of the brain states, not representations of the world.

Since representational theories "have the brain states as the represented world and the theoretical structures as the representing world" (ibid.), the figure presented above may be completed with a theory of representation as dipicted in Fig. 6.2.

Figure 6.2 shows that representational theories are not theories about human experience but theories about brain states. Thus Rumelhart and Norman (1987, p.18) argue that it is often mistakenly believed that representation describes the relationship between experience and reality. They state that this relation is a secondary one:

> There are objects of the world and there are objects of experience. The objects of experience are not the same as objects of the world, but they seem to reflect much of the structure of the world. In this way, it probably does make sense to speak of our experiential "representation" of the world.

However, if brain states reflect the external environment and the representational theory tries to account for these brain states through a description of them in representational terms, then it is not odd to claim that the descriptions arrived at through investigations reflect the world. Rumelhart and Norman (1987) themselves admit that the object of experience seems to "reflect much of the structure of the world" (ibid.). Thus Rumelhart and Norman (1987) seem to be ready not only to make a distinction between "the structure of the world", and brain states as different metaphysical entities, but also to be ready to conceive of phenomenal experience as something else than brain states. We will return to the question of how the relation between experience and brain states may be defined (the ontological problem).

The idea that it is reasonable to make a distinction between a world as such and experiences of this world is supported by a wide variety of researchers within the field. McShane (1991, p.97) claims likewise that:

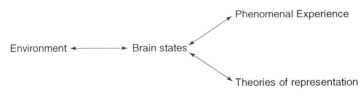

FIG. 6.2. Relations between environment, brain states, phenomenal experience and theories of representation within representational theories of cognition.

"Mental representations are symbolic encodings of the environment". This is also the conclusion that Winograd and Flores (1986, pp.30–31) have arrived at in summarizing fundamental assumptions shared by cognitivists:

1. We are inhabitants of a "real world" made up of objects bearing properties. Our actions take place in that world;
2. There are "objective facts" about that world that do not depend on the interpretation (or even presence) of any person;
3. Perception is a process by which facts about the world are (sometimes inaccurately) registered in our thoughts and feelings;
4. Thoughts and intentions about action can somehow cause physical (hence real-world) motion of our bodies.

How is Information Represented?

The concept of representation is a core concept in cognitivism, although there is a variation in how information is represented, e.g. by semantic networks, frames (Minsky, 1975), scripts (Schank & Abelson, 1977), production systems (Newell & Simon, 1972) or mental models (Johnson-Laird, 1983).

As the concept of schema has been of the utmost importance in cognitive psychology and has heavily influenced the cognitivist stance, we will approach the problem of how information is represented by analysing this concept. However, as we previously noted, the concept has been used by different theorists, which makes it more difficult to handle. In contemporary literature the schema concept is nonetheless often seen as "a theoretical construct which refers to the format of organized knowledge" (Glaser, 1987, p.403). It contains "prototypical information about frequently experienced situations" (ibid.). Rumelhart and Norman's (1987, p.36) definition is similar:

> Schemas are data structures for representing the generic concepts stored in the memory. There are schemas for generalized concepts underlying objects, situations, events, sequences of events, actions and sequences of actions ... Schemas in some sense represent the stereotypes of these concepts. Roughly, schemas are like models of the outside world.

According to Rumelhart and Norman (1987, pp.36–37) the most important features of schemas are the following;

1. *Schemas have variables;* which means that a concept has "a fixed part (characteristics which are always true of exemplars of the

concept and a variable part). The *colour* of a dog exemplifies the variable part and the *number* of legs the fixed part" (ibid.)
2. *Schemas can embed, one within another;* this means that "a schema consists of a configuration of subschemas" which "in turn consist in new configuration of subschemas. Some schemas are assumed to be primitive and to be undecomposable" (ibid.)
3. *Schemas represent knowledge at all levels of abstraction;* meaning that "schemas can represent knowledge . . . from ideologies and cultural truths, to knowledge about what constitutes an appropriate . . . sentence in our language" (ibid.)
4. *Schemas represent knowledge rather than definitions;* means that "schemas are our knowledge" (ibid.)
5. *Schemas are active recognition devices* whose processing is aimed at the evaluation of their goodness of fit to the data being processed.

In learning the knowledge structures (i.e. the schemata), a subject has one major job—"the construction of an interpretation of a new situation" (Glaser, 1987, p.403). A new representation is formed by the triggering of schemata; "if a problem is of a very familiar type, it can trigger an appropriate schema; if not, some more general schema is triggered . . . Once a schema is triggered it can control learning; it may contain precisely the right conceptual and procedural knowledge to solve a problem" (ibid.).

This is almost identical to what Ulric Neisser wrote in 1976. But according to Neisser the schema is not only a mechanism for recognizing but also a mechanism that actively directs the individual's interest in his surrounding world. Yet a schema is limited, since information can only be received if there is some representational format that is ready to do the job (Neisser, 1976, p.53). We may thus say that Neisser's schema contains a plan for receiving information and that it is active in doing this.

In any case, the result of the learning process may be expressed in terms of a mental representation consisting of some kind of symbolic structure representing an external world. However, it should be clearly noted that this structure is constructed on the basis of sensations supplied by the sensory system. Thus, the conceptual structure developed cannot be conceived of as a mirrorlike picture of the external world.

The Learning Paradox and Representational Epistemology

The concept learning paradox has been used to refer to the problem of how individuals are able to construe a more complex model of reality than they already have access to. I argue that in fact this is not a paradox or, to the extent that it is a paradox, the argument is based on a very specific idea of the relation between mind and external reality.

The problem called the learning paradox seems to stem from the inability to include the concept of construction in a theory which simultaneously holds that the world exists as such. Or the other way round—the concept of acquisition is an awkward one in constructivist theory, for how can one acquire knowledge by constructing it? If one constructs knowledge, one constructs it, one does not acquire it. In a constructivist account of learning there seems to be no place for acquisition.

One reason for this paradox is the belief in two ultimate, metaphysically different worlds, a world of objects and events and a world in which these objects and events are represented. Learning in this view is, roughly, the transformation of information from one system into another. This dualist position is described by Bredo (1994, p.24):

> . . . one assumption common to many members of the family is the assumption of a separately defined individual and environment, which must somehow match one another. Inside and outside, person and environment are viewed as separable, as independently definable, and then in need of being related.

Ference Marton, the leading phenomenographer, has for years criticized cognitivism for this position (Marton, 1981).

The problem is close to that of critical realism. According to critical realism, the world out there is given and preconstructed but nevertheless unknowable as such since we perceive it from our subjective point of view, being active in constructing an understanding of the world, making sense of it. Like critical realism, constructivism is situated in the tension between these poles (belief in some kind of autonomous existence of the world out there and the individual's subjective ordering of experiences). Yet it is not clear that constructivism or cognitivism manages to handle this tension successfully.

This suggests that the learning paradox might be solved in terms of how the relation between construction and acquisition is defined. As I see it, the paradox for cognitivists emanates from the difficulty of believing in a given world out there and at the same time constructing new knowledge about this world. It is obvious that a stipulation allowing these two contrasting positions is needed.

Conclusion

It seems evident that cognitivists and constructivists do not always realize the following two relations concerning the epistemological problem. On the one hand we have the relation between the physical world and human ability to receive sense impressions of it. On the other hand we have the relation between these sense impressions and our awareness of these impressions. As long as these distinctions are not made, the debate will be extremely confused.

The aim of the following chapter is therefore to investigate the epistemological problem by asking the traditional question of epistemology, i.e. what object do we have access to in perception? I will suggest that cognitivism accepts a dualist position concerning the relation between presentations and representations, but a monistic position on the relation between physical objects and presentations.

COGNITIVISM AND REPRESENTATIONAL EPISTEMOLOGY

I will now try to summarize the position cognitivism represents concerning the epistemological mind–world problem by relating it to the classical question of perception and to how the role of a scheme is understood.

The kernel of the epistemological problem can be summarized in the following question: "Which is the real object of perception, the object in the external world or the form within the perceiver's mind?".

Medieval scholastics (e.g. Anselm of Canterbury) made this distinction on the basis of Aristotle's work (Sajama & Kamppinen, 1987, p.12). The point was that after having been perceived, an object can be said to exist in two ways; as a form in the mind and as a combination of form and matter in the material world. The similarity between the real object and the mental content would then consist in the form the object has in these realms. No similarity, however, was to be identified with respect to the matter of the object in the two realms. The problem can be visualized as in Fig. 6.3.

The answers given since have, exactly as the question presupposes, been presented in an either–or fashion. According to the first alternative (conception A in the figure below) the perceived reality is considered to be the object per se. Within the second answer (conception B in Fig. 6.3) it is the content of the subject's perception that is conceived.

The Real Object—the Experienced Object or the Object in the World?

The information-processing approach clearly resembles the second position, i.e. that the perceiver has access only to perceptual information provided by the senses. In accordance with this the individual is aware of perceptions, not of the reality as such.

6. FEATURES OF COGNITIVISM   177

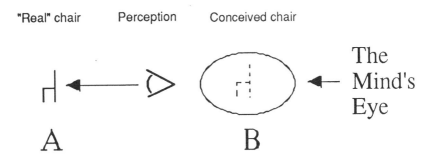

A The chair itself is perceived but by means of a mental image
B The chair itself is not perceived, only its appearance in the mind is perceived

FIG. 6.3. What do we have access to—the real chair or the conceived chair?

The sceptics of antiquity (e.g. Sextos Empeirekos) belonged to those who first argued that what we have access to in experience is a mental picture of an object and not external things (conception B above). The idea was that we cannot know the things themselves, only their appearances; we can be sure that we really are aware of a certain mental content, but we cannot be sure of a possible objective referent ("I am sure that I see a cat, but how can I be sure that there really is a cat?"), i.e. one can be sure that there *seems* to be an object before us, but not that there really *is* an object. The problem is thus how sure we can be that our experiences have external, objective correlates.

This sceptical interpretation (B) was carried further by the British empiricists. John Locke (1632–1704) represented the causal theory of perception, according to which perceiving was to have sensations caused by the things themselves (Locke, 1961). More specifically the primary qualities of objects were received by the perceptual system (Hamlyn, 1967, p.23). Simple ideas did not receive any contribution from the mind. The construction of complex ideas, i.e. knowledge, was possible as the mind was capable of repeating, comparing and uniting simple ideas. One can say that Locke was a clear empiricist concerning the sources of ideas but a rationalist with regard to knowledge, as human reason was able to construct complex ideas. It is useful to note that Locke conceived of inner experience, called reflection, as a type of experience in addition to outer sense experience (sensation). Also, the simple ideas stemming from reflection could be combined into complex ideas.

The point in the present context is that according to Locke human knowledge was not a copy of the external world. However, although we do not have access to the essence of the things themselves, Locke postulated the existence of primary qualities as the foundation for his empiricism (see Haag, 1988, pp.57–58).

In defining reflection, i.e. thinking about one's own thinking, Locke clearly stressed the individual dimension, the knowing subject. Locke argues that reflection upon simple ideas results in the creating of the self. Remembering how I was aware of something earlier and comparing that awareness with my awareness of something present is the foundation of personal identity. Identity is thus the result of correspondence between two conceptions of myself. By this identification the subject becomes a recognizing subject.

The existence of personal identity has its foundation in a state of consciousness. The Cartesian man can thus be seen as a reflecting man, not as an acting man (cf. Marková, 1982). Reflection is thus prior to action in the sense that to be sure of our existence we must be conscious of our acts. As Marková (1982) puts it, to say that "I walk, therefore I exist" must refer to the awareness of doing this. More precisely one should say: "I am aware that I walk, therefore I exist".

George Berkeley (1685–1753) again advanced one step from Locke's position; not only were the secondary qualities constructed by the mind as Locke had argued, but also primary qualities (extension, shape, etc.). His position is condensed in the new principle, "Esse est percipi", according to which the objects of experience only exist as being experienced. This position is usually called epistemological or subjective idealism (Hamlyn, 1967, p.25). Berkeley's position should not be misunderstood—he did not argue that the outer world does not exist. What he asserts is that unexperienced reality does not make sense (Marc-Wogau, 1983, p.219). Consequently, objects not experienced by individuals exist anyway, as they are experienced by a God.

Like Berkeley, David Hume (1711–1776) argued that man in direct experience is aware only of his ideas. Thus, Hume denies the causal role of primary qualities accepted by Locke. As ideas were the only objects of certain knowledge, the existence of external objects, causal relations etc. had to be inferred from perceptual evidence. The associative rules guaranteed the coherence of perception.

Rationalists (e.g. Descartes) argued that absolutely certain knowledge is possible only in conceptual domains like logic and mathematics, which are not dependent on empirical reality. The empiricists thought that sources of knowledge consist in our experience, and true knowledge of the outer reality should thus be possible (Uljens, 1994b, pp.40 ff.). The empiricists (Hume), however, did not succeed in reaching true knowledge of the world because they were trapped in the sceptical tradition and made a distinction between the world as such and the world as perceived. The empiricist conclusion was thus extremely close to Descartes' position; only propositions about the world as perceived were possible.

The difference between Locke's and Hume's empiricism is crucial in this context. Whereas Locke preserved the idea of a causal theory of perception concerning primary qualities, Hume did not accept this position. Therefore it appears that present-day cognitivism is closer to Lockean than to Humean empiricism as a causal theory of perception is accepted. While Locke accepted that the mechanism by which simple ideas were combined into complex ideas was an innate capacity to unite, compare and repeat ideas, contemporary cognitivism is often silent about what is innate, although the question is debated. Cognitivism rather emphasizes the individual's capacity to construct new methods of connecting simple ideas with each other.

The Kantian Impact

Finally there is reason to briefly consider the Kantian solution, which in a certain sense combined the rationalistic and empiricist traditions. In accordance with the empiricists, Kant (1724–1804) thought that knowledge of empirical reality must be possible. Further he thought, like the empiricists, that the only reality we have access to is the experienced, phenomenal, reality. The reality-as-such is impossible to reach in direct experience but nevertheless exists. In order to avoid the risk of solipsism or idealism in both rationalism and empiricism he locked the mind by introducing aprioristic categories and relational concepts which organize sense impressions. The forms of perception (*Formen der Anschauung*), like time, space and rational categories (possibility, necessity, causality, etc.), were used by the subject to synthesize sense impressions with these forms. The access to this synthetic a priori knowledge guaranteed knowledge of experienced objects. Kant thus introduced the idea that the mind had a constitutive function in perception but, as Meyering (1989, p.114) points out, these activities of the mind did not affect what was perceived:

> [A]lthough the mind's operations concerning the data of sense are certainly constructive, they do not constitute free rational activities. Rather, the mind interprets data supplied by *Anschauung* through the necessary automatic application of a priori categories. Thus the content of perception is not in any way affected by the mind's constructive operations. In this sense the old Cartesian dualism of sensing and judging, though considerably modified, is yet retained after all in the Kantian dualism of thought and intuition.

Helmholtz

Once the operations of the mind were known, one could assume that the knowledge reached concerning the phenomenal world can be considered as valid for outer reality. It is, however, important to identify a difference between classical empiricists and the Kantian use of synthetic a priori knowledge. While Locke accepted a causal theory of perception concerning an object's primary qualities as the ground for believing that perceptually based knowledge was about the world (although this cannot be proved by reference to experience), Kant, for his part, used synthetic a priori knowledge in the same manner. But Kant's categories have only an assimilative function. As such they are necessary for experiencing but they themselves do not change.

In an impressive reconstruction of the historical development of the cognitive paradigm, Meyering (1989) shows how the research paradigm on the theory of perception developed by Herman von Helmholtz (see Kahl, 1971) constitutes a move beyond the Kantian stable system of categories towards a view where these constructive categories themselves are "capable of gradual and adaptive development" (ibid., p.113). In describing the Helmholtzian project, Meyering concludes:

> [I]n agreement with Reid that what we perceive is indeed objects (and not ideas or sensations) he [Helmholtz] maintained, contrary to Reid (and to Kant), that the epistemic transition from sensation to perception was due not to fixed principles of our human constitution nor (contrary to Hume) to natural imagination but to pragmatically controlled hypothesis subject to change.

Meyering (1989, pp.211–213) also argues that the reason why Helmholtz's theory admitted of access to the noumenal reality (Kant) was that although we do not have access to the metaphysical reality through our sense impressions, the impressions are still "signs of something":

> The relation between the symbols [qualities of sensations] and what they represent is only confined to this: that the same object operative under the same conditions will produce the same phenomenal sign and thus different signs must correspond to different causes. This rock-bottom relation—which is ... a formal relation of purely symbolic representation—makes the system of phenomenal signs into an extremely powerful cognitive tool. For, after all, this relation does copy the external reality, if only its lawlike structural aspects, its regularities and the sequential order of its events.

Meyering's (1989) conclusion is then that Helmholtz's hypothetical realism, with respect to the noematic reality, means that "the resulting harmony holds between the real world and our conceptions thereof and not merely (as in Kant) between reason on the one hand and a formally ordered a priori conceptualized reality on the other" (p.219).

The similarity between Helmholtz and Kant was that Helmholtz also emphasized the psychic processes producing knowledge, but he was much more modern in his idea of the role of these cognitive processes. Meyering (1989, p.217) concludes: "Contrary to Kant, Helmholtz did not conceive of these mediating processes as necessary restrictive fixed structures, but rather as goal-directed adaptive mechanisms."

The Role of the Cognitive Mechanism

A Lockean sceptical position on the epistemological problem means that knowledge of reality is constructed on the basis of sense impressions. Given this, the question of how sense impressions are related to each other becomes extremely important. While Locke suggested innate abilities like comparison, uniting etc., Hume suggested associative laws, Kant proposed innate categories, and cognitivists have emphasized the development of schemata.

Now, precisely because human rational thought is emphasized as the ultimate guarantee for reaching true knowledge, the mental processes become a central problem for cognitivist theory. The mental processes manipulating the information in the system thus become a key question in explaining how individuals reach knowledge of the world. Observe that when Kant claimed that the innate category system is equal for everybody, he assumed that different individuals can reach a similar conceptual structure. Cognitivists again allow the information processing strategies (including the encoding of received information), and schemata used to define what information means, to vary. This means that research must be directed both to the strategies used and the schemata constructed. Given a causal view of the relation between information in the external world and information received by the system (although it may be differently encoded among individuals), it is guaranteed that individuals experience the same reality.

THE ONTOLOGICAL MIND–BRAIN PROBLEM

Introduction

The relevance of the ontological mind–brain problem in understanding the process and result of learning is as follows. Assuming that learning is related to a change in an individual's competence, insight, skills or the like, the question is how we should describe that change. Even though it is argued in cognitivism that learning is primarily a change in an individual's mental representation and that this mental reality is causal with respect to behaviour, the question of how the changes in this representational level should be described is unanswered. Consequently, the result of learning could be similarly approached by asking in what language we ought to express what a person is aware of, when they are said to know something.

THE PROCESS OF LEARNING

Briefly one may say that orthodox information processing psychology compares minds with computational systems. One feature of computational systems is that the processes of the system operate solely on syntactic features of mental states (representations), not on semantic or pragmatic properties. In this conception syntactical features of symbols manipulated are not defined in relation to the semantics of the symbols. Even though syntactic properties are close to physical properties, they are not considered identical. An important feature of the cognitivist view is thus the efforts to specify the rules or mechanisms through which symbols are manipulated within the mind.

Regardless of whether such a computationalist view is understood literally or metaphorically in cognitivism, thinking is seen as the manipulation of an internal representation of an external domain (Hunt, 1989, p.604). The information content is seen as autonomous since it is thought that it can be explicated independently of physical instantiation. The analogy with the mental is that as an ordinary computer program will run on any machine independently of how the machine is built, it is thought that a mental programme can be described independently of individual or neurological aspects, i.e. that we do not have to deal with the neurological implementation when trying to understand how the information is processed in the brain.

One of the first explicitly arguing for this was Putnam (1960). Putnam's point was that different programs on different machines could carry out structurally identical problem-solving operations. Thus the logical operations themselves (the software) could be described apart from the hardware. The analogy with the human cognition was that the human brain (bodily states) corresponds to the computational hardware, and the patterns of thinking or problem solving (mental states) could on the other hand be described separately from the particular constitution of the human nervous system.

We can thus see that this version of cognitivism represents a dualist position on the ontological mind–brain problem. The representational level can be approached methodologically, independently of its brain–

physiological base. However, it is simultaneously thought that other physical systems, like computers, might perform cognitive operations. In this sense again the computationalist position is best described by calling it mind–physical instance dualism in this study. It would thereby represent a weak token identity theoretical position.

Before a more detailed specification of the cognitivist position concerning the ontological problem is presented, it is necessary to explicate fundamental features of the approach in more detail from this ontological perspective, i.e. how we should describe the content of mental states. A typical feature is that even though it is consistently argued that a representational symbol-manipulation level is necessary in describing learning, most theories are silent with respect to how these changes occur on this descriptional level.

The Level of Representation

One main feature of cognitivism is the belief that it is legitimate to posit a level of analysis which can be called the level of representation. It is claimed that the level of mental representation is necessary when we are interested in studying human cognitive activities. It is thus necessary to deal with representational entities as symbols, rules or images and to study how these representational entities are joined, formed or contrasted with each other. It is argued that this level is necessary to explain human thought, action and behaviour (Gardner, 1987, p.36). Usually these representations have been described in terms of schemas, images, models, or ideas. It may be useful to pay attention to the fact that internal representations are often divided into symbolic and distributed representations, though it has been argued that distributed representations are just symbolic representations on a more detailed level (Eysenck & Keane, 1991, p.202).

It is important that the representational and computational perspective is kept totally separate from a biological–neurological and from a sociocultural or socio-historical level of analysis. This means that the level of representation falls between culture and the nervous system. It is, however, often thought that representations and rules operating on these symbols ultimately exist or can be mirrored through the central nervous system. Within representational and computational theory it is nonetheless argued that the neurological level is not the most suitable for describing human cognition.

It is also important to make a distinction between representations on the one hand and plans, intentions and beliefs on the other. Thus, a person can have mental representations of plans, intentions and beliefs.

The Capacity of the Memory

Variation in cognitive achievement has been explained in terms of variations in the short-term or working memory. For example Brown and Van Lehn (1980) argue, on the basis of their empirical work on children's arithmetical achievement, that variation in this achievement is partly due to the children's memory capacity. According to the explanation provided, certain schemata, necessary for solving problems, are sufficiently developed, as a result of which the activity of solving problems may load the working memory to such an extent that central arithmetical operations are forgotten or overlooked. This is not of course the explanation of all differences in cognitive achievement. Other aspects that are considered important are how information is structured, how individuals interpret situations and how heuristic rules are applied. For example, when it comes to heuristic rules, it is thought that these help the individual to restrict the total number of possible ways of acting. Thus, if an individual does not succeed in correctly solving a problem, it is argued that the individual has not formed a sufficiently complete representation of the situation. Again, when the individual tries to diminish the load on the memory by restricting the problem space, important information is lost, which leads to illusions (bugs). If an individual's memory capacity, especially the working memory, were larger, it would be possible to make more rational decisions, it is claimed. This view, represented by e.g. Brown and Van Lehn (1980) and Chandler and Sweller (1991), represents the class of theories that may be called limited capacity theories (Goldman, 1991, p.334).

Learning as Problem Solving

A central feature of the cognitive paradigm is the rule system applied in solving problems or in cognition in general. In this view, a symbol structure is always manipulated according to some rule system. There are primarily three rule systems that cognitivism historically draws upon. These are the idea of the algorithm, logic, and grammar. The principle of formal logic covers these rule systems. In short this means that an individual looks for the most suitable strategy of actions in order to achieve a goal. In this context formal logic thus deals with the question of what a correct strategy or conclusion is like. It is the structure of the conclusion or strategy which guarantees the validity of a result. A strategy consists of elementary operations in the representational system.

Problem solving is considered a typical situation where it is thought that an individual's symbol structure is used and eventually changed. It should be observed that solving a problem is a performance, not necessarily learning something new. To solve a problem and to learn to solve a problem are two different things (see Uljens, 1992b, p.23).

A problem is defined as a situation where an individual has a goal or an understanding of a situation that is not present, but lacks the means of reaching that goal or future state (Newell & Simon, 1972). Thus a problem has an initial state and a terminal state. A problem is solved when an individual has moved from the initial to the terminal state by applying a number of elementary operations. These operations follow some rule-system. The problem thus consists of elements which can be dealt with, with the help of elementary operations. A game of chess is often used as an example of this procedure. The initial state and the terminal state are well-defined. The elements and rules can be identified. The problem is to carry out such operations as lead to the terminal situation.

The Role of Previous Knowledge in Problem Solving

In cognitivism it is usually explained that individuals make use of their previous schemata in order to restrict the problem space. Thus there are not necessarily any differences between individuals with respect to the strategies as such, applied in solving a problem. The difference does not depend on "the use of different or more powerful heuristics, but on initial representation that allows the expert to succeed in pursuing the better path to solution without considering all the others" (Glaser, 1987, p.401).

A schema thus functions as the knowledge structure directing attention. In addition, it may contain information in terms of a plan. Expressed in the terminology above, a plan is the way the subject moves from the initial state (a task) to the solution of it (goal-state) (Miller, Galanter, & Pribram, 1960). Winne (1987, p.501) summarizes the concept of a plan:

> [A] plan can . . . be described as a set of sequenced cognitive operations that the student applies to information to complete a task. In essence, a plan is a schema the student activates to perform a particular task. The plan progresses through a succession of cognitive operations on information.

When a student moves towards the goal-state in a stepwise manner, the results of discrete operations are stored in the working memory as is the student's position in the plan. This means that the student is thought to be aware of the discrepancy between their present state in the plan and the goal-state.

However, it appears that cognitivism has not paid much attention to the acquisition or change of schemata (Eysenck & Keane, 1991, p.280):

Many theorists are either silent about how schemata are formed or assume that some type of ill-specified induction is used in which specific experiences are concatenated . . . This is a fairly loose account and reflects the underdevelopment of theoretical proposals on schema learning.

THE RESULT OF LEARNING

Different Ways in Which Information is Represented

All representational theories accept the following two assumptions as necessary in cognition; the existence of the data structures, which are stored according to some representational format and the processes that operate upon the data structures (Rumelhart & Norman, 1987, p.59).

These assumptions are apparent within three representational accounts of research on cognition. These are propositional, procedural and analogical representational systems (Silver, 1987, p.37).

The propositional representational systems view knowledge in terms of a set of symbols or propositions in the sense that concepts are represented by formal statements.

In the procedural systems, knowledge is assumed to be represented in terms of procedures. In some cases the representation cannot be separated from the process it represents.

Within the analogical systems the correlation between the represented and representing world is as direct as possible. Typical examples of these kinds of representations are maps that may be seen as analogical representations of geographical features or two-dimensional pictures which represent a three-dimensional reality.

It is thus assumed that information is represented in the human mind mainly in three different ways, depending on what happens to be the object of representation. In propositional systems, meaning expressed in symbols is represented, in analogical systems images are represented, and in procedural systems procedures are represented.

Here it may be noticed that the process that operates upon data structures is as important as the representation itself, i.e. one of them cannot exist without the other. Some representational format always has to exist with some process that corresponds to that format (McShane, 1991, p.163).

There are, however, many controversies on the differences and similarities between these types of representations. It is debated whether there really is any difference between analogical and propositional systems (Kosslyn, 1987) and how analogical and representational systems do relate to continuous and discrete representations (Rumelhart & Norman, 1987). Thirdly, it has been debated whether declarative and procedural representations correspond to declarative and procedural knowledge

(McClelland, Rumelhart, & the PDP Research group, 1986; Rumelhart & Norman, 1987, p.59).

How is the Result of Learning Stored in the Memory?

We concluded earlier that all representational and information processing theories of the mind regard the problem of *how* information is stored in the mind as important. The contemporary cognitive view of memory is that memory consists in encoding, storage and retrieval of information. Further it is maintained that one must also acknowledge both the structure and process of memory (Eysenck & Keane, 1991, p.133). With respect to storage of information, Broadbent (1971) suggested that information might be stored in the memory as it is stored in a library, i.e. organized according to semantical features.

The view according to which information can be found in the memory only according to some specific rules of storage has been criticized as too limited. Multi-store theories have been developed as a solution to these problems.

Nevertheless, the view of memory presented by Atkinson and Shiffrin (1968) has become, at least metaphorically, the dominant model. According to them there are a sensory register receiving (modality-specific) information, a short-term store and a long-term store. Furthermore, there are control processes that operate on both the short- and the long-term memory.

Tulving's (1972, 1983) distinction between a procedural memory and a cognitive memory came to be an additional cornerstone of this paradigm. According to Tulving, in the procedural memory motoric and cognitive skills are stored. Often these skills are automatized. The cognitive long-term memory is then divided into an episodic and a semantic memory. The episodic memory covers limited episodes or events in time and space, while the semantic memory covers organized conceptual, often general or principal knowledge or symbolic systems (Tulving, 1972, pp.385–386).

Baddeley and Hitch (1974) revised Atkinson and Shiffrin's model. Their point was that the short- and long-term stores should be replaced by one store; a part of which is activated and becomes working memory when information is being processed (cf. McShane, 1991, p.162). This working memory in turn consists of different components (a visual component, a phonological component and a "modality free central executive resembling attention", Eysenck & Keane, 1991, p.143). The Baddeley and Hitch (1974) model was later developed into a more complex model (see Baddeley, 1986), but the main ideas are the same. The multi-store model with a specific structure and specific processes has nevertheless remained as a metaphor in cognitivist memory research.

Type of Knowledge

What kind of knowledge does the cognitivist view of learning then result in? In cognitive psychological literature, two types of knowledge are frequently referred to: declarative and procedural knowledge. Many of the contemporary theories on cognition explicitly develop their theory within the framework of propositional theories of knowledge (Anderson, 1983; Minsky, 1975; Newell & Simon, 1972; Schank & Abelson, 1977). In fact this is not very surprising, since these are similar to those forms of knowledge that are needed in artificial systems. A declarative symbol structure is thus conceived of as having a propositional content which may be evaluated with regard to the extent to which this propositional content represents an outer reality.

It is also enlightening to relate these forms of knowledge to two different concepts of information. Declarative knowledge is close to the idea of semantic information and deals with the question of how symbols are related to their reference or meaning. Procedural knowledge is close to syntactic information, which is connected with the syntactic (grammatical) dimension of language, i.e. with the relations between the signs or symbols of a language.

Nativism

It is clear that, in cognitivism, Kant's a priori synthetic categories regulating perception are replaced by continuously changing schemes or other forms of conceptual structures. It seems, however, that many cognitivists ultimately find nativism necessary because it offers either a fundamental category system or an innate symbol system enabling humans to develop culturally relevant categories (e.g. Carey, 1985; Chomsky, 1965; Fodor, 1975; Piaget, 1953). This by no means implies an acceptance of Piaget's genetic epistemology. On the contrary, modern cognitivists seem by now to have completely abandoned Piaget's genetic epistemology, i.e. the idea that the development of fundamental schemes goes through identical steps irrespective of individual experience. Only some form of initial inborn set-up enabling individuals to develop schemes later seems to be accepted.

THE ONTOLOGICAL POSITION OF COGNITIVISM— PROPERTY DUALISM AND FUNCTIONALISM

By now we have seen that many different positions and directions exist within what has been called the cognitive paradigm. Primarily we have investigated representational and information processing theories.

It appears reasonable to claim that two different ontological positions are actualized within this research. The positions represented by the different versions of the information processing framework are property dualism and functionalism.

Property Dualism

Many advocates of the representational school of conceptual change (e.g. Rumelhart, Carey) represent what is called a property dualist position on the ontological mind–brain problem.

The main feature of the dualistic conception of the nature of mind is that the mental is of a qualitatively different character than the physical world, and hence irreducible to physiological processes in the brain or to any other physical system (Uljens, 1994b, pp.51 ff.).

When we talk about traditional Cartesian dualism, we talk about it in terms of a substance dualism, i.e. holding the radical view that fundamentally reality consists of two different substances. A modern and weaker form of dualism holds that the world is fundamentally of one substance, material things, but that some material objects (e.g. brains) also have mental properties. This position, property dualism, allows mental phenomena to be of a distinctive nature but rejects the idea that a second substance must exist in the world to make the existence of the mental possible. Property dualism is also called emergent interactionism, emergent materialism (Bunge, 1980) or interactionist property dualism (Churchland, 1988, p.12). Interactionism implies that the mental is seen as having causal power, and is thus different from e.g. epiphenomenalism. Property and emergent refer to the idea that the mental is a property that has emerged from complex processes in the brain; it therefore contrasts with Cartesian substance dualism. Dualism stands for the idea that the mental cannot be reduced to neurological processes. The main difference from Cartesian two-substance dualism is that mind is not considered to be of another kind of substance compared with matter. It is conceived of as a property that some physical objects (systems) have.

When we classify the position described above as representing dualism, we must remember that this is in no way unproblematic. On the contrary, we could conveniently argue that property dualism is a materialist theory since the neuronal reality is absolutely necessary for the mind to exist. In this sense property dualism is closer to materialist positions than to Cartesian two-substance dualism.

Functionalism

Of the previously discussed theories of learning, Anderson's (1983) ACT together with Fodor (1975, 1983) represent what is here referred to as functionalism.

A distinctive feature of functionalism is the idea that it is possible to study the mind independently of its physical constitution. According to a functionalist definition anything that realizes an identified functional role in a particular system is identical with the original mental state. Functionalism does not have any requirements with respect to the structure, form, chemistry or any other physical feature concerning the functional system (Dennett, 1990; Churchland, 1988, p.36). Instead, the functional role of mental states is emphasized. It means that mental states are identified in terms of the functional role they have in the system.

When representations are individuated in functionalist theory (in terms of a network of functional roles), two relations are identified. First, the relation between different representations and second, the relation between a representation and reality. This identification is guided by the interactive relation a particular representation has with respect to other representations and reality.

Since the computational form of functionalism is close to the computationalist view of mind, I will only briefly point out what makes this a specific version of functionalism. In this version mental activities are characterized in terms of symbols and rules manipulating these symbols. The point is to explicate both the symbols and the rules so precisely that it is possible to determine when two physically differently instantiated systems apply the same symbols and rules to produce the same outcome (thus avoiding the behavioural Turing criterion).

One approach which very well exemplifies this is the concept of functional architecture developed by Pylyshyn (1984). In short, the idea is to identify a set of basic procedures which can be executed by minds and computers. Pylyshyn thinks that the human brain is constituted of a biologically given basic cognitive architecture which it is possible to discover. This is possible through experimental simulation using the computer. Since the computer does not have an absolute architecture, it is thought that this can be modified to become comparable with human cognitive activities.

The main difference between property dualism and computational functionalism is that property dualism is silent concerning the mechanisms through which the representational symbols are manipulated. Thus, strictly speaking, it would be possible to view functionalism as a specification of property dualism.

Mind–Physical Instance Dualism

Functionalism thus argues with token identity theory that all mental states (each token) must always consist of one or another state of the brain, i.e. that no mental state is a non-physiological, non-neurological event. From this position it is argued that it might very well be that a functional system with another physical constitution compared with the human one, can be in an identical functional state (Fodor, 1975). This way of defining mental states gives hope for work within cognitivism since this ontology also allows an artificial system to "be" in a functional state; the artificial system would be the "subject" of a mental state. Thus functionalism rejects the Type identity theory since it is supposed that one specific mental state can be realized in several physical systems, i.e. there does not have to be any identity between a mental and a physical position so that every mental state must correspond to some specific physical instantiation. This means that functionalism represents a kind of "mind–physical instance dualism".

The point is that, as in identity theory generally, every mental state must correlate to *some* kind of physical state. Functionalism is thus liberal where the relation between mental and physical states is concerned. Type identity theory requires *specific* types of physical states as counterparts of certain types of mental states; token identity theory limits the demands, requiring that every mental state has to have *some* brain–physiological correlate. Functionalism again accepts *any* kind of physical state as a correlate to mental states, i.e. both physiological and physical.

The previous distinctions also show in what sense functionalism is dualistic. Functionalism is not dualistic in the sense of Cartesian two-substance dualism but it represents Cartesian dualism in that genuine human experience should not be described on a neurophysiological level although cognition is dependent on the human brain. Functionalism, like neurophysiological psychology, thus represents a kind of mind–physical instance dualism in that physical states other than physiological brain states can be said to be in experiential states.

A reason for the popularity of functionalism is that according to this view psychology remains methodologically autonomous, i.e. it cannot be reduced to the neurophysiological structure of the brain. Thus there is a logical difference from the eliminative materialist position represented by physical-level psychology, which tries to explain mental events in purely physicalistic or neuroscientific terms (see Churchland). It is against this background that it becomes interesting to construct systems of functional states in terms of computer simulations to be compared with human behaviour aiming at discovering the functional organization of humans.

A second positive feature of this view is that it offers a quite simple way of dealing with the notion of the unconscious mind. The position accepted is that one may view conscious awareness as the usage of a limited part of the information stored in the memory. As Jackendoff (1989, pp.16–17) says: "inactive information can be regarded as unconscious—but still mental . . . Thus, the conscious and unconscious parts of the mind are of the same character, built of information and the processes that operate upon it".

SUMMARY

In the previous analysis, the process and result of the cognitivist view of learning were systematically related to the ontological and epistemological problem within the philosophy of mind. The analysis was reported in accordance with the four relations identified. The process and the result of learning were thus discussed both in terms of the epistemological problem and in terms of the ontological problem. In short, the result revealed the following.

Learning in the Light of the Epistemological Problem

The epistemological problem actualized the relation between the content of awareness and external reality. The first question was how cognitivist theory conceives of this relation when an individual has knowledge of something. The second question was how the process of learning may be understood in terms of changes in the so-called mind–world relation.

The results of the analysis concerning these questions revealed the following. During the learning process an individual receives information about the surrounding world via the sensory systems and the brain. This information has a subject-independent existence, i.e. it exists independently of an experiencing individual. This information is then received and manipulated by the human information-processing system. Often some type of causal relation between external reality and the receiving sensory system seems to be accepted. This information is then encoded and manipulated by the cognitive system.

The result of this process is conceptual knowledge which may be described in terms of individual systems of information stored in some representational format. This conceptual structure, a scheme, mental model or the like, is then an individual representation of the surrounding world. The correspondence between the individual conceptual structure and the structure of the external reality may consequently be evaluated.

The epistemological analysis thus shows that the cognitivist position may be described in terms of a representative epistemology or a dualist epistemological position. In some cases it seems that this dualist epistemology is based upon scientific critical realism according to which the world has independent existence, but that its meaning is to be established in terms of a relation between the experiencing subject's previous knowledge and their sensory input of the world.

However, there seems to be an unsolved conflict between the view of the individual as an active agent constructing interpretations and the view according to which the individual receives and treats information. On the one hand, the cognitivist thinks that it may be possible to obtain a true picture of the world by relating pieces of information to each other. This view often occurs in connection with the implicit assumption of a causal theory of perception. On the other hand, in cognitivist-oriented positions supporting a view of learning as a constructive process, experiences do not have any straightforward relation to external reality. On the contrary, a constructivist cannot evaluate their experiences by comparing them with a world as such, precisely because experiencing is always a constructive process. In this respect constructivism represents some version of epistemological idealism.

Finally it should be noted that the result of the learning process is discussed in a much more detailed way compared with the process of learning. From an epistemological perspective on the mind–world problem, learning is close to the assimilative process through which information is incorporated into the individual's conceptual structure. In order to discuss how the content of mind changes in learning, the ontological level was a necessary level of analysis.

Causal Theory of Perception and Epistemological Dualism. It seems reasonable to conclude on the basis of the previous analysis that the information processing approach to human cognition shares a representational position on the epistemological problem.

According to this view, information would exist in the world independently of a perceiver. This information systematically affects the individual's sensory system. This received information forms the stuff manipulated by the cognitive system.

The mental world is thus constructed on the basis of sensory information, i.e. using perceptual inputs as the building blocks. In order to be able to assume that a conceptual knowledge structure, a scheme or the like, is about the real world, a causal relation is accepted between the system receiving information and the external world.

On the basis of the previous discussion it may be concluded that cognitivism represents a dualist understanding of the relation between perceptual presentations and cognitive representations. Furthermore, cognitivism seems to accept some kind of non-dualist or causal relation between the properties of physical objects and the individual's sense impressions.

Learning in the Light of the Ontological Problem

The second set of questions concerning learning was investigated in terms of the ontological mind-brain problem aiming at an understanding of how human cognitive life should be described. The first question was how a mental state as such should be described regardless of what the individual is aware of, i.e. regardless of the answer to epistemological questions.

The analysis showed that the cognitivist approach includes many approaches to learning, but is primarily a representational and computational approach.

The first question of the two within the ontological mind–brain problem was how the change in a mental state should be described.

The answer suggested by all cognitivist approaches to learning was that manipulation of information received was stressed. Learning was conceived of as a cognitive activity whereby the individual treats information according to some patterns or strategies. Learning is thus equated with processing of information.

Two different ontological positions on the mind–brain problem were identified among the investigated approaches. The first was property dualism and the second functionalism.

Property dualism was considered close to such representational models as approached learning in terms of restructuring schemata or conceptual change models. These theories do not explicate the process of change in any great detail although they emphasize the usefulness of strategy instruction. They also seem to feel comfortable with describing cognition in a non-reductionist manner with respect to the physiology of the brain although they accept an interactive relationship between the brain and the representational level.

The second position identified within cognitivism is functionalism, representing mind–physical instance dualism on the ontological problem. This means that functionalist cognitivism accepts a dichotomy between the phenomenological reality and the physiological level of description. This separation refers to the fact that physical processes other than brain-physiological ones might model or represent mental processes and states, i.e. that phenomenological states may be represented by any physical system.

This version was more explicit in its effort to specify the mechanisms or the process through which learning occurs. It appears that most present-day cognitivism applies the fundamental ideas of assimilation, accommodation and equilibration in approaching learning though applying a slightly different terminology (restructuring, knowledge representation). Yet there are fundamental differences between the traditional Piagetian view and the information processing approach.

Concerning the result of learning in an ontological perspective, all approaches argue that it should be described on a representational level, i.e. on a level independent of the physiology of the brain. Learning was claimed to result mainly in descriptive, propositional and analogical knowledge structures stored in the long-term memory. The information could be stored as concepts, propositions or schemata. Therefore the structure and function of different types of memories were emphasized.

7 Pedagogical Implications of Cognitivist Learning Theory

INTRODUCTION

In this chapter, results of the analysis of pedagogical implications of the cognitivist approach to learning are reported. Pedagogical implications refer to questions of instructional method and content of teaching.

The following discussion of pedagogical implications will be based on the analysis presented in Chapter 6. Thus, the epistemological mind–world problem and the ontological mind–brain problem are used as the two main sections of this chapter. The pedagogical implications of the cognitivist approach are then seen in relation to how the process and result of learning were understood.

One Method—Many Learning Theories

Assumptions about learning are often used as the point of departure in developing instructional methods to be used by teachers. However, although a specific view of learning may suggest some specific instructional procedure, this instructional method is seldom unique to that theory of learning only (Silver, 1987, p.54). Many instructional methods are common to many learning theories, but the way these methods are argued for may vary with the assumptions regarding the learning process and the nature of knowledge reached. Thus, the motive for applying specific pedagogical methods may vary across theories. Because of this I think it would be fruitful to focus on the relation between how basic assumptions behind cognitivist theory of learning and pedagogical implications are advocated.

A Comment Concerning the Approach

There is a large amount of literature dealing with pedagogical implications of different cognitivist approaches to learning. In the 60s many influential books based on a cognitivist view about learning were published (e.g. Ausubel, 1963; Bruner, 1966; Gagné, 1965; Taba, 1966).

Some of the early ideas have remained, some are refined, others, again, are less emphasized today and new ideas of teaching have developed as the cognitivist approach has developed. For example, more recently, the shift from content- or domain-independent strategies to content-related strategies has had educational consequences. Contextual aspects of the learning process are rapidly affecting the way teaching is understood as well. In addition, the view of the actors in the pedagogical process has changed in some respects with the student seen as an active decision-maker to an increasing extent (Gallagher, 1994, p.171 f.).

Joyce and Weil (1980) note in their extensive work on models of teaching that the variety of models based on different views on information-processing is large: "The range of information processing models is considerable ... Grasping the entire family of available models is a formidable task" (p.23). In this study I do not intend to present even a structural map of these different approaches. The focus of interest is instead on frequently occurring pedagogical implications in the light of the previous analysis.

The approach in this study differs in some fundamental ways from that in Joyce and Weil's (1980) study. While they discuss existing models of teaching developed on information-processing theories of cognition, the point of departure of the present study is the two criteria pointed out earlier—the ontological and the epistemological problems.

The level of analysis chosen thus goes beyond the level on which the information-processing theories are usually explicated. This means that when pedagogical implications are discussed, these implications (pedagogical principles) can be considered valid for several models of teaching based on the information-processing view of learning. Thus, the choice of a more fundamental level of analysis leads to a more general level of discussing pedagogical implications. The negative result is that differences between competing models will remain invisible, while the positive result is that attention is turned towards essential implications of this approach to the TSL process.

A second difference from Joyce and Weil's (1980) approach is that the present study does not treat learning as a superordinate category on the basis of which instructional principles are developed. Although the idea in this chapter is to present pedagogical implications of this school of thought, the overall approach of this study was to start from a theory of didactics and then ask what role a theory of learning could play within the descriptive-normative model of didactics that was developed.

A third difference, related to the previous ones, is that although the description of the pedagogical implications of cognitivism may view the teacher as a rationalist decision-maker (Shavelson, 1987) or as a regulator of information-processes in the classroom (Joyce & Weil, 1980), this view of the teacher is not adopted by the present didactic approach to the TSL process. The didactic model developed earlier was not assumed to reflect an individual teacher's thinking, rather it was developed as a scientific (research) model of didactics. In what respects and to what extent a teacher is able to make use of such a model is another problem. Some aspects of it were discussed in Chapter 3 and will be returned to in Chapter 8. However, it should be more than clear that the school didactic model in Part One conceived of the TSL process as something more than the application of prescriptive recommendations derived from learning theory.

The Epistemological and Ontological Problems in Relation to the Mediational Approach to Learning from Teaching

It may be instructive to note how the instruments of analysis, i.e. the epistemological and the ontological problems, correspond to the cognitivist approach to learning from teaching. Winne (1987, p.457) has neatly summarized a model synthesizing "mainstream research from cognitive and instructional psychology with recent research on learning". For the sake of clarification his visual figure is reprinted below (Fig. 7.1).

The model is divided into two major components, the students' cognitive processing system and the classroom environment. The students' system is in turn described in terms of four sites "through which information is moved and processed" (ibid. p.499). Firstly, there is the sensory system which is "the gateway through which information from the environment enters the cognitive system. Here, energy from the environment such as light reflected from print on a page, is transformed into a neurally coded representation of the print" (ibid. p.499).

The second system is the memory system including working- and long-term memory. The third site is the processing system. Finally, the response system "is the gateway for the products of students' cognitive processing to be manifested as performances. It consists of a storage area that temporally holds information before it is transferred into neural messages for motor action" (ibid. p.499).

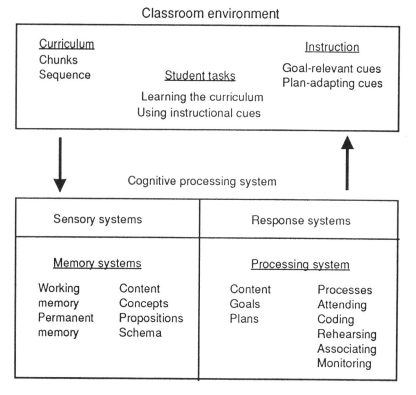

FIG. 7.1. A cognitive model of learning from teaching according to Winne (1987, p.497). A model very similar to this, though emphasizing the social interaction, is presented by Norman (1987). Reprinted from Winne, P.H. (1987). Students' cognitive processing. In M.J. Dunkin (Ed.), The international encyclopedia of teacher education, p. 497. Copyright (1987), with permission from Elsevier Science Ltd.

Winne divides the classroom environment into three dimensions: the curriculum, student tasks, and instruction. These dimensions will be of specific interest in this chapter.

The core idea of this cognitive model of learning from teaching is basically that cognitive processing is reciprocal with respect to the instructional environment. This means, according to Winne (1987, p.497) that (a) "students cannot be passive recipients of teaching. They participate in creating what teaching means to them" and that (b) it is "improper to declare teacher behaviors as the sole cause of students' achievement".

It is argued (see Doyle, 1978) that the mediational model of research on the TSL process is fundamentally different from the process–product paradigm. In the process–product model much attention was focused on the idea that specific teaching activities would be connected with specific learning processes, which in turn would lead to specific learning outcomes. Instructional research on teachers' questions was based on e.g. Bloom's (1956) taxonomy of educational objectives[1] (Winne, 1987, p.498). The idea was that instruction demanding more complicated cognitive processing would result in qualitatively better learning. The cognitive mediational model developed partly as a result of growing insights relative to the fact that students experienced instruction differently, contrary to what was previously assumed. The cognitive mediational model (Winne, 1987, p.498) thus emphasizes the interactionist relation between learning and teaching:

> The cognitive mediational model characterizes learning from teaching as a series of interactions between events in the instructional environment and the students' cognitive processing system. It is hypothesized that there are instructional cues or stimuli in the environment that have a potential to influence each student's cognitive processing.

A comment to be made with respect to the mediational approach concerns the absence of interest in the students' response system. To say that knowledge about "the response system and its role in the cognitive processing system ... is outside the domain of most classroom phenomena" (Winne, 1987, p.499) casts a shadow on the interactionist orientation of the teaching–learning process. If the students' response system is neglected, as it apparently is, then on what does a teacher react when teaching? Should not the students' response system be developed in the model in order to reach a truly interactionist approach? The students' response system clearly plays a crucial role for the teachers' cognitive processing system. As it is now, the attention in Winne's model is turned towards the students' internal cognitive processing system and the instructional environment. But the teacher as an intentional subject acting upon students' studying–learning processes is not included in Winne's model. This is, in fact, one major difference between Winne's model and the school didactic model presented in Chapter 3 of this study.

In fact, research on students' experience of teaching is also limited within the mediational approach (Winne, 1987, p.506):

> Classroom research identifying the kinds of instructional cues students attend to and how their plans are influenced by instructional cues is scant.

> [R]esearch has shown that students can be taught to identify and use instructional cues, but the effects of this training in classrooms are not yet consistently predictable.

However, with these limitations the *aim* of the mediational approach is to approach the TSL process from an interactionist perspective.

Norman (1980, 1987) is another representative of the mediational paradigm. The view of the student as an interpreter of the instructional environment connected with the learner's way of acting upon perceived information is supported. Norman (1980, 1987) stresses, however, that learning in classrooms cannot be fully understood on the basis of mediational models which neglect social interaction. Yet he argues (Norman, 1987, p.315) that a cybernetic view of the individual's activity or information processing works as the basic unit of social interaction:

> [I]f one wishes to understand the particular responses of the teacher or of an individual child to a particular classroom event, then it is necessary to have an information processing view of the person ... But the model is only going to be useful if it is coupled with an understanding of the several simultaneous (and possibly conflicting) goals and motivations of the various participants.

The relation between Winne's (1987) model of learning from teaching presented in the figure above and the approach of this study is that the epistemological problem actualizes the relation between the individual and the instructional environment in terms of the process and the result of learning. The ontological problem again actualizes how we should describe or characterize the individual's psychic reality, its changes and products.

Finally, in order to avoid misunderstandings—there are also other fundamental philosophical aspects through which learning theory may be investigated. One such aspect is the social and cultural dimension of learning and its products, a second is the question of ideology in learning theory, a third concerns the ethics of knowledge acquisition or construction and teaching.

The Structure of this Chapter. The approach adopted in this part of the study parallels the approach in the previous chapters, i.e. the cognitivist paradigm and its implications for teaching are not limited in a very narrow-minded way. This was not considered fruitful, since a very strict limitation of the interest to only one line of thought within the cognitivist paradigm (e.g. to the computational approach) would have given a too limited picture of the cognitivist paradigm and its pedagogical implications.

Finally, attention in this study is mainly limited to dealing with acquiring conceptual knowledge, not with learning practical skills, ethical reasoning or the like. However, the school didactic model as such allows for such an analysis of learning.

In order to avoid misunderstandings it should also be said that the main function of this chapter is to organize the pedagogical implications in accordance with the previous analysis, i.e. many of the implications occur frequently in the literature in the field and are thus not constructed within the frames of this study.

TEACHING AND THE EPISTEMOLOGICAL MIND-WORLD PROBLEM

The epistemological mind–world problem focuses on the relation between an individual's psychological reality and the (semantic) structure of some external learning content. The pedagogical problem is how a teacher may influence the relation between an individual's understanding and external reality in order to assist learning.

The following two subsections consider this problem from the perspective of the process and result of learning. Let me repeat here that the result of learning is identified both with the initial stage of the learning process and with the result of a process.

TEACHING AND THE LEARNING PROCESS

The major question actualized by the epistemological perspective on the process of learning concerns how the individual receives or chooses information from the external world in order to build up a mental representation of this world. In particular, the question of how this process is connected with the learning process identified as radical restructuring is important. This kind of learning was identified as accommodation, because the learner's model undergoes a radical shift comparable to a shift in the scientific world-view, e.g. the shift from a geocentric to a heliocentric world-view.

The subject-matter taught and learned in schools may in turn be seen as an externalization, or a representation of a curriculum maker's representation of some subject matter.

The fundamental feature of cognitivist theory in this respect is that there is a causal relation between the stimulus input from the environment and the individual's sensory system. The encoded information is a lawful representation of the stimulus input. However, as Miller (1987) reminds us, the stored information is not necessarily equal to the environmental stimulus. This again has to do with the learner's initial cognitive structure and information processing strategies; previous representations direct what is attended to in perception.

Teaching—Facilitating the Construction of a Goal-model

One of the most general pedagogical implications of the cognitivist approach is that teachers should help the learner to build up an internal model that corresponds to the goal-model as well as possible.

The Explication of the Students' Initial Model

One of the important steps in teaching which aims to achieve conceptual change is that the teacher should clarify the students' initial model.

It is argued that a teacher has a very distinct role in the instructional setting as this view "involves an active teacher who is interested in understanding the students' point of view, proposing alternate frameworks, creating conceptual conflict, and leading students into constructing conceptually consistent theories of [knowledge] domains" (Vosniadou & Brewer, 1987, p.61).

Teaching by Helping the Learner to Reflect on Their Own Model

Many of the instructional implications developed on the basis of the cognitivist view of learning are related to the idea that the learner should be made aware of their own understanding or conceptual structure. By this means, it is argued, it is possible to compare different ways to perceive one and the same instructional content, as well as to test different models of explanation of the same experiences.

Vosniadou and Brewer (1987, p.61) have argued in favour of what they call socratic dialogues to bring about the transformation termed radical restructuring, which was discussed previously. They mean that these dialogues help the students to become aware of problems with the schema they have:

> Socratic dialogues are used mainly to facilitate the awareness of inconsistencies in an individual's current schema, which appears to be a necessary step for those types of changes that require that old beliefs are abandoned and replaced with a fundamentally different conceptual structure.

Cognitive Conflicts—Anomalies on the Individual Level

According to the idea of learning as an accommodative process, and comparing learning with Kuhn's idea of scientific revolutions through a number of anomalic observations, Posner, Strike, Hewson and Gertzog

(1982) suggest that the creation of cognitive conflicts may be seen as a useful instructional method. Therefore the teacher's role is to point out the consequences of and inconsistencies within individual students' cognitive structure, and to show in what respects a student's understanding is not satisfactory, again with the motive of helping students to become aware of their own way of perceiving the subject-matter at hand (see also Hewson & Hewson, 1984; Nussbaum & Novick, 1982).

Posner et al. (1982) argue that the degree of the individual's dissatisfaction with their conception affects the learner's willingness to change their understanding. The less satisfied, the more willing the individual is to change, so to speak: "The more the students consider the anomaly to be serious, the more dissatisfied they will be with current concepts, and the more likely they may be ready ultimately to accommodate new ones" (ibid., p.224). The idea of dissatisfaction as a driving force creating willingness to learn shows obvious similarities with Piaget's concept of equilibration.

Besides creating cognitive conflicts teaching could, as Posner et al. (1982) suggest, be organized so that enough time is spent "in diagnosing errors in student thinking and identifying defensive moves used by students to resist accommodation" (p.226).

The Goal-model or the Student's Model as a Starting Point?

Sometimes the student may not have any model at all of some specific subject matter or a very ill-structured model of some specific content. Therefore the teacher should sometimes just start with the goal model (Glaser, 1987, p.407) and sometimes with the student's own model:

> One can explicitly teach new models of understanding or one can build on models presently held by the individual. The determination of which approach is most facilitative must be made in consideration of learners' existing model or understanding and its relation to the to-be-attained model.

Previous Knowledge and Freedom in Interpretation

A view concerning the development of an individual's mental schema is that a well-developed model held by the learner makes the individual more free in determining the meaning of new information. This would explain partly why experts should be taught differently than novices; the more experienced a learner is, the more responsibility they may be given for the learning process as they have become more free to interpret the information received.

However, Neisser (1976, p.179) showed that this is not necessarily the right conclusion. In fact, he showed that adults are often more conventional in their interpretation than children. He writes: "Children are spontaneous, unpredictable, and free of convention: how can they also be stimulus bound?" Neisser's (1976) point is that the more experienced individual is not necessarily more free to interpret the information as they like. More recent research has also shown that previous models or alternative frameworks may be highly resistant to change (Champagne, Gunstone & Klopfer, 1985). Neisser's point is that the expert's experience allows them to see the world differently in comparison with the novice, but does not necessarily make them more free in their way of seeing.

In answering the question of what we would have to know in order to control what a skilled person does, Neisser (1976, p.183) says that only a person who has access to the same information as the individual whose behaviour will be predicted is able to predict what this person is most likely to do. To improve one's behaviour then means to improve one's knowledge of a subject matter and not to improve in psychology:

> This means that the psychologist cannot predict and control anyone who knows more about the situation than he does, or who picks up information that he has left out of the reckoning.

Consequently, a teacher who wants to influence the learner's study activity should focus on controlling how the learner understands the world as well as on how the learning environment is arranged, not on controlling the psychological processes by which the individual is thought to treat the information received.

If we accept what Neisser (1976, p.185) says, i.e. that "real manipulation occurs all the time without benefit of psychological theory", of which lying and misinformation are just two examples, then we may ask what a teacher needs (mentalistic) psychological theory for in order to teach successfully.

Naturally Neisser's (1976) conclusion is at odds with the cognitivist school, where the psychological processes are considered crucial in the process of receiving and treating information. Neisser's position conflicts with the idea of monitoring one's own cognitive processes.

Teaching by Choosing and Providing Relevant Information

It is generally accepted within the cognitivist paradigm that a mental model, a scheme or the like, directs the individual's mode of attending to some learning content, although we also saw that bottom-up processing is advocated to some extent (e.g. Fodor, 1986). Given this, the teacher, being familiar with the student's initial understanding of a content item, should help the student to focus on specific and important aspects of that item. The teacher can do this, for example:

1. By choosing some relevant learning content or material from the perspective of the students' understanding and thus reduce the students' information seeking processes;
2. By presenting the problems or content in such a way that the student understands what is expected;
3. By asking relevant questions helping the student to "see" relevant aspects. As representations serve to direct attention, the teacher can help the learner to direct his/her attention to crucial aspects of the content. Consequently, the student may also be made more aware of why certain aspects of the content is crucial;
4. Finally the examination as such once again reminds the student of what were considered the main points of a specific subject. In this respect the examination can function as a learning experience as well.

Providing relevant information may be compared to the assimilative aspect of learning—the student's model becomes more refined although it does not necessarily undergo any radical changes.

One frequently occurring idea in the literature resembles the familiar Piagetian advice: information to be presented must be familiar enough in order to be successfully identified or recognized (i.e. assimilated) at some level. On the other hand, it should be different enough from the individual's present state of knowledge so that there is reason to learn. It is thought that only when an existing scheme fails to successfully assimilate information can accommodation occur (Hergenhahn & Olson, 1993, p.284).

This idea resembles Comenius's idea of the school as a miniature of the external real world—the school reality is arranged in a complex enough manner so that there really are problems to be solved. However, this pedagogical reality should not be too complex for the student, as this may hinder meaningful learning experiences from occurring.

Modelling Expected Competence

Brown and Palinscar (1989) have presented many different instructional strategies based on the cognitivist school of thought. "Scaffolding" and reciprocal teaching are two of these. In both strategies the idea is that the teachers model the expected competence. In scaffolding, the teachers' help gradually diminishes with the learners' increasing insight during the learning process.

To Track the Development of Conceptual Change

Glaser (1987, p.408) has for his part suggested that research on teaching could be directed to "track the development of models during the transition from initial learning to proficient performance". The pedagogical equivalent would be that the teacher would actively pay attention to the pattern of changes in the students' representations.

The Learner as a Scientist

A widely accepted model of the learner is that of working as a scientist (Brewer & Samavapungavan, 1991). Pintrich, Marx and Boyle (1993, p.169) summarize this dominant metaphor:

> This standard individual conceptual change model assumes that ontogenetic change in an individual's learning is analogous to the nature of change in scientific paradigms that is proposed by philosophers of science.

The general model accepted by the information processing approach to elements of learning presents a theory using an inductive method summarized in the list below:

- Collecting data;
- Organizing data;
- Generating hypotheses;
- Relating data to hypotheses;
- Stating concepts;
- Relating data to concepts;
- Stating theories;
- Relating data to theories.

Joyce and Weil (1980, p.494) summarize:

> The skills important to the information-processing family have to do primarily with collecting and organizing information, generating and testing hypotheses and theories, and moving back and forth from data to more abstract concepts and ideas. Unless these skills are developed, the student is extremely dependent on the teacher.

Glaser (1987, p.397) describes in more detail the learners' "theories" and functioning as the hypothesis testing researcher:

The knowledge that students bring to their studies or acquire early in instruction can be thought of as theories of informal models that are used and tested as they encounter new learning experiences. The theory held by the student becomes a basis for hypothesis generation and induction of new relationships and predictions that can be tested. During instruction, as in scientific work, the theory is compared with observations and the results of experience, and if it fails to account for certain aspects of these observations, it is rejected, modified, replaced or given only temporary acceptance. This process is a central feature of school learning and of life in general and should play a significant role in instruction.

Although this is beyond the scope of the present study, it is worth noting that as our understanding of what the scientific discourse is about changes, the educational applications of the scientific method change also. If we were to accept a pragmatist (Dewey) or falsificationist (Popper) idea concerning the role of experience in developing theories and in valuing the status of scientific theories, then, naturally, the educational programmes developed would vary according to the conceptions of the scientific project accepted. Because of this, Swartz (1982) argues in favour of educational programmes allowing for methodological pluralism as this better reflects what the scientific way of creating new knowledge is about.

The Social Dimension of Knowledge and the Learner as Scientist

The cognitivist models of conceptual change discussed in this study often make use of the metaphor of the learner as scientist. One of the leading ideas has been to view the learner as a goal-oriented learner applying different forms of plans.

One of the fundamental problems with this view of the learner as scientist is the individualistic position adopted. When the learning process, including the accommodative and assimilative dimensions, is compared with a scientific development of knowledge, both the learning and scientific development are seen as something individual. It is, however, perfectly in order to emphasize that the learner is always an individual subject—only individuals learn.

The problem with the comparison of learner with scientist is that while learning is always an individual change, a scientific change or invention is both an individual change and a collective change. Reaching an insight new only to the individual in question is not regarded as a scientific development. It must at the same time be new on a collective level. Therefore, in order to be new a crucial step in creating scientific knowledge is to relate it to previous collective knowledge (Bereiter, 1994, p.8):

Hands-on school science has emphasized discovery, what has been missing . . . is the discourse into which experimental findings need to be brought and critically analyzed if they are to contribute to progressive understanding.

Although a scientific invention may be seen as an individual learning change, it is, by logical necessity, to be related to the collective level of knowledge in the community.

This difference may be expressed in terms of learning as invention and learning as discovery discussed in Chapter 2 (see also Reif & Larkin, 1991). Learning as invention refers to the fact that the result was not known to the learner in advance, i.e. the learner did not identify a goal state or a competence before they were engaged in a learning process. Learning as discovery would then refer to reaching insight or competence new not only to the learner but to the (research) community at large.

One of the differences between learning as invention and learning as discovery may be discussed in terms of contextual awareness. In learning as invention, the learner is not aware of the state of the art while this is the case in learning as discovery. However, as discussed before, it is not necessarily the learner who must be aware of the relation between results reached and the collective state of the art; the learner is not able to say whether or not the competence reached goes beyond what is known. Somebody else can do this instead. For example, a teacher may recognize a student's achievement as extraordinary in some respects even though the learner himself is not aware of the relative value of that achievement.

During recent years we have witnessed a move in the philosophy of science towards the question of the social and cultural validity of scientific results. Today, knowledge in social and human sciences is seen as more contextually dependent than it was earlier thought to be. The belief in universal truths has been questioned to a growing extent (e.g. Rorty, 1979). We better understand today that creating scientific knowledge is guided by certain interests (Habermas). Insight into the sociology of knowledge has also increased parallel to this (e.g. Bourdieu, 1991). By and large scientific discourse has abandoned the idea of the scientist as pure observer objectively constructing theories about the existing world. When Hanson (1958) taught us that scientific observation is always theory-laden, this was simultaneously strongly advocated within the psychology of cognition and perception. Today we more clearly understand that scientific knowledge represents one form of knowledge and that it does not necessarily offer us the only true picture of reality. With Habermas (1971) we see that creating knowledge is connected with certain interests. Similarly teaching and learning in institutionalized settings must be understood in this light.

It may be that the previously indicated contextual and content-oriented changes in recent cognitivist research on learning should be taken as signals of a parallel move (paradigm shift) in the field of main stream research into learning.

Conclusion

The epistemological perspective on the process of learning draws attention to the assimilative aspect of learning, i.e. how the individual receives information provided. Thus, the major question concerning teaching from the epistemological perspective on the learning process was how the teacher can provide new and relevant information for the learner.

However, as cognition is considered to direct perception, the individual's previous understanding is naturally a crucial factor. Therefore it is important, for pedagogical purposes, to analyse the relation between the learner's initial model and the goal-model of teaching.

Thus teaching is not only to support the increase of new information in the learner's cognitive system, but also, and rather, to facilitate a change in the individual's mental representation. The major method of doing this was to turn the learner's attention to their own model and in various ways to help the learner to reflect upon the differences between it and the goal model.

On the basis of the analysis of the epistemological foundations of cognitivism carried out in the previous chapter, it should be clear that when the individual is engaged in relating new information to an initial representation, this information is something perceived by the sensory system. In other words, the individual relates perceptions to representations. In cases where previous mental representations do not assimilate new perceptions into existing representations, the question of fit concerns the relation between perception and the cognitive scheme, not the relation between a scheme and the external world as such. However, if one accepts something like a causal theory of perception, then it appears easier to conceive of a more direct relation between schemas and reality.

In order for teaching to be meaningful in such a perspective, the teacher's role is both to provide information to be processed and to suggest how it could be interpreted. In cases where relevant schemes are missing or where they are not adequate to handle information presented, such schemes must naturally be worked out first.

The causal theory of perception accepted also makes it easier to teach; there is a regularity with respect to how the learner's sensory systems receive information, although there is no guarantee of how the received information is attended to or how attended information is encoded.

TEACHING AND THE LEARNING RESULT

Evaluation—How the Logical Structure of a Discipline is Represented Mentally

As we have already seen, the dominating view concerning the result of learning, e.g. conceptual knowledge, within the cognitivist school of thought is that this knowledge is seen as an internal representation of an external world.

Granted that conceptual knowledge is considered a mental representation of an external domain, one of the main pedagogical implications of the analysis of the learning result from an epistemological perspective concerns evaluation.

Evaluation of learning results means evaluating the differences and similarities between external reality and internal models. Thus evaluation does not mean measuring the number of facts or pieces of information in the long-term memory, but describing this inner psychic structure in relation to the structure of some specific content.

As has been shown, the individual is viewed as an active constructor of his representations: cognition directs perception. Although this is generally accepted as more or less self-evident, it seems that the teacher is conceived of as a subject having access to the true picture of the world. Consequently it is thought that this is the reason why teachers are in a position to evaluate the students' mental representation in relation to a true one. However, this assumption is not as straightforward as it first appears. Naturally a teacher is also an active constructor of their own internal representations. If both the teacher and the students are in a constructivist position with respect to the world, the question is on what grounds the teacher is given the right to evaluate the correctness of the students' representation.

A first answer could be that the teacher has access to scientific knowledge of the world and that this knowledge is not just any representation of the world: it is the true picture of the world. And moreover, if the teacher's representation corresponds to the scientific picture, then the teacher is able to evaluate and correct the learner's representation as well as support its development. However, this view presupposes that learning in the ordinary sense and scientific discovery belong to two different epistemological spheres; learning only leads to representations of which some may be true, others false, while scientific research always, at least ideally, leads to a true picture of the world. Yet few would accept such a conclusion. On what grounds then should a teacher be given the evaluator's role if both the learner and the teacher are in a constructivist position, and if the teacher's supposed scientific view is not true in an epistemologically deeper sense than the learner's understanding (personal theory) of the world?

Against this background a second answer would be that the teacher represents the socially accepted and dominant view of reality, although not necessarily the true picture of the world.

Accepting such a relativistic view of knowledge constituted by the insight into the historical and social dimensions of knowledge, it is difficult to claim that any knowledge, scientific or not, would "mirror nature" (Rorty, 1979). Under such conditions the teacher is not only a simple reflector of truth. If the teacher's understanding of the world does not represent an absolute and unquestionable standard, parts of the responsibility and freedom of defining the goals of education as well as the evaluation of whether they have been achieved must be transferred to the learner.

Accepting a constructivist position of knowledge also changes the relation between the teachers and the collective. It presupposes that responsibility for evaluation in institutionalized education must also be controlled more by teachers, compared with collective evaluation procedures. The reason is that only by being functionally responsible for evaluation, can teachers decide when and how the learner can participate in the planning and evaluation of learning achievements. White (1992, p.161) correctly notes this:

> [According to the view of learning as construction of meaning] any examination system must allow for a large amount of, if not total, control being in the hands of individual teachers or even to some degree of students, because that is the only way in which the depth of *diverse* understanding can be plumbed.

White (1992, p.162) suggests essays as tests as they can reveal "whether students know other things that the teacher does not". Another method would be concept mapping "which shows the patterns of relations respondents see between key terms" (ibid.). Prediction–observation–explanation tasks, again, ask the students "to predict how a situation will turn out following a given change, and later to explain any discrepancy between what they predicted and what they observed or were told happened" (White, 1992, p.161).

Observe, however, that even though a relativist view of knowledge and a constructivist view of learning are accepted, this does not automatically lead to a more democratic educational process in the above-described sense (where the right to decide on the standards is regulated by the person who is able to decide on the correct picture of the world). The reason is that even though no objective reference to correct school

214 SCHOOL DIDACTICS AND LEARNING

knowledge exists, what remains as the standard is what is contemporarily regarded as the most rational, coherent and intelligible explanation of experiences. This is most evident when subjects like history or religion are discussed as these subjects almost solely rely on what is culturally accepted as relevant and true knowledge. Accepting a constructivist view of learning and a relativist view of true knowledge should not prevent us from realizing that evaluation in schools is to be seen as a cultural process by which the studying individual is primarily supported in the construction of the culturally desired picture of the world.

On Using Behavioural Data in the Evaluation of Students' Cognitive Structures

Many different methods have been used to evaluate cognitive structures, (see Goldsmith, Johnson & Acton, 1994).[2] All of these evaluative processes face the same problem that may be identified in research on cognitive structures. This problem concerns the extent to which it is possible to use behavioural data in determining the kind of cognitive structure represented by students in cognitive learning research. Among others, Phillips (1987) and Kieras (1980) have actualized some fundamental problems in such empirical research as intends to describe both actual cognitive structures and changes of these through learning (see also Wenestam, 1993).

In what sense and to what extent are cognitive structures described through the kind of research done within cognitivist psychology?

The problem arises from the idea that when a person masters a certain discipline (a language, biology, or engineering), it is attractive to think that this person has internalized the structure of that discipline. This would mean that the person's cognitive structure, for example by learning, becomes isomorphic or shows close resemblance with the structure of the discipline. Now what is problematic about this? Is it not reasonable to think of learning as a change in a person's cognitive structure in relation to the extent to which it resembles the structure (conceptual or logical) of a certain discipline?

The debate can be tightened up by using Popper's three-world idea. For a moment we will leave the somewhat problematical metaphysical assumptions underlying this terminology out of account and focus on the sense in which these worlds can be used as analytical instruments for the intersection of the idea of change in cognitive structure.

To begin with, it is necessary to repeat what Popper's worlds are thought to be. World 1 consists of material or physical objects, World 2 is a subjective world, a psychological world of the content of minds, while World 3 is the place for cultural products like knowledge and scientific theories. The subjective psychological reality thus belongs to World 2, the physical brain processes belong to World 1, while the products of individual psychological and cognitive efforts often result in World 3 products, collective ideas. Consequently, theories about cognitive structures belong to World 3. These World 3 products, produced by individual subjects, can also be stored in World 1 objects, books.

In this terminology, individual cognitive structures thus belong to World 2, while structures of different disciplines are World 3 objects. The point made here is that it might be fruitful to discuss the relation between a subject's cognitive structure and the content or structure of a discipline as a relation between World 2 and World 3 objects.

Phillips (1987, p.121) notes that what led Popper to distinguish the three worlds was "his recognition of the distinction between a person's thought processes and the content of those thoughts". Popper writes in *Unended Quest* that: "thoughts in the sense of contents or statements in themselves and thoughts in the sense of thought processes belong to two different 'worlds'" (1976, p.181).

It is important to note Popper's specific stand on the question at this point. He writes:

> (1) That every subjective act of understanding is largely anchored in the third world.
> (2) That almost all important remarks which can be made about such an act consist in pointing out its relations to third world objects. This, I suggest, can be generalized, and holds for every subjective act of "knowledge": all the important things we can say about an act of knowledge consist of pointing out the third world objects of the act—a theory of proposition—and its relation to other third-world objects, such as the arguments bearing on the problem.

Thus, according to him, any psychological process that leads to understanding "must be analyzed in terms of the third-world objects in which it is anchored. In fact, it can be analyzed *only* in these terms" (op. cit., p.163, italics in original).

This statement implies that it would not be possible to discuss the mind in terms of the processes of the mind. Instead this should be done in terms of the content of the mind. In this interpretation Popper's ideas cannot function as a point of departure for the cognitivist. But what does Popper then mean by saying that there is this distinction between the processes and contents of thoughts? The main point made by Phillips (1987) is that researchers in cognitive psychology (a) often mix up the concepts of the cognitive structure of an individual and of the content structure of a discipline and (b) draw conclusions from data that are not included in the premises, i.e. the data are considered to indicate things which are not discussed in the premises, thus leading to a logical gap in the argumentation.

As regards the first point, that the psychological realm and the public realm are mixed up, the following notes can be made. Even if it is clear that the third world of knowledge is arrived at by creative thinking by researchers in a discipline, one should not necessarily draw the conclusion that the structure of the result of this work is isomorphic with the cognitive structure of the researchers. How a person publicly structures his understanding of reality is not of necessity identical with the mechanisms or the structure of this person's psychological reality. How we express our understanding of a subject matter is concerned with numerous factors such as the person we are discussing it with, rules of discussions in different contexts etc. (cf. Phillips, 1987, p.140). Another point made by Phillips, relying on Popper, is that when students are trained in a discipline, they are not trained to reproduce the structure of the discipline but in how the discipline is handled in World 3 terms. The critique launched here is thus that there has often been a confusion between the logical and the psychological realm, i.e. between concepts and their internal relation versus the cognitive domain. This argumentation falls back on a critical attitude towards the assumption that it is possible to distinguish internal representations from behavioural data. As noticed by Kieras (1980):

> It should be clear that internal representations can not be uniquely identified from behavioral data. Unfortunately, many in cognitive psychology have not understood or recognized this basic limitation on cognitive theory. Apparently their problem lies in a basic confusion on the logical status of various sources of knowledge used in the process of constructing psychological theories.

Another objection is related to the possibility of describing performance in World 3 terminology. As Phillips (1987, p.145) notes, even though both successful and unsuccessful performance is describable in World 3 terms, it is not reasonable to suppose that the cognitive processes which generate the performance have the same structure as the public subject-matter. This can be exemplified by an analogy from the computer world. It is quite possible that several different computers with different programs can generate the same set of answers given the same stimulus-word. Thus the structure of the generated answer does not tell us about the structure of the system generating the answer. The reason why it is possible to describe these performances is one of conceptual necessity: there has to be a public framework in relation to which performances are evaluated.

When we consider the way in which conclusions are drawn in empirical research within some cognitive science research, Phillips (1987, pp.148–149) has shown how logical gaps between premises and conclusions have been accepted without sufficient reflection. The analysis is concluded in the following way:

Premise: (in summary) Data gathered during the research indicate certain differences in performance on probability problems between students of differing ability taught in different ways; etc.

Conclusion: Therefore, cognitive structures of students have changed in certain ways (e.g., discovery learning increases the integration of cognitive structure).

What is lacking between the premise and the conclusion is "at the very least some premise referring to cognitive structures ... [as well as] a premise referring to how these structures become well-integrated" (p.149). The point is that even if it is difficult to suppose anything at all regarding cognitive structures from behavioural data, since these two dimensions belong in two different worlds, this is done.

In sum, this kind of criticism suggests that it might be more fruitful to limit research in human cognition to a description of how individuals publicly perform certain domains of knowledge. This limitation does not suggest that there would not be some cognitive mechanisms functioning within learners, but it seems that in an educational setting insights into these mechanisms are not required. The argument for this is that since it is possible to determine how a person publicly manages in some knowledge domain without knowing how this performance is generated, insights into these processes are not necessarily interesting from an instructional point of view. According to this view, teachers would need insights into how students publicly perform in a certain area. This has for example been stressed by Hirst (1965, p.59): "Concepts are acquired by learning the complex use of terms in relation to other terms and their application in particular cases." Hamlyn (1967, p.43) also has argued in this way:

> That is to say that the best person to say how the teaching of, say mathematics, should proceed is the mathematician who has reflected adequately, and perhaps philosophically, on what is involved in his own subject.

Hirst and Hamlyn especially use arguments from the instructional field in explaining why the kind of knowledge produced by some branches of cognitive psychology is uninteresting.

The question of how teachers conceive of human learning apparently has consequences for their instructional and educational work. Both cognitivists and their critics like Hamlyn answer the question of how human learning is to be understood. Even if the answers are heavily conflicting, they are still answers to the same question. Therefore, the question of how the epistemological mind-world problem is solved has implications for instruction.

TEACHING AND THE ONTOLOGICAL MIND–BRAIN PROBLEM

TEACHING AND THE LEARNING PROCESS

Learning Strategies as Explaining Differences in Learning

The difference between high- and low-achieving students is often explained by differences in the learning strategies used.[3] Weinstein and Mayer (1986, p.323) conclude:

> [W]hereas many children may gradually acquire the processing skills needed for good comprehension, poor comprehenders appear to be relatively deficient in the use of active monitoring strategies.

Learning strategies are sometimes defined as "behaviors that the learner engages in during learning that are intended to influence affective and cognitive processing" (Weinstein & Mayer, 1986, p.315). Learning strategies are often defined in terms of intellectual skills. Encoding in turn refers to how the learner selects, organizes and integrates new information.[4] Therefore it should be made clear that what makes a cognitive strategy different from other intellectual skills is the object. Gagné and Briggs (1979, p.72) clearly explain the difference:

> [It] is the *object* of the skill which differentiates cognitive strategies from other intellectual skills. The latter are oriented toward environmental objects and events, such as sentences, graphics, or mathematical equations. In contrast, cognitive strategies have as their objects the *learner's own thought processes*.

If it is accepted (a) that a learner makes use of thought processes in learning, and (b) that a learner can be aware of these processes during learning, then it seems reasonable to make such processes the object of instruction.

In agreement with this, Wittrock (1986) concludes that there is reason to distinguish between (a) teaching and student cognition and (b) student cognition and learning: "That is, teaching influences student thinking. Students' thinking mediates learning and achievement" (p. x).

The aim of teaching students learning strategies is thus to affect the way in which the learner selects, acquires, organizes or integrates new knowledge. These are also called encoding processes (Weinstein & Mayer, 1986, p.315). Weinstein and Mayer also claim that the encoding processes called selection and acquisition determine how much is learned. This view matches the dualistic stance on the epistemological problem in that a causal theory of information was accepted, implying that pieces of information were received by the perceptual system.

Hieberg and Lefevre (1986, p.4) support this view:

> The development of conceptual knowledge is achieved by the construction of relationships between pieces of information. This linking process can occur between two pieces of information that already have been stored in the memory or between an existing piece of knowledge and one that is newly learned.

The encoding process called construction and integration would "determine the organizational coherence of what is learned and how it is organized" (Weinstein & Mayer, 1986, p.317).

Five distinct categories of strategies are then pointed out by Weinstein and Mayer (1986): rehearsal strategies, elaboration strategies, organization strategies, comprehension monitoring and affective strategies.

Winne (1987, p.502) in turn distinguishes between the following five ways in which information is manipulated: attention, coding, associating, rehearsing and monitoring.

Paying attention means focusing on some specific item of information in the long-term memory. Paying attention to a concept in the long-term memory activates this concept and transfers it to the working memory.

Coding means that information received by the sensory system is changed "into a form that is manipulable by the cognitive system" (Winne, 1987, p.502). Information can also be recoded. In recoding, existing information in the working memory is simply given another code, e.g. a visual image may be changed into a symbolic code.

Associating refers to forming propositions. "Chunking" is the association of several concepts on the basis of one shared feature. Associating new information with information in the long-term memory is called encoding (Winne, 1987). Also concepts like elaboration and organization are used to define how an individual connects new information with previous knowledge (McKeachie, Pintrich & Lin, 1985). Garcia and Pintrich (1994, p.141) define elaboration as follows:

Elaborative strategies include paraphrasing or summarizing the material to be learned, creating analogies, generative note-taking (where the student actually recognizes and connects ideas in their notes in contrast to passive, linear note-taking), explaining the ideas in the material to be learned to someone else, and question asking and answering.

Organizational strategies again include "behaviors such as selecting the main idea from a text, outlining the text or material to be learned, and the use of a variety of specific techniques for selecting and organizing the ideas in the material" (ibid., p.141).

Rehearsing is a strategy for keeping information active in working memory without changing it. According to Garcia and Pintrich (1994, p.140): "Rehearsal strategies involve the reciting of items to be learned or the saying of words aloud as one reads a piece of text". According to Winne (1987, p.502) "Rehearsing seems to transfer information to permanent memory by a method of brute force, but this may produce information that is less interconnected with other information stored here."

Monitoring, finally, refers to the process of evaluating the match between a schema (a prototype) and a current state of information. The following-up of the relation between a goal-state and the results of an intermediate cognitive process can thus point to continuous discrepancies. When this occurs, a discrimination is achieved which is thought to lead to the activation of an executive plan. By this procedure, other relevant information is looked for and other strategies are tested.

As claimed earlier, individual variation in applying strategies like these are used to explain differences in learning achievements. Consequently an important instructional implication is to teach such strategies to the learners (see also Gagné & Briggs, 1979).

On the Teaching of Strategies

As learning is thought to occur as the result of applying the strategies indicated above to different forms of information (concepts, propositions, schemata), a general educational equivalent is to teach effective information processing strategies to students, especially to weak learners (Uljens, 1989, pp.59–62).

First, the teacher has to decide how new information should be structured in advance and presented to the students, i.e. if teaching should be started by introducing new concepts, propositions or schemata. These decisions should be related to the students' previous knowledge of the subject-matter in question.

The second major problem is deciding what information processing strategy is the most appropriate for manipulating the information presented. For example, as regards teaching students how to make inferences, Glaser (1987, p.308) suggests that "abilities to make inferences can be fostered by instruction that demands that their current knowledge is restructured". This is most conveniently achieved if the students are "placed in a constructivist position in which they build new knowledge from existing information" (ibid.).

McKeachie, Pintrich, Lin and Smith (1986, p.30) emphasize the following principles in teaching learning strategies:

1. The instructor should teach different learning strategies for different tasks;
2. [S]trategies should be able to be decomposed into multiple components related to particular information processing variables and operations . . . Students can learn the components and then adapt and combine them in different ways depending on the task;
3. Learning strategies must be considered in relation to students' knowledge and skills . . . Students must have the prerequisite skills to master certain strategies;
4. Learning strategies that are assumed to be effective must be empirically validated . . . There must be empirical data on the effectiveness of various strategies and general strategy programs if we are to learn more about how to teach learning strategies;
5. Direct instruction in strategies is not only useful for students, but almost required;
6. Modelling the strategies for students and providing guided practice in the use of strategies.

Evaluation Affecting the Use of Strategies

The issue of evaluation has been discussed in more detail earlier in this study. In the present context it will suffice to make it clear that within the cognitivist paradigm it is thought that the form of evaluation affects the way information is processed.

Among others, Winne (1987, p.506) supports the view that the form of evaluation may affect the students' learning strategies:

> Students process curriculum differently if told they will be tested by a multiple-choice test than by an essay test. Though the same basic set of propositions may be required to answer questions on both tests, multiple-choice items require information to be chunked differently than essay items.

Metacognition—A Method of Learning Learning Strategies

The concept of metacognition or metacognitive processes reflects an important part of the cognitivist paradigm on learning. In the literature the term has been defined in various ways. In fact it is still called a fuzzy concept (Braten, 1993). It has been taken to refer both to individuals' knowledge of learning and cognition, and to individuals' self-regulation of this process (Brown, Bransford, Ferrara, & Campione, 1983; Flavell, 1979).[5] A major idea in metacognition is that the individual may turn their attention to the learning strategies used in learning: "When students monitor how they are cognitively processing information, they are said to be engaged in meta-cognition" (Winne, 1987, p.507).

Recently the concept of metacognition has aroused considerable interest. However, an earlier model of metacognition was presented by Atkinson and Shiffrin (1968) when they talked about control processes helping the learner to remember. Another early version was presented by Miller, Galanter, and Pribram (1960) and their TOTE-unit (test/operate/test/exit).

The educational equivalent is naturally that the cognitive processes made use of in learning are dealt with as curricular contents to be learned. As a correct and relevant understanding of the goal-state itself is not sufficient to guarantee successful learning, knowledge of and abilities to use these strategies effectively become important, it is argued. However, to have knowledge of strategies does not necessarily mean one is able to make use of them (Garcia & Pintrich, 1994, p.142).

Several models of metacognition include the following three strategies: planning, monitoring and regulating (e.g. Corno, 1986; Corno & Snow, 1986; Garcia & Pintrich, 1994). Although it is argued that they may be explicated separately (Garcia & Pintrich, 1994, p.143), it is more than evident that they are closely interrelated. Planning would "include setting goals for studying, skimming a text before reading, generating questions before reading a text and doing a task analysis of the problem" (Garcia & Pintrich, 1994, p.143). Brown and Pressley (1994, p.156) discuss how monitoring would then refer to how students cognitively process information:

> Good thinkers monitor their progress, shifting strategies when they sense problems and moving forward when subgoals are accomplished. Thus, once the good writer senses that sufficient planning has occurred so that good progress can be made in drafting a manuscript, writing begins. When the writer senses an impasse due to conceptual gaps, the skilled writer plans and researches some more.

Regulation strategies are almost identical with monitoring strategies (Garcia & Pintrich, 1994, p.144). McKeachie et al. (1986, p.28) write that "as learners monitor the comprehension of a text, they can regulate their reading speed to adjust for the difficulty of the material. This continuous adjustment and fine-tuning of cognition is an important component of metacognition".

It is evident from the treatment of cognitive and metacognitive strategies above that the distinction is not always kept strictly. For example, while Winne (1987) sees monitoring as one central cognitive strategy, McKeachie et al. (1986) and Garcia and Pintrich (1994) conceive of monitoring as a metacognitive strategy. Yet the pedagogical implications are similar.

Content Independent and Content Dependent Strategies

A pedagogical question posed simultaneously with the growing awareness of the importance of domain-specific learning strategies has been whether teaching should focus on the development of the previously discussed content-neutral general abilities or whether more domain-specific strategies should be emphasized. A majority of earlier training programmes can be seen as aiming at the development of general strategies (McKeachie et al., 1986). Glaser (1987, p.409) concludes:

> A further instructional problem for investigation is whether to teach general model-building strategies independent of specific domain knowledge, so that this capability is developed for use as a general learning skill, or whether to concentrate on building up specific knowledge structures which should aid in the construction of domain-specific models, and which may eventually result in a more generalized model-building ability.

During recent years the cognitivist approach has, to a growing extent, moved away from the metaphor of the learner as the possessor of general problem-solving or learning strategies. Research indicates that domain- and context-specific strategies have been considered effective while general strategies are considered weak "because their application does not, in and of itself, ensure problem solving success" (Ashman & Conway, 1993b, p.74). Consequently it is claimed that advocates of general cognitive skills "have overlooked the importance of a rich knowledge base upon which learning and problem-solving operates" (ibid., p.74). The interest has moved towards domain-specific learning skills (Gallagher, 1994, p.173):

> When teachers try to encourage the mastery of thinking skills, the most successful programs appear to be organized around particular bodies of

knowledge and interpretation—in other words, particular subject matter—rather than around general abilities.

In more recent research both domain-specific knowledge and strategies are emphasized more evenly. The issue has been called the strategy-knowledge interaction issue (Siegler, 1990).

A compromise position has developed focusing on content-specific strategies and the need for generalizing the knowledge reached in one situation to other situations (Marfo, Mulcahy, Peat, Andrews & Cho, 1991; Reid & Stone, 1991).

One example of a recent approach to instruction based on both specific and general strategies is the so-called model for process-based instruction (Ashman & Conway, 1993a). The idea of process-based instruction (PBI) is, in short, to teach students about the process of planning. The idea is that students can use plans as metacognitive instruments to become aware of their learning process. When teachers make use of this approach (Ashman & Conway, 1993b, p.75) they

> assist students to understand the constellation of learning and problem solving events that are appropriate at their particular developmental level, and assist them to develop their ability to anticipate where planning successes or failure may occur.

A widely accepted view is that research on strategy instruction is by no means a finished chapter, quite the contrary. For example, research on implementing strategy instruction in classroom contexts is still considered an open field of research (Bråten, 1993).

What Learning Strategies are Effective in Learning Learning Strategies?

In order to learn learning strategies, both general and domain-specific, these strategies must naturally be treated as part of curricular contents. In fact it is often claimed that not only subject-matter contents but also strategies as such should constitute a substantial part of the curriculum (Weinstein & Mayer, 1986, p.325).

The problem here is that the student naturally makes use of a learning strategy in order to learn an effective learning strategy. Thus we can assume that learners applying effective learning strategies in their learning of learning strategies will learn these strategies more effectively compared with students applying weak strategies. The instructional implication would then be to begin with teaching supporting effective learning of good learning strategies (Uljens, 1989, pp.59 f.). These first-order learning strategies should, in the name of consistency, be called content-specific learning strategies, the content being learning strategies. However, such a position is clearly problematic; accepting this view would in fact lead to endless regress. Firstly the learner had to learn effective learning strategies in order to learn and then learn how to learn strategies that could be applied in order to effectively learn "first-order" learning strategies. If this seems problematic it is not the only fundamental problem in cognitivist learning theory. We may in fact ask if it is possible, in principle, to be aware of one's cognitive learning process at all.

Is Awareness of the Learning Process Possible?

It is a fundamental idea of the cognitivist approach to learning that an individual may be aware of her cognitive processes. The concept of metacognition discussed earlier clearly revealed this. By being engaged in metacognitive processes, the learner is thought not only to be aware of the content of their thoughts but also of thinking process. In addition, the learner is expected to be able to influence these cognitive activities (see e.g. Säljö, 1995, p.15).

However, there is reason to ask: Are we really able to be aware of the way we are aware of something? If we accept awareness of cognitive processes, this position seems to suggest the existence of something like a consciousness that would have the capability of being aware of all subordinated cognitive processes and schemas (Eckblad, 1981).

I will argue that we are not, in principle, aware of our cognitive processes, through which the world presents itself to us.

What is Consciousness? According to a recent dictionary of philosophy (Filosofilexikonet, 1988, p.360), the term consciousness is traditionally used in three different ways. First, consciousness is used as a collective concept for what is called mental states and acts including sense impressions, perceptions, ideas, feelings, thinking, etc. In short this sense of the term refers to the experience of something.

Secondly, consciousness refers to theories about consciousness. These two positions may be identified in terms of consciousness as object consciousness, i.e. as mental states that are directed towards something. Consciousness thus covers both the experience of something and the meaning of this something.

Thirdly, consciousness may be discussed in terms of self-consciousness or as awareness of one's own consciousness. In discussing self-consciousness it is useful to make the distinction between self-consciousness and self-reflection.

Self-consciousness would then refer to the individual's immediate awareness of themselves, which means that the individual is not the object of reflection. The individual is just conscious of their own existence.

In self-reflection again, the individual reflects upon personal experiences (mental states, conceptions). In self-reflection, mental states are made the object of reflection. Von Wright (1992, p.61) summarizes:

> Self-reflection implies observing and putting an interpretation on one's own actions, for instance, considering one's own intentions and motives as objects of thought.

Often a mental state is taken to exist in terms of a correlation between the cognitive act (the process) and its semantic content. In cognitivism self-reflection is then taken to mean that individuals are able to make their own mental states the object of reflection. Furthermore, it has also been frequently argued that individuals can reflect upon the act of a mental state and the content of a mental state separately. My argument will now be that we are *not* able to make the act-aspect of a mental state the object of our reflection.

Can We Be Aware of the Way We Are Conscious of Something? Defining self-consciousness as awareness of one's own consciousness, we may now ask if it is possible to be aware of one's own act of consciousness? In other words, can we be aware of that specific cognitive process in virtue of which we are aware of something?

We have previously accepted that we may be aware of ourselves and that we may be aware of something external or internal, i.e. that we can be aware of what we are conscious of. Thus, when we think about what it is that we are aware of, in being aware of something, we think of the content aspect of our experience, not the act aspect of our experience.

Therefore, when we are aware of something (e.g. when we see a car in the street, hear a bird singing, when we are happy or sad), we are not aware of the very act through which we experience this something as something, rather we are aware of this content and its constitutive properties. In experiencing, there certainly is an object of experience. In addition we experience something *as* something, i.e. the experienced content in conceiving having specific features constituting the very content. But it is hard to see what it would be like to be aware of the cognitive act through which the content of an experience is experienced.

Then, when we have an experience (e.g. that we saw a red car in the street, when we reflect on being happy), the same constellation seems to be true; we have difficulties in directing our attention to the act-aspect of the original experience.

In the literature on what metacognition is supposed to be, it is difficult to avoid the impression that metacognition often seems to refer to the learner's awareness of his way of studying, i.e. the learner's reflection on what they are doing in order to learn. Thus, metacognitive activity often seems to be about thinking about *what* one is doing or trying to do rather than about thinking about (or being aware of) *how* one is thinking during the learning process.

Metacognition as Awareness of Subject Matter and the Act of Studying—Implications for Teaching. If it is true that we cannot be aware of the process through which we are conscious of something as something, and if we accept that learning is to be described on a representational level, as cognitivists argue, then what pedagogical implications would this have?

If we are not aware of the cognitive act through which we experience the world, then what are we aware of during the study process? I would say that we are, principally, aware of two things. Firstly, we are aware of what we are studying, i.e. some content or competence. Secondly, we are aware of what we are doing in trying to reach insight or competence.

This position accepted in this study supports Marton's (1981, 1988) phenomenographic[6] approach concerning how human experience should be empirically described. In discussing differences between cognitivism and phenomenography and their pedagogical implications, Marton (1986b, p.220) thinks that learners should pay attention to the content, not to the strategies applied:

> They [the learners] should focus on what they are learning about. In order to catch a ball, for instance, we have to focus on the ball and not on the movement of our arms . . .

It is then argued that the content aspect of an experience is what we should turn our attention to in learning. In addition when we are aware of a content item, Marton says that we are always aware of this content item in some way. Using Gurwitsch's (1964) words, we are always aware of something as something. Experiences thus have a content-aspect and a form-aspect.

It is of crucial importance to understand that the mentioned form-aspect of an experience should not be confused with a psychic act. The phenomenographic form-aspect or the how-aspect of a human experience has nothing to do with psychic processes (Uljens, 1992a, pp.97 ff.). Rather, the how-aspect refers to the structure constituting an object of experience. The experienced object always has some form organically intertwined with the content-aspect of an experienced content. The phenomenographic how- or form-aspect has thus necessarily nothing to do with psychic processes.

Returning to the metaphoric description of what one should pay attention to in learning, I would say that we can, in fact, focus our attention on both the ball *and* the movement of our arms. In other words, we can pay special attention to *what* we are trying to learn and what we are *doing* in trying to learn this something (Marton, 1974; 1982). But to direct one's attention to the movement of one's arms is not to be aware of the psychic act through which we are aware of how we move our arms. This last point is what cognitivism argues in favour of and something which I, as well as Marton (1986), argue against.

In line with Marton's (1981) phenomenographic position, Pramling (1990) has argued for an additional approach to metacognition compared with Flavell (1979) and Brown (1978). Pramling's position is not to increase the subjects' knowledge of their own cognition, which Flavell argues for, nor is the idea to focus on the strategic dimension as such, which Brown argues for. The idea is instead to help the students to pay attention to how they themselves reflect on some specific subject-matter, i.e. to make the students aware of how they experience curricular contents in relation to other individuals or in relation to the school's intended way of understanding the content.

In a limited respect, Pramling's (1990) position is supported by Gunstone & Northfield (1994, p.526) as they argue that conceptual change and metacognition are closely related to each other, and that it is consequently not possible to train thinking skills separately from learning tasks:

> Any such suggestion is the antithesis of our view of the intertwined nature of metacognition and conceptual change. We assert that the development of metacognitive skills and knowledge must be in the context of learning tasks perceived by learners to be appropriate and valuable.

On the basis of the arguments presented concerning the impossibility of being aware of cognitive processes as such (if such processes exist), Pramling's position on metacognition is supported.

A second pedagogical implication is related to the fact that we must be aware of what we are doing and what we are trying to do in order to reach insight. We may be aware of our study activity, i.e. what we have done in order to reach some competence. An act of studying is thus something completely different from a psychic act of learning, which we are, in principle, not aware of.

The act of studying can be related to a reflective mode of thinking. We can be more or less aware of what we do in a goal-oriented study process; we can consciously try to apply different approaches or styles or strategies. A study strategy thus belongs to the cognitive domain. It is metacognitive in the sense that the student may direct their attention to the way in which they try to reach competence. But a study strategy does not include awareness of one's own psychic act of learning.

In addition we, as intentional learners, can be aware of the meaningfulness of either the content or our efforts in trying to reach insight. Often the degree of experienced meaningfulness can be understood in terms of motivation.

The Neuropsychological Alternative. If we accept that we, as individuals, cannot be aware of our own learning processes, does this mean that nobody can be aware of these processes?

What if we are successful in describing learning on a neurological level? Could we not say that the neurologist is then aware of this process even though we ourselves are not aware of it, in a similar sense that we may measure the haemoglobin of our blood without otherwise being aware of it?

It may very well be possible in the future to describe psychic processes in neurological terms. In fact this may even be the only reasonable way of describing psychic acts as we ourselves are not aware of the processes which make experience possible. However, from a pedagogical perspective the neuropsychological alternative is of less, almost negligible importance.

So, if we deny the relevance of the neuropsychological alternative because it is pedagogically useless and still admit that we ourselves cannot, in principle, be aware of our own acts through which we experience reality, it means that we seriously question the pedagogical implications of the cognitivist view of the process of learning.

TEACHING AND THE LEARNING RESULT

The Level of Description and Teaching

The main result of the previous ontological analysis in Chapter 6 supported the view that the cognitivist paradigm accepts a dualist position on the ontological mind–brain problem. This means that the content of awareness, i.e. mental representations, constitutes an autonomous level of description not reducible to any other level.

This position thus claims that there is both room and need for an autonomous science of the mental world. In other words, mental reality is not treated in any reductionist manner. Consequently eliminative materialism as well as different forms of contextual reductionist positions are refuted.

We have previously drawn attention to the methodological problem of accepting an autonomous representational level of description. Accepting the criticism from Wittgenstein, Ryle, Popper, Hirst and others leads us to the point where it becomes interesting to limit our descriptive ambitions to how individuals publicly structure their experiences (for a discussion on the Wittgensteinian perspective on private languages see Uljens, 1994b, pp.11–17).

If the representational level may be questioned from such a perspective, it is easier to defend it against the neuropsychologist attack. Accepting a neuropsychological level of describing learning would be more difficult from a pedagogical point of view; only the neurologist would be able to express himself in scientific terms when referring to the process and result of learning.

The Nature of Memory and Teaching

Accepting that the aim of teaching is to facilitate learning, which hopefully will lead to learning processes called radical restructuring and that these changes should be described on a representational level, there is reason to look at the implications of the result of this process.[7]

As the result of the learning process is stored in the long-term memory, there is reason to pay attention to how such representations form part of memory. Here I will limit the discussion to commenting on Tulving's (1983) distinction between different types of long-term memory.

Tulving (1983) distinguishes between a procedural memory and a cognitive memory system, together constituting the long-term memory. In the procedural memory, both motoric and cognitive procedures are stored, most of which are automatized and many of which are combined cognitive–motoric skills (e.g. playing the piano). The second part of the long-term memory is called the cognitive memory, in which knowledge is stored both semantically and analogically.

In addition, Tulving (1983) divides the cognitive memory into two subsystems: episodic and semantic memory. In the episodic memory, episodes and events, limited in time and space, are stored regardless of whether they are individually experienced or indirectly experienced, e.g. through reading. In some respects episodic memories can be compared with narrative knowledge, which is organized in terms of stories. The semantic memory again contains formalized knowledge where concepts, symbols, principles and the like are related systematically to each other. This knowledge is not as clearly content-related or context-dependent as episodic knowledge.

One pedagogical question raised by these distinctions is whether a teacher should start their teaching with a general principle or an event exemplifying such a principle. In other words, should the teacher try to support the construction of knowledge to be stored in the semantic or episodic memory?

The question of how the semantic and episodic memory are interrelated thus has pedagogical implications. For example, if the teacher is expected to organize meaningful learning environments, then one question is how relevant content (episodes) is chosen from the student's perspective and from the perspective of the general principles that are the goal of teaching. In other words, how are general principles (semantic knowledge) embedded in specific contents (episodic knowledge)? In Willman's (1903) terminology we deal here with the question of what the educational substance is in some specific educational content. In Willman's view the teacher's job is to search for the educational substance. The cognitivist approach would emphasize the student's previous conceptual model as an important factor to take into account in deciding what is to be considered this educational substance. By emphasizing the student's model in this way, it is possible to see a relation between the formal human science theory of education (see Klafki, 1963, p.23 on *formale Bildungstheorie*) and the cognitivist position.

The Format of Information and Teaching

A second, related pedagogical problem is that of the form in which some specific content should be presented to the students.

We stated earlier that information is stored in the long-term memory in "codes that reflect different modalities in the environment" (Winne, 1987, p.499) and that this information is organized in terms of different kinds of models or networks.

Concerning the nature of the information stored, the literature in the field often distinguishes between concepts, propositions and schemata. A concept is "the basic unit of information that represents a category" (Winne, 1987, p.499). Propositions are then combinations of concepts. Propositions can contain factual information, reflect feelings, describe static relations, and describe procedural knowledge. It is in fact claimed that descriptive factual propositions "make up the majority of academic curricula" (Winne, 1987, p.500). Finally a schema is a collection of propositions describing prototypes of events or phenomena. These three forms of information structures are then thought of as being highly interrelated. The fundamental pedagogical question naturally concerns what form of information students lack in some specific subject matter. Winne (1987, p.501) notes that the teacher's job is thus to decide what information should be presented in teaching and how this teaching should be organized:

One goal of teaching is to add properly organized information of all three forms [i.e. concepts, propositions, schemata] to students' permanent memories.

Students can also fail to learn a specific content-item if their schema (their prototypical understanding) of a certain type of content or process is not well developed. Thus teaching may in some cases be focused on the schema needed for proper understanding of a more specific event or curricular content (Winne, 1987, p.501).

[S]tudents whose schemata for stories are underdeveloped often fail to comprehend fully stories that they read. This suggests that teachers may need to teach a schema for stories.

Parameters Influencing Learning

The cognitivist view of mind includes the idea of so-called parameters. Parameters are those conditions of the information processing system that limit the scope of the individual's cognitive system's work. Examples of parameters occurring in the literature are the amount of information that can be held in the working memory for processing and the degree of automaticity of processing.

The first type of parameter limits the amount of information the individual can deal with at one and the same time (Miller, 1956). The implication is that teachers should try not to overload the capacity available. Chunking and taking notes are strategies suggested to reduce the load (Winne, 1987).

More recently Chandler and Sweller (1991) have argued for a so-called cognitive load theory[8] focusing on respects in which problem-solving is demanding and results in an extraneous cognitive load which, in turn, may have negative learning consequences (Ward & Sweller, 1990). In a series of experiments, Chandler and Sweller (1991) showed how reducing redundant information from self-explanatory learning material enhanced learning.

A second pedagogical implication developed on the basis of cognitive load theory is that teachers should make use of worked examples in their teaching as these allow the students to direct their attention more appropriately (see also Sweller, 1994). A related suggestion is to use partially completed problems that students have to complete as this reduces the cognitive load (Paas, 1992).

Third, it was argued that "information that needs to be mentally integrated in order to be understood should be restructured into integrated formats" (ibid. p.331). In other words, if texts and diagrams are presented in an integrated form, it reduces the cognitive load and thus enhances learning.

The second parameter affecting the learning process was the degree of automaticity of manipulating information (Shiffrin & Schneider, 1977). As the primary way in developing automaticity is rehearsing a plan (or strategy), the pedagogical implication is to organize occasions for practising central processes in order to reach the level of automaticity (Winne, 1987). It is thus argued (Winne, 1987, p.504) that drilling is an acceptable method as long as the content is meaningful to the student:

> Drill results in rote or nonmeaningful learning only when the information being drilled is not integrated with other propositions that could be peripherally activated during drill . . . Thus, it is what is drilled and not the drill as such that influences whether learning is meaningful.

Information about the Goal State

As plans are more or less automatically applied to different learning contents, the teacher can be helpful in various ways when the students carry out their plans. According to the cognitivist view of learning instruction then means providing students with relevant information that helps them in their monitoring or associative processes.

As the goal-state of a task is important to this view of learning, a teacher's task is to present information concerning the goals of teaching. Understanding the goals and comparing them with the initial state helps the students to handle these discrepancies. Winne (1987, p.506) points out how important it is for the learner to have relevant information describing the goal-state. An unclear picture of the consequences of the knowledge reached hinders the student from judging whether the goal is worth striving for or not.

NOTES

1. "[T]he choice of method must be dependent on the objectives of the instruction. Didactic teaching is likely to be very effective for the lower mental processes, although dialectical teaching will probably be necessary for the higher mental processes." (Bloom, Hastings & Madaus, 1971, p.16)
2. Little attention has been paid to methods of evaluating cognitive instructional systems (Royer, Cicero & Carlo, 1993, p.202).
3. Naturally differences at the cognitive level have not been considered the only relevant factor. Often affective and motivational aspects are also emphasized (e.g. Pintrich & DeGroot, 1990; Seegers & Boekerts, 1993) as well as many others like the students' socio-cultural home background.
4. It should be noted that the present discussion excludes a consideration of learning *approaches* and learning *styles* to the extent that these concepts do not deal with strategies for selecting and treating information during the learning process.

234 SCHOOL DIDACTICS AND LEARNING

5. Wittrock (1986, p.310) writes: "Metacognition refers to the learners' knowledge about and control over their cognitive processes."
6. See Marton (1981, 1988) and Uljens (1989, 1992a, 1993c).
7. "Successful instruction is thought to result in qualitative changes in the organisation of knowledge and in the fluency and efficiency with which the knowledge is used." (Royer, Cicero & Carlo, 1993, p.202).
8. This theory is an example of what is called "limited capacity theories" (Goldman, 1991).

III DISCUSSION

8 Closing Thoughts and Perspectives

INTRODUCTION

The following discussion primarily intends to deal with issues which have not been previously touched upon but which are closely related to the conclusions arrived at. The motives for such a structure are that there is not much point in repeating what has been said thus far, and that the reflective and analytic nature of the study makes it less meaningful to discuss the results in a traditional sense.

Another way of characterizing the following discussion is to say that in the first part of the discussion the didactic model is treated in terms of its role as a research model. The descriptive model was assumed to frame the empirical analysis of the pedagogical implications of learning theory.

In the second and more extensive part of this chapter the model is viewed from the practitioner's perspective. In other words, its role as a thought model for the individual teacher is discussed.

THE SCHOOL DIDACTIC MODEL AND THE PEDAGOGICAL IMPLICATIONS ARRIVED AT

A general aim of this study was to develop a model of didactics valid for the intentional, interactional, institutionalized pedagogical processes and then ask how learning could be approached within the frames of such a model.

The problem was approached through an analysis in two stages. In the first part a descriptive model of didactics was outlined. The model was designed to be valid for institutionalized education framed by a politically accepted curriculum. Because of this, the model presented was called a school didactic model.

In the second part of the study cognitivist learning theory was investigated in order to discuss pedagogical implications emanating from it. The position adopted was that it is reasonable to develop and investigate prescriptive implications of learning theory as long as this is done within the framework of didactic theory. Didactic theories accepting the complexity of pedagogical reality were expected to be able to show what role learning theory, among numerous other important factors, has in the pedagogical process. By such a procedure we avoid the reductionist view that educational theory is based on psychology.

According to the school didactic model developed the fundamental features of an institutionalized pedagogical process consist in the intentional, interactional, TSL process that is culturally and historically developed and situated. As the present model was an analytical model, it did not explicitly formulate goals nor the means of educational practice. Rather, the model emphasized the teacher and student as reflective and intentional subjects where the teacher is acting as the representative of the collective, but also as the learners' advocate. Thus the normative and prescriptive decisions necessary to carry out a successful pedagogical practice had to be made by the teacher.

Some of these normative-prescriptive decisions are made on the basis of the teacher's understanding of what human learning is. It was thought that a teacher's understanding of human learning functions prescriptively in directing the teacher's decisions concerning a wide variety of questions.

Since the theory of learning is subordinated to the theory of didactics in the sense described above (although human learning as a phenomenon is always prior to a theory of didactics), it became interesting to investigate what kind of practical pedagogical implications different approaches to human learning may have.

The second part of the study attempted to investigate pedagogical implications of cognitivist theories of learning. In order to carry out such an analysis it was considered important to find a suitable level of analysis—such a level was found in the philosophy of mind. Two questions were regarded as fruitful. The first was how the relation between the human mind and the external world is defined, i.e. the epistemological mind–world problem. The second was the ontological mind–

brain problem, i.e. how one should describe the content of the human mind and changes in it.

The Cognitivist View of Learning

Concerning the epistemological problem, the analysis revealed that cognitivist learning theory is characterized by a causal theory of perception, implying that the sensory system systematically receives information which exists in the external world independently of a perceiver.

However, concerning the relation between perception and cognition, a dualist position seems to be accepted in cognitivism. This was called representational epistemology. The dualism between presentations and representations means that individuals use presentations as the building blocks in actively constructing conceptual structures. These structures do not correspond as such to any external reality. As in empiricism, it is assumed that the individual's structure is about the empirical reality precisely because the causal theory of perception is accepted. When it is claimed that the individual's mental structure directs perception, this seems to mean both (a) that the cognitive structure regulates what sense impressions the individual registers and (b) that the cognitive structure may determine what information the individual's sensory system receives in the first place.

Concerning the ontological mind–brain problem, cognitivist theory emphasizes that human knowledge should be discussed on a representational level. More specifically, a property dualist position was accepted, assuming that the mental processes have a brain–physiological basis and that some of these processes possess mental properties. Functionalist cognitivism again accepts a mind–physical instantiation dualism according to which physical systems other than brains can also possess mental properties. The common feature of both is that the human mind is conceived as constituted of cognition, i.e. thinking, implying that every mental act is a process by which individuals manipulate perceived information. It is also thought that these processes may be described as such, disembodied from any content.

The learning process is often discussed in terms of radical restructuring or accommodation, implying that an individual's cognitive structure undergoes a radical change. As a consequence, the strategies by which individuals treat or manipulate information were stressed.

It may also be observed that even though the cognitivist theory of learning was investigated in this study it does not mean that it is supported without reservations. In fact, cultural historical theory of learning (e.g. Engeström, 1987) could also have been the object of analysis in this study.

TEACHING AS INTENTIONAL ACTIVITY AND TEACHING AS SUCCESS

The school didactic model may be seen as a special case of a rather general model involving human action which follows the formula: intention—action—reflection on results. One feature of the model was that the evaluative phase of the pedagogical process was acknowledged. One way of showing how it is possible to include the evaluative phase in a model aiming at understanding the process as such and accepting teaching as intentional is to make use of the classical distinction between viewing teaching as success and teaching as intentional activity (e.g. Smith, 1987).

Teaching as Success—the Perspective of the Collective Level. In the teaching as success model, the pedagogical process is understood as a factor explaining learning results. Teaching is reduced to a predictor variable in a process–product paradigm. In this view teaching is seen as the primary cause affecting learning. Accordingly, evaluation of the learning results is assumed to reflect the quality of teaching.

While the view of teaching as intentional activity is suitable from the perspective of the individual teacher, the model of teaching as success is primarily designed to serve the interests of educational planning and administration on the collective level and reveals something about teacher effectiveness (Fenstermacher & Soltis, 1986, p.17).

Teaching as Intentional Activity—Focus on Classroom Processes. The role of evaluation is different in the teaching as intentional activity model. According to this view, teaching does not necessarily lead to intended learning results. Or to put it differently: teaching does not guarantee that learning will occur. If teaching does not automatically lead to learning, the motive of including evaluation is different from that of the teaching as success model. Evaluation is now motivated precisely because teaching as such cannot guarantee learning. To accept evaluation as a fundamental feature of pedagogical activity does not mean that attention is diverted from the process. On the contrary—one form of the teacher's reflection during the TSL process is reflection on the teacher's own experience of the students' intentional efforts to learn as well on the results of learning. This was thought to lead to situated didactic experience.

Evaluative reflection is thus primarily aimed at regulating the process in relation to the intentions. To see teaching as intentional activity is most natural from the perspective of the individual teacher working in the classroom. As this model admits that teaching does not guarantee learning outcomes, the role of evaluation is to give the teacher information about the respects in which intentional efforts to support the learner's intentional study process have succeeded.

The School Didactic Model Covers both Teaching as Success and Teaching as Intentional Activity. In the model of teaching as intentional activity, attention is directed towards understanding and explaining the pedagogical process as such. In the model of teaching as success, the purpose is not to explain the process but to use the process in order to explain the results, as something like a causal relation is assumed between teaching and learning. Even though we have shown that there are severe contradictions between the models discussed, it is possible to handle both of these analytically within the school didactic model presented.

The solution is that the model of teaching as success may be considered attractive from the perspective of decision-making concerning planning and evaluation on the collective level, as the effectiveness of both schools and teachers is measured by students' achievements. From the perspective of the individual teacher, the model of teaching as success is of less use. As pointed out earlier, the intentional model of teaching does not see only the teacher but also the student as an intentional subject in the classroom. This allows us to explain variation in learning outcomes not only in terms of teacher activities and students' studying but also in terms of interaction between these intentional subjects. Thus, the school didactic model offers a conceptual structure by which we may handle the movement from a testing culture to an assessment culture in education (Nisbet, 1992).

TEACHERS' INTENTIONS, THE CURRICULUM AND STUDENTS' INTERESTS

Intentionality is a complex term. Sometimes it is used to denote human goal-orientation, meaning that an individual has intentions and is aiming at something that is not present. On other occasions again, primarily within the phenomenological tradition, it refers to the nature of human consciousness. Human consciousness is claimed to be intentional, since it is always directed towards an object or some content. Here, only the goal-oriented aspect of the concept will be discussed.

In the presented model, teaching is seen as a conscious, deliberate activity; teaching cannot generally be characterized as being unintentional or non-intentional.

A specific feature of teaching in schools compared with teaching outside schools is that a curriculum frames the teaching process. A consequence previously discussed is that the goals explicated in the curriculum are realized in the schools only to the extent that the individual teacher accepts them. We may thus identify intentionality as goal-orientation on several levels of the school system. As this is one of the fundamental problems in trying to understand the TSL process in the institutionalized schools, the discussion on intentionality is here limited to this issue.

A model of didactics which, like the present one, takes intentionality as its point of departure, is not automatically a rationalist model in the sense that it would claim that all educational activity takes the goals of education as its point of departure. As far as I understand, such a rationalist model presupposes that the teacher plans on the basis of the goals, i.e. that the content and form of instruction are deduced from the goals. To accept intentionality or purposiveness as a starting point does not mean accepting this sense of rationality. Even though planning is a fundamental category, it is easy to accept that a teacher may let the available resources affect the goal-setting, since there is seldom any point in setting goals that cannot be attained.

The interdependence between intention, content, method and media, as well as the context-relatedness of these concepts, has already been discussed. The present model accepts the thesis of interdependence but argues that the question of intention is different in character compared, for example, with methods.

A further reason why this model is not a rationalist model in the narrow sense, is that the choice of goals and the relating of them to the teacher's own personal educational philosophy is done both before an actual pedagogical situation and within it. The goal-setting may thus be parallel to, for example, the choice of content and of form of representation. And the goal-setting is naturally closely related to the students' intentions and activities.

Intentionality as Purposiveness

When the school didactic model of this study was presented, it was claimed that the teachers' planning (P2) may transcend planning on the collective level (P1). This relation contains a wide spectrum of problems and only a few principal questions can be touched upon here. One important problem is how teachers follow the collective curriculum. In other words, how can we conceptually deal with the tension between the collective intentions and the individual teacher's intentions?

Applying a teleological mode of discussing goal-orientation and intentionality, Kansanen and Uusikylä (1983, pp.73 ff.) make a distinction between purposive and intentional pedagogical activity; pedagogical activity is always intentional when the teacher's intentions are based on the teacher's own goals. But it may be called purposive if the teacher's intentions are based on the predetermined goals and if the teacher is aware that this is the case. Again, if the teacher were to pursue a predetermined goal without being aware of doing this, it would be a quasi-teleological activity and not purposive in the sense described above. Thus, awareness is required in order for some activity to be purposive.

In order to handle the relation between the intentions of the curriculum and the teacher, Kansanen (1993b) has suggested how the notions of deontological and teleological ethics may be used in solving this problem. Deontological ethics is generally seen as dealing with the intention of an act when it is evaluated while the act itself is considered as a duty to be performed. Teleological ethics again stresses the consequences of an act when it is valued. In Kansanen's (1993b) interpretation the deontological dimension is present when the teacher internalizes the goals and intentions of a curriculum. He claims that when "the teacher knows the curriculum, its purposes, aims and goals, it is possible for [the teacher] gradually to make them become a part of [their] thinking and internalize its content as part of [their] responsibility" (p.58). When external values are internalized by the teacher these values and norms become a kind of internalized intention with moral obligations: "With the internalized purposes as [the teachers'] intentions, the aims and goals gradually receive the character of some kind of a deontological theory with moral responsibilities" (ibid., p.58). Having reached this point the teachers' intentions are "identical" with the aims and intentions of the curriculum. This is one of the cornerstones of Kansanen's (1993b) model of teachers' pedagogical thinking.

According to Kansanen's (1993b) interpretation of deontological ethics, we are offered an instrument by which we can handle the relation between norms and goals on the collective level and the teacher's individual intentions. The teleological aspect again makes it possible to discuss the already internalized intentions of the teacher and to focus on the effects of teaching, i.e. the students' achievements. This model offers the possibility of analysing how an individual teacher's intentions function as the mediation between collective goals and their effects. To limit ourselves to one of these perspectives severely restricts our possibilities of understanding the process as a whole, it is argued. As such the deontological dimension seems to be close to traditional normative positions in didactics and offers as such no possibilities of discussing the results of the teaching process.

To Kansanen the described process is a constitutive element of pedagogical awareness: "combining the deontological aspect with the teleological aspect reflects the teacher's conscious understanding of the totality of the instructional process inside the curricular frame" (1993b, p.58). Further, Kansanen argues that "if" the teacher knows the curriculum "it is possible" for teachers to internalize the collective goals. We agree with this but we also note the open nature of the assumption; teachers do not necessarily internalize the goals of the curriculum because they only know the curriculum and know what is expected. In order to understand why certain collective goals are internalized while others are not, we must investigate under what circumstances and conditions an individual acts as a teacher. Thus, as was said before, it is important to understand *who* the subject is and even more important to observe *why* he is acting as a teacher in an institutionalized school. If we want to understand the relation between the collective curriculum and the individual teacher's intentions, we must acknowledge the problem of commitment. This argument may thus be seen as an additional aspect of Kansanen's (1993b) argumentation of deontological ethics and its relevance to understanding the internalization of collective goals.

A second comment concerning the otherwise valuable model described above is connected to the problem of responsibility. When we try to explicate the teacher's intentional activity in the institutionalized school, it is necessary to reflect on the relation between the teacher's rights and obligations with respect to both the curriculum (collective) and the individual. Kansanen's approach is structurally effective and valuable, but its point of departure seems to be primarily the curriculum, not the individual student. Let me develop this point.

We noted at the beginning of this study that attending the institutionalized school is one of the ways in which an individual grows into society. Often the school is conservative in that it educates subjects to become members of the existing community; schooling is a way of upholding and preserving the community. Yet we must remember that students partly themselves decide about their participation. We also know that pupils or a group of students can easily ruin a lesson or a course if they do not accept the contract proposed by the teacher or the educational system of which they are a part. Thus the students' interest cannot be neglected.

This is not to say that there is or could be some kind of symmetry between students' and teachers' intentions in institutionalized education. That kind of symmetry is in principle not possible in an institutionalized school like the Nordic comprehensive school—the teachers' moral obligation towards the collective makes this impossible. The teacher is an authorized gatekeeper. This is the reason why a therapist model of teaching (Fenstermacher & Soltis, 1986, pp.23 ff) is also insufficient in understanding teaching in institutionalized education.

This actualizes an additional fundamental aspect of the relation between students and the individual teacher that I want to stress—the teachers' moral obligations towards the students. We may in fact take the students' interests and needs as the point of departure in addition to the intentions behind the curriculum. We may, in other words, interpret the students' interests as a kind of curriculum. Applying the kind of deontological reasoning discussed above, the teacher could internalize these interests and needs. In other words, the teachers could accept them as legitimate and reasonable; taking the students' needs and interests into consideration would be a kind of moral obligation to be fulfilled by the teacher in the same sense as the collective curriculum would be seen as a responsibility. As a consequence, teleological ethics then offers us the possibility of discussing the teacher's intentions and analysing the consequences of the teacher's activity in terms of students' learning results; the teacher who manages to help the students to learn what *they* want to learn has succeeded.

Making use of the distinction between intentional and purposive teaching we may conclude that if the teacher's intentions are based on students' interests, then we can talk not only about the teacher's intentional activity but of his purposive activity with respect with the students' intentions. Purposiveness here means a unification of the teacher's individual intentions with external goals, in this case the students' interests. The conclusion is that the principal structure proposed by Kansanen (1993b) is considered valuable in that students' interests may be conceived of as functioning as moral obligations for the teachers' intentions in the same sense as the collective curriculum.

The position adopted in the model presented in this study is that both these lines of argumentation are legitimate. Restricting ourselves to only one of them leads to problems. Kansanen's (1993b) model reminds us of the existence of the national curriculum and the boundaries imposed by it. I take this to mean that when conceptual systems in didactics are developed, this fact must be taken into account. However, limiting ourselves to the curriculum means that we may forget the student as an intentional subject. Thus, adopting the principal structure of Kansanen's (1993b) reasoning but extending it in the above described sense, we reach a position like the one visualized in Fig. 8.1.

Students' Interests and the School Based Curriculum. Finally, the usefulness of the school didactic model will be indicated by relating it to more recent trends in curriculum development. A general trend in western countries since the end of the 70s has been a decentralization of the responsibility of planning education on the local level. Accordingly so-called local curriculums on community level were introduced into Finland a decade ago, the last step being the school based curriculums (1994). This has been called the second wave of decentralization of curriculum planning (Kansanen & Uljens, 1995a, 1995b, 1996).

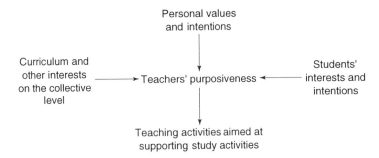

FIG. 8.1. Teachers' teleological purposiveness as a result of a deontological incorporation of students' interests and values explicated in the curriculum.

One of the major differences between a local (community specific) and a school based curriculum for the compulsory school is that teachers and parents are more directly involved in the process of producing school based curriculums, i.e. the curriculum makers are closer to the school itself (Clandinin & Connelly, 1992). The parents whose children visit the schools thus also control, in principle, the activities in the schools. Compared with a situation with a national, wide curriculum which only vaguely limits the teacher's responsibility, the teacher's degree of freedom to educate may decrease considerably in following school based curriculums. This may appear as a paradoxical statement, but acknowledging that evaluation procedures are simultaneously being centralized it is evident that teachers will probably increasingly be conceived of as civil servants.

The positive result of decentralization of curriculum planning is the possibility that the teacher has of participating in the construction of the curriculum more directly than previously (see e.g. Gundem, 1995). This again increases the teacher's possibilities of acting as an educator. Under these circumstances we may ask to what extent the students' interests may be considered as a kind of curriculum as was suggested above. Considering the school based curriculum we may thus observe that the teachers take part in the construction process, i.e. they agree together with parents on a plan or, say, about a contract to be followed in the schools. Having done this, it is probably more difficult than it used to be for the teacher to follow the students' interests in a specific pedagogical situation if these interests go beyond the curriculum agreed upon, as a deviation from the contract could violate the parents' interests. The difference with respect to a national curriculum is obviously that in the local and school-based version of curriculum making, the teacher has moral obligations towards specific individuals (or clients)—the parents of the pupils visiting schools.

Against this background it is reasonable to argue that the vagueness of a national curriculum includes more freedom for the teachers—because of its vagueness many interpretations are possible. Under such circumstances it is easier for teachers to pay attention to the students' interests as a very detailed control of how the teacher follows the curriculum is not possible. As the local curriculums are more specific and as centralized evaluation procedures appear to increase in order to measure the quality of teaching, the teachers' personal freedom of choice decreases, which also means that their possibilities of directly paying attention to the students' interests may decrease.

REFLECTIVE PEDAGOGICAL PRACTICE AND THEORY OF DIDACTICS

The school didactic model presented should not be limited to being used as a research model in investigating the TSL process in schools. It may also be used by teachers as an instrument for reflecting on pedagogical reality in order to increase the self-understanding of their pedagogical activity and the conditions under which they are working.

In this respect the model may be used both in analysing the pedagogical reality in schools, i.e. as a research model, and by teachers as a thought-model in their reflection on instruction in the institutionalized school.

To claim that the present model offers a language for analyzing the TSL process in the institutionalized school is naturally also a limit to what the model is supposed to be useful for. It has, for example, not been claimed that teachers' professional competence in general should be equated with what is covered by school didactics. The model is too narrow and limited for a discussion of all aspects of what is counted as belonging to teachers' professional competence. Of course this depends on how professional competence is limited (Terhart, 1991, 1994).

It should also be clearly observed that the aim of this study has not been to explicitly address the question of student teachers' or teachers' professional development (see Bennett, Carré & Dunne, 1993; Calderhead, 1989; Carter, 1990; Doyle, 1990; Eraut, 1994; Gilbert, 1994; Järvinen, 1989; Kagan, 1992; Myrskog, 1993; Sundqvist, 1995). This is a most interesting and important issue, and it may very well be developed in the future in relation to the model presented here. Most models of teachers' professional development almost completely neglect what role educational or didactic theory might play in this development: therefore the next section touches upon the role didactic theory may play in teachers' pedagogical reflection.

The School Didactic Model as a Thought Model

The position advocated is that the descriptive model of school didactics presented may be used as an instrument dealing with problems which require normative reflection and decisions. This is the main function of a descriptive theory of didactics in relation to teaching. According to the model, the teacher reflects in a normative fashion both in the pedagogical situation and in the planning and evaluation of a pedagogical sequence (Schön, 1983). But in order to understand what one is doing one needs to get a perspective, a long view of this activity. Descriptive theory of school didactics offers such a perspective. Thus the model presented here supports the view that a teacher may reflect on his practice on different levels and in different phases. The model is proposed as a conceptual instrument in this reflective process. Thus the presented model can be used both by a single teacher as a thought model and by a researcher investigating the pedagogical process (Giesecke, 1992, pp.161 ff.).

The teacher is thus seen both as a reflecting and a position-taking subject. In fact, pedagogical practice is characterized by these very aspects—a continuous shifting between reflection and decision-making, planning and action, evaluation and action, distance and closeness. But one may reflect in different ways. Consequently, to use the present model means that the teacher reflects on activities theoretically or scientifically.

A part of teachers' professional competence thus consists both in ability to reflect on the constituents of pedagogical reality (analytic self-reflection) and also in readiness to make the decisions required and identified in the model (normative reflection) as well as to act in accordance with these decisions. The teacher is thus an analytically reflecting practitioner, as well as an ethically reflecting and culturally acting practitioner, among students within an institutionalized school (Uljens, 1994a).

The teacher is conceived of as an actor with moral responsibilities towards the individual student and the collective. The teacher is able to reflect rationally (analytically) and critically on this culturally embedded practice by using a descriptive theory of didactics. Through this analytical reflective process distance is created to practice. This distance may be identified as a space which enables the teacher to decide e.g. on what norms and values should be followed. This space gives a teacher the opportunity to decide autonomously and in a responsible manner on the values to be realized.

A MODEL OF TEACHERS' PEDAGOGICAL REFLECTION AND DIDACTIC THEORY

The relation of individual teacher's didactic or pedagogical reflection related to didactic theory is suggested in Fig. 8.2. The figure consists of three circles, each of which refers to different types of reflection.

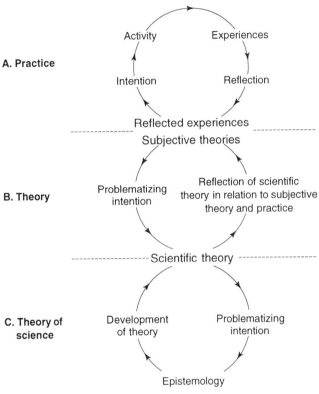

Circle A: The teacher's contextual reflection on various aspects of the pedagogical process.

Circle B: The teacher's theoretical reflection where the reflected experience is compared to a didactic theory or a colleague's subjective theory of the pedagogical process. This reflection may result in:
a) that the practitioner's subjective theory, understanding or the like may change or that;
b) the conceptual model with which the comparison is done is required to be changed.

Circle C: Epistemic reflection on the nature of the didactic theory made use of including reflection on the nature of this theory and the nature of one's beliefs in practice.

FIG. 8.2. The three circles—a scheme for how didactic reflection may be related to didactic theory.

Reflection on Experiences in Relation to Intentions in Institutionalized Practice—Circle A. The first level of reflection is equal to the circle that constituted the kernel of the previously presented school didactic model. That circle consisted of the following steps: intention—activity—experience—reflection—preunderstanding. In some respects it also reminds us of the hermeneutic circle (*Gadamer*). Yet this reflective process should always be understood in relation to the cultural context and the specific activity in question.

Kolb's (1984) model was previously criticized for being neutral to the type of activity and the context within which this activity both occurs and partly constitutes. The expression teaching–studying–learning process was taken to indicate the organic relation between the teachers' and students' intentional and contextual inter-activity. In some respects the concept of activity-system used in activity theory reflects this view (Engeström, 1987). The first circle in the figure thus reflects the students' and the teachers' processes in this respect. The following discussion is, however, delimited to the relation between the teacher's activity and didactic theory.

To be more specific "reflection" refers here to thinking about one's experiences (German *Erlebnis*, Swedish *upplevelse*, Finnish *elämys*). This type of reflection may result in reflected experience (German *Erfahrung*, Swedish *erfarenhet*, Finnish *kokemus*).

The next step, reflecting on one's reflected experience (*Erfahrung*) may then be called self-reflection. In other words, the thought processes involved may be the same, but the object of reflection varies. In reflection (i.e. in thinking about one's experiences), the *Erlebnis* is the object of reflection. In self-reflection again the *Erfahrung* is the object.

To reflect on one's continuous experiences during action may then be called reflection on action (Schön, 1983). Observe, however, that reflection on action here means that a teacher may, in the course of teaching, stop for a while to reflect. In doing this the teacher changes his attention from being engaged in the world or from his beingness to his experience as such. Thus reflection on action does not refer here to awareness of the ongoing TSL process (Bengtsson, 1993, pp.29 ff.) but to reflecting on one's own experience of the process.

It should be said that this reflection is situated within the institutionalized practice of teaching regulated by its own norms.

Making Use of Didactic Theory in Reflecting on One's Didactic Experiences—Circle B. A teacher, as any practitioner, may circle around on the first level for an hour or for decades. Sometimes, however, there is a need to take what is called a problematizing attitude towards one's own experiences. The reasons for this may be of different kinds. Primarily, though, this need to change evolves from either experienced changes in the external reality or changes in the individual's internal world. Both changes may result in an incongruence between previously reflected experience and present experiences or in an incongruence between reflected experience and possibilities to realize intended future activity.

This problematizing attitude can mean that a teacher systematically tries to focus on why one's understanding of a pedagogical process does not work. On this second level the private experiences may be compared with another teacher's, a colleague's experience or with a model or theory of didactics. To use didactic theory as an instrument in reflecting on one's experiences (*Erfahrungen*) is thus one form of self-reflection—theory is thus used as a conceptual tool in developing one's understanding and activity. This kind of self-reflection naturally includes the teacher's evaluation of some specific model or theory.

Even though teachers do not necessarily *act* in accordance with didactic models but rather in accordance with their experiences of the pedagogical process, traditions, implicit norms and values in a certain practice etc. these didactic models may still be valuable in reflecting on and discussing situated activity. This way of understanding didactic theory is different from seeing the model as a model *of* something, i.e. as a picture of reality (Rorty, 1979). According to the view adopted in this study, didactic theories are not models in this respect. Instead the constructive nature of didactic theory is emphasized: making use of a didactic model in reflection may help the teacher to construct an understanding of pedagogical reality. This constructing activity primarily refers to organizing one's experiences.

This position supports the idea that an explicit and reflective process preceding normative decisions is more valuable than a non-reflective and uncritical acceptance of norms. Such a process increases the subject's self-awareness, which is in itself a positive value. It also leads to more conscious decisions on the teacher's part. In Koskenniemi's terms the teacher becomes a didactically reflecting professional (Koskenniemi, 1968, pp.223–224; 1978, p.197). Reflecting systematically on one's work may also be conceived of as a modified version of investigating one's own work.

When a model is used as an instrument for reflection, it is often called a thought model (German *Denkschema*, *Denkmodelle*). However, in reflecting on one's pedagogical experiences using a didactic model, it is not necessarily the model that develops but rather the individual's own way of thinking. This may be especially true in a practitioner's perspective; a teacher has the opportunity to develop a personal theory in confronting scientific models. In fact one may ask if didactic theory can have any other function for the practitioner than this (see Jank & Meyer, 1991, p.42).

When a conceptual model is made use of in reflecting on one's experiences, the attention may be turned either to the original experience (as it is remembered) or to the reflected experience (*Erfahrung*). The aim may also vary in using a conceptual model as an instrument of reflection—it can be oriented both to future practice or to organizing one's own experiences. In any case a theory of didactics is made use of. This view also suggests that in making use of a conceptual model, teachers may be seen as researchers evaluating didactic theory (Girmes-Stein, 1981; Weniger, 1990).

Epistemic Reflection—Circle C. Sometimes, however, a conceptual structure (e.g. theory) is also changed as the result of an individual's reflection upon it—the person using a model as an instrument may come to the conclusion that the instrument in question is not suitable or useful for handling the individual's experiences. When a teacher comes to the point where he criticizes some theory for being useless for understanding or guiding his practice he has taken a problematizing attitude on the third level, which is here called epistemic reflection. This is a critical point in the professional's reflection, as the teacher may take steps towards developing the theory as such. However this is often very difficult, even for researchers in the field, and requires insights in the epistemology of didactic theory. Questions such as the following must be answered: What is required in order for something to be a scientific theory? Should a theory say something about the goals of teaching, i.e. should it be normative and prescriptive? Yet it is not an impossible task, especially if the teachers are educated at universities and are familiar with didactic theory.

The presented model, containing the three reflective dimensions, is not questioned by the fact that teachers in their practice and researchers developing didactic theory partly make use of different language and represent two different societal practices. In fact in part this problem falls back on the researchers—if the theories developed are not useful for teachers, although they are expected to be useful, this may tell us more about the theories than about the teachers. But we also know that the education of teachers differ very much internationally and therefore teachers in different cultures may also be differently prepared to make use of didactic theory in developing their practice.

A specific feature of the model presented is that epistemic reflection (Circle C) is also directly connected to the circle describing situated reflection on action (Circle A). In the figure above they are not visually connected in this respect—the reader must make use of her imagination here! This means that the teacher may very well start by asking about the nature of one's own beliefs and subjective experiences without first moving to scientific theory as such. To question one's understanding in this respect is what Mezirov (1991) means by his concept of critical reflection i.e. to reflect on the premises for one's beliefs of central concepts constituting one's professional competence.

The epistemic reflection partly keeps together didactic reflection on practice (Circle A) and reflection using didactic theory (Circle B). The point is that by clarifying the nature of one's didactic knowledge-in-practice and the nature of so called theoretical knowledge of didactics one may better see how one's own understanding of the practice might be developed or how the theory in question could be developed. This type of reflection also helps the teacher to critically evaluate different types of theories available. Understood in this way, epistemic reflection offers the tools for reflecting and investigating the relation between practical and theoretical knowledge—it is a bridge between these two worlds. The development of reflection on practice and development of didactic theory really belongs to two different cultural worlds, as they form different societal practices with their own history and culture. Without accepting this difference we are never able to unite them, even by epistemic reflection.

CONCLUSION

If we conceive of education as a science of enlightened reflection and discussion, then teachers who are used to formulating their experiences in a shared language could participate in the scientific discourse more authentically. They would also be better equipped to evaluate critically pedagogical research aimed to be useful in their practice. Through such a process teachers can better support students in realizing the opportunities they have to develop with regard to their own intentions (Nohl, 1949, p.152).

Conscious, enlightened reflection and discussion in educational sciences is a continuous process and a major goal in itself. Giroux's (1988) view of the teacher as an intellectual is thus supported. The descriptive nature of the model presented in this study sits well with the view of the teacher as an ethically and intellectually reflecting actor.

The position represented here is coherent with the research-oriented paradigm of teaching and teacher education (Zeichner, 1983) according to which the teacher is seen as reflecting on the content of their work in relation to the cultural-historical context within which it is embedded, as well as problematizing the curricular contents, goals and methods of instruction.

The descriptive character of the school didactic model does not take a stand on what goals education should aim at. Rather it is claimed that it is reasonable to limit the interest to an identification of central dimensions, in order to understand the pedagogical process. This is however not to say that a theory of didactics could be value neutral; it has been shown how the model is value-related. Yet a descriptive position does not mean that an information-theoretical model (cybernetics) would be accepted. There is a position midway between cybernetic and emancipatory positions in didactics and that position implies offering the teacher a critical, reflective role by not explicating in the didactic model what values the teacher should choose.

The problem with accepting a normative perspective is that such a didactic approach may be considered an ideological programme which may compete with the ideas expressed in the national curriculum. What function would an ideological theory of didactics have if its goals were realized, e.g. accepted as the norm for a national curriculum? Would a normative theory, one may ask, have *any* function in such a situation, i.e. any function that goes beyond a scientific support of an ideological programme? Obviously the critical power of a normative theory would be eliminated in a community in which the values of normative didactics were accepted. Finally, observe that even if the present model is open with respect to educational goals, the model is not value-neutral. There are specific knowledge interests connected with the model. It is thus important to make a distinction between these two ways in which didactic theory can be value-related.

References

Adl-Amini, B. (1993). Systematik der Unterrichtsmethode. In B. Adl-Amini, T. Schulze, & E. Terhart (Hrsg.), *Unterrichtsmethode in Theorie und Forschung* (pp. 82–110). Weinheim: Beltz.
Adl-Amini, B. & Künzli, R. (Hrsg.) (1991) *Didaktische Modelle und Unterrichtsplanung*. Weinheim: Juventa.
Adl-Amini, B., Schulze, T. & Terhart, E. (Hrsg.) (1993). *Unterrichtsmethode in Theorie und Forschung. Bilanz und Perspektiven*. Weinheim: Beltz.
Aebli, H. (1983). *Zwölf Grundformen des Lehrens. Eine allgemeine Didaktik auf psykologischer Grundlage*. Stuttgart: Klett-Kotta.
Aitkenhead, A. M. & Slack, J. M. (1987). *Issues in cognitive modeling*. Hillsdale, NJ.: Lawrence Erlbaum Associates Inc.
Anderson, J. R. (1982). Acquisition of cognitive skill. *Psychological Review*, 89, 369–406.
Anderson, J. R. (1983). *The architecture of cognition*. Cambridge, Mass.: Harvard University Press.
Andersson, H. (1979). *Kampen om det förflutna. Studier i historieundervisningens målfrågor i Finland* (Ser. A. Humaniora, vol. 57, nr. 1). Åbo: Acta Academiae Aboensis.
Andersson, H. (1995). Fostran och tillhörighet. *Kasvatus, (26)*2, 97–100.
Anthony, M. & Biggs, N. (1992). *Computational learning theory*. Cambridge, Mass.: Cambridge University Press.
Apel, H.-J. (1993). Was ist Schulpädagogik? *Pädagogische Rundschau*, 47, 389–411.
Arfwedson, G. (1986). *School codes and teachers' work. Three studies on teacher work contexts*. Malmö: Liber/CWK Gleerup.
Arfwedson, G. & Arfwedson, G. (1991). *Didaktik för lärare*. Stockholm: HLS Förlag.
Arfwedson, G. B. (1994a). *Allmändidaktikens kunskapsintressen och forskningsfrågor*. Stockholm: Didaktikcentrum, Lärarhögskolan i Stockholm.
Arfwedson, G. (1994b). *Nyare forskning om lärare. Presentation och kritisk analys av huvudlinjer i de senaste decenniernas engelskspråkiga lärarforskning*. Stockholm: HLS Förlag.
Arfwedson, G. B. (1995a). Den tyska didaktiken—tankevärld och strukturer. *Utbildning och Demokrati*, 4(1), 97–115.
Arfwedson, G. B. & Arfwedson, G. (1995b). *Normer och mål i skola och undervisning. Några perspektiv hämtade från tysk didaktik*. Stockholm: HLS Förlag.

Ashman, A. F. & Conway, R. N. F. (1993a). *Using cognitive strategies in the classroom.* London: Routledge & Kegan Paul.

Ashman, A. F. & Conway, R. N. F. (1993b). Teaching students to use process-based learning and problem solving strategies in mainstream classes. *Learning and Instruction, 3,* 73–92.

Atkinson, R. & Shiffrin, M. (1968). Human memory: A proposed system and its control processes. In G. H. Bover & J. T. Spence (Eds.), *The psychology of learning and motivation: Advances in theory and research* (Vol. 2). New York: Academic Press.

Ausubel, D. (1963). *The psychology of meaningful verbal learning.* New York: Grune & Stratton.

Ausubel, D. P., Novak, J. D. & Hanesian, M. (1978). *Educational Psychology. A cognitive view* (2nd ed.). New York: Holt, Rinehart & Winston.

Baddeley, A. D. & Hitch, G. (1974). Working memory. In G. H. Bower (Ed.), *The psychology of learning and motivation* (Vol. 8). London: Academic Press.

Baddeley, A. D. (1986). *Working memory.* Oxford: Oxford University Press.

Bannister, D. (1982). Personal construct theory and the teaching of psychology. *British Psychological Society Education Section Review, 6,* 73–79.

Bartlett, F. C. (1932). *Remembering.* London: Routledge & Kegan Paul.

Bechtel, W. (1988). *Philosophy of mind. An overview for cognitive science.* Hillsdale, NJ.: Lawrence Erlbaum Associates Inc.

Beckman, H.-K. (1981). Über die Grenzen der Allgemeinen Didaktik und die Notwendigkeit einer Schulpädagogik. In H.-K. Beckman (Hrsg.), *Schulpädagogik und Fachdidaktik.* Kohlhammer.

Bengtsson, J. (1993). Theory and practice: Two fundamental categories in the philosophy of teacher education. *Educational Review, 45*(3), 205–211.

Benner, D. (1991). *Allgemeine Pädagogik. Eine systematisch-problemgeschichtliche Einführung in die Grundstruktur pädagogischen Denkens und Handelns.* Weinheim: Juventa.

Benner, D. (1995). *Studien zur Didaktik und Schultheorie.* Weinheim: Juventa.

Bennett, N., Carré, C. & Dunne, E. (1993). Learning to teach. In N. Bennett & C. Carré (Eds.), *Learning to teach* (pp. 212–220). London: Routledge & Kegan Paul.

Bereiter, C. (1985). Toward a solution of the learning paradox. *Review of Educational Research 55*(2), 201–226.

Bereiter, C. (1994). Implications of postmodernism for science, or, science as progressive discourse. *Educational Psychologist, 29*(11), 3–12.

Bereiter, C. & Scardamalia, M. (1989). Intentional learning as a goal of instruction. In L. Resnick (Ed.), *Knowing, learning and instruction. Essays in honour of Robert Glaser* (pp. 361–392). Hillsdale, NJ.: Lawrence Erlbaum Associates Inc.

Bergqvist, K. (1990). *Doing schoolwork. Task premises and joint activity in the comprehensive classroom.* Linköping: Linköping University.

Bjørndal, H. & Lieberg, S. (1979). *Nye veier i didaktikken.* Oslo: Aschehoug.

Blankertz, H. (1987). *Didaktikens teorier och modeller.* Stockholm: HLS Förlag.

Bloom, B.S. (Ed.). (1956). *Taxonomy of educational objectives: The classification of educational goals. Handbook 1. Cognitive Domain.* New York: McKay.

Bloom, B.S., Hastings, J. T. & Madaus. G.F. (1971). *Handbook on formative and summative evaluation of student learning.* New York: McGraw-Hill.

Bock, I. (1994). Pädagogische anthropologie. In L. Roth (Hrsg.), *Pädagogik. Handbuch für Studium und Praxis* (pp. 99–108). München: Ehrenwirth.

Bourdieu, P. (1991). *Kultur och kritik [Questions de sociologie].* Göteborg: Daidalos.

Bransford, J.D. (1979). *Human cognition: Learning, understanding and remembering.* Belmont, Calif.: Wadsworth.

Bredo, E. (1994). Reconstructing educational psychology: Situated cognition and Deweyan pragmatism. *Educational Psychologist, 29*(1), 23–35.

Brewer, W. F. & Samavapungavan, A. (1991). Children's theories vs. scientific theories: Differences in reasoning or differences in knowledge? In R. R. Hoffman & D. S. Paterno (Eds.), *Cognition and the symbolic processes* (pp. 209–232). Hillsdale, NJ.: Lawrence Erlbaum Associates Inc.

Brezinka, W. (1978). *Metatheorie der Erziehung.* München und Basel: Reinhardt.

Broadbent, D. E. (1958). *Perception and communication.* Oxford: Pergamon.

Broadbent, D. E. (1971). *Decision and stress.* London: Academic Press.

Brown, A. L. (1978). Knowing when, where and how to remember: A problem of metacognition. In R. Glaser (Ed.), *Advances in instructional psychology* (pp. 177–165). Hillsdale, NJ.: Lawrence Erlbaum Associates Inc.

Brown, A. L., Bransford, J. D., Ferrara, R. A. & Campione, J. C. (1983). Learning, remembering and understanding. In P. H. Mussen (Ed.), *Handbook of Child Psychology. Vol III. Cognitive development* (pp. 77–166). New York: Wiley.

Brown, A. L. & Palinscar, A. S. (1989). Guided, cooperative learning and individual knowledge acquisition. In L. Resnick (Ed.), *Knowing, learning and instruction. Essays in honour of Robert Glaser* (pp. 393–452). Hillsdale, NJ.: Lawrence Erlbaum Associates Inc.

Brown, J. S., Collins, A. & Duguid, P. (1989). Situated cognition and the culture of learning. *Educational Researcher, 18*(1), 32–42.

Brown, J. S. & VanLehn, K. (1980). Repair theory: A generative theory of bugs in procedural skills. *Cognitive Science, 4*, 379–426.

Brown, R. & Pressley, M. (1994). Self-regulated reading and getting meaning from text: The transactional strategies instruction model and its ongoing validation. In D. H. Schunk & B. J. Zimmerman (Eds.), *Self-regulation of learning and performance. Issues and educational applications* (pp. 154–179). Hillsdale, NJ.: Lawrence Erlbaum Associates Inc.

Bruhn, K. (1935). *Uppfostran hos de nordiska nomaderna. Det europeiska uppfostringsväsendets förhistoria I.* Helsingfors: Söderströms.

Bruhn, K. (1953). *Didaktik.* Helsingfors: Söderströms.

Bruner, J. (1960). *The process of education.* Cambridge, Mass.: Harvard University Press.

Bruner, J. (1966). *Toward a theory of instruction.* Cambridge, Mass.: Harvard University Press.

Bruner, J. & Haste, H. (1987). *Making sense. The child's construction of the world.* New York: Methuen.

Bråten, I. (1993). Cognitive strategies: A multicomponent conception of strategy use and strategy instruction. *Scandinavian Journal of Educational Research, 37*(3), 257–272.

Bunge, M. (1980). *The mind–body problem.* Oxford: Pergamon Press.

Calderhead, J. (1989). Reflective teaching and teacher education. *Teaching and Teacher Education, 5*(1), 43–51.

Carey, S. (1985). *Conceptual change in childhood.* Cambridge, Mass.: MIT Press.

Carey, S. & Gelman, R. (1991). *The epigenesis of mind: Essays on biology and cognition.* Hillsdale, NJ.: Erlbaum.

Carter, K. (1990). Teachers' knowledge and learning to teach. In W. R. Houston (Ed.), *Handbook of Research on Teacher Education* (pp. 291–310). New York: Macmillan.

Champagne, D. B., Gunstone, R. F. & Klopfer, C. E. (1985). Instructional consequences of students' knowledge about physical phenomena. In L. H. T. West & A. L. Pines (Eds.), *Cognitive structure and conceptual change* (pp. 61–90). New York: Academic Press.

Chandler, P. & Sweller, J. (1991). Cognitive load theory and the format of instruction. *Cognition and Instruction, 8*(4), 293–332.

Chi, M. T. H., Glaser, R. & Rees, E. (1982). Expertise in problem solving. In R. Sternberg (Ed.), *Advances in the psychology of human intelligence* (pp. 17–76). Hillsdale, NJ.: Lawrence Erlbaum Associates Inc.

Chomsky, N. (1959). Review of B. F. Skinner's Verbal Behavior. *Language, 35*, 26–58.

Chomsky, N. (1965). *Aspects of the theory of syntax*. Cambridge, Mass.: MIT Press.
Churchland, P. (1986). *Neurophilosophy*. Cambridge, Mass.: MIT Press.
Churchland, P. (1988). *Matter and consciousness*. Cambridge, Mass.: MIT Press.
Clandinin, D. J. (1986). *Classroom practice: Teacher image in action*. London: Falmer.
Clandinin, D. J. & Connelly, F. M. (1992). Teacher as curriculum maker. In P. W. Jackson (Ed.), *Handbook of Research on Curriculum* (pp. 363–401). New York: Macmillan.
Clark, C. M. & Yinger, R. J. (1979). Research on teacher thinking. *Curriculum Inquiry*, 7(4), 279–294.
Cleve, Z. J. (1884). *Grunddrag till skolpedagogik*. Helsingfors: Edlunds.
Cole, D. J. (1990). Cognitive inquiry and philosophy of mind. In D. J. Cole, J. H. Fetzer, & T. C. Rankin (Eds.), *Philosophy and cognitive inquiry* (pp. 1–46). Dordrecht: Kluwer.
Comenius, J. A. (1990). *Didactica magna. Stora undervisningsläran*. Göteborg: Daidalos.
Corno, L. (1986). The metacognitive control components of self-regulated learning. *Contemporary Educational Psychology*, 11, 333–346.
Corno, L. & Snow, R. E. (1986). Adapting teaching to individual differences among learners. In M. C. Wittrock (Ed.), *Handbook of Research on Teaching* (3rd ed.). New York: Macmillan.
Cummins, R. (1989). *Meaning and mental representation*. Cambridge, Mass.: MIT Press.
Dahllöf, U. (1967). *Skoldifferentiering och undervisningens förlopp*. Stockholm: Almqvist & Wiksell.
Dale, E. L. (1981). *Vad är uppfostran?* Stockholm: Natur och Kultur.
Dale, E. L. (1989). *Pedagogisk profesjonalitet*. Oslo: Gyldendal.
Danner, H. (1989). *Methoden geisteswissenschaftlicher Pädagogik*. München: Reinhardt.
Dennett, D. C. (1990). Current issues in the philosophy of mind. In D. J. Cole, J. H. Fetzer, & T. C. Rankin (Eds.), *Philosophy, mind and cognitive inquiry* (pp. 49–74). Dordrecht: Kluwer.
Desforges, C. (1985). Training for the management of learning in the primary school. In H. Francis (Ed.), *Learning to teach. Psychology in teacher training* (pp. 120–134). London: Falmer.
Dewey, J. (1934). *How we think*. Boston, Mass.: Heath.
Diederich, J. (1988). *Didaktisches Denken. Eine Einführung in Anspruch und Aufgabe, Möglichkeiten und Grenzen der Allgemeinen Didaktik*. Weinheim: Juventa.
Dilthey, W. (1958). Über die Möglichkeit einer allgemeinen pädagogischen Wissenschaft. In W. Dilthey (Hrsg.), *Gesammelte Schriften*. Bd. VI (pp. 56–82). Stuttgart, Göttingen: Teubner, Vandenhoeck, Ruprecht.
Doyle, W. (1978). Paradigms for research on teacher effectivness. In L. Schulman (Ed.), *Review of Research in Education*, (Vol 5). Peacock.
Doyle, W. (1986). Classroom organization and management. In M. C. Wittrock (Ed.), *Handbook on research on teaching*. 3rd ed. New York: Macmillan.
Doyle, W. (1990). Themes in teacher education research. In W. R. Houston (Ed.), *Handbook of Research on Teacher Education* (pp. 3–24). New York: Macmillan.
Doyle, W. & Westbury, I. (1992). Die Rückbesinnung auf den Unterrichtsinhalt in der Curriculum- und Bildungsforschung in den USA. *Bildung und Erziehung*, 45(2) 137–157.
Dweck, C. S. & Bempechat, I. (1983). Children's theories of intelligence: Consequences for learning. In S. G. Paris, G. M. Olson, & H. V. Stevenson (Eds.), *Learning and motivation in the classroom*. Hillsdale, NJ.: Lawrence Erlbaum Associates Inc.
Eckblad, G. (1981). *Scheme theory. A conceptual framework for cognitive-motivational processes*. London: Academic Press.
Egglestone, J. (1977). *The sociology of the school curriculum*. London: Routledge & Kegan Paul.
Einsiedler, W. (1978). *Schulpädagogischer Grundkurs*. Donauwirth: Ludwig Adenauer.

Eisner, E. (1964). Instruction, teaching and learning. An attempt of differentiation. *Elementary School Journal, 65*, 115–119.
Engelsen, B. U. (1990). Didactics: Swedish and Norwegian understandings compared by a Norwegian. *Scandinavian Journal of Educational Research, 34*(4), 285–299.
Engelsen, B.U. (1995). Læreplananalyse og analytisk kompetanse. Nytt perspektiv på kvalifikasjonsteorien. *Nordisk Pedagogik, 15*(1), 2–10.
Engeström, Y. (1987). *Learning by expanding. An activity–theoretical approach to developmental research.* Helsinki: Orienta-Konsultit.
Englund, T. (1984). *Didaktik—vad är det?* (Arbetsrapport 85). Uppsala: Uppsala Universitet, Pedagogiska Institutionen.
Englund, T. (1986). *Curriculum as a political problem. Changing educational conceptions with special reference to citizenship education.* Lund: Studentlitteratur.
Englund, T. (1990). På väg mot en pedagogisk dynamisk analys av innehållet. *Forskning om utbildning, 17*(1), 19–35.
Eraut, M. (1994). *Development of professional knowledge and competence.* London: Falmer.
Eysenck, M. W. & Keane, M. T. (1991). *Cognitive psychology. A student's handbook.* Hove: Lawrence Erlbaum Associatres Ltd.
Fend, H. (1980). *Theorie der Schule.* München: Urban & Schwarzenberg.
Fenstermacher, G.E. & Soltis, L. (1986). *Approaches to teaching.* New York: Teachers College Press.
Filosofilexikonet (1988). Medvetande. In P. Lübcke (Red.), *Filosofilexikonet* (pp. 360–361). Stockholm: Forum.
Flavell, J. (1979). Metacognition and cognitive monitoring. *American Psychologist, 34*, 906–911.
Fodor, J. (1975). *The language of thought.* Cambridge, Mass.: Harvard University Press.
Fodor, J. (1980). Fixation of belief and knowledge acquisition. In M. Piatelli-Palmarani (Ed.), *Language and learning: The debate between Jean Piaget and Noam Chomsky* (pp. 142–149). Cambridge, Mass.: MIT Press.
Fodor, J. (1981). *Representations: Philosophical essays on the foundations of cognitive science.* Brighton: Harvester Press.
Fodor, J. (1983). *The modularity of mind.* Cambridge, Mass.: MIT Press.
Fodor, J. (1986). The modularity of mind. In Z. W. Pylyshyn & W. Demopoulos (Eds.), *Meaning and cognitive structure* (pp. 3–18). Norwood, NJ.: Ablex.
Francis, H. (1982). *Learning to read. Literate behaviour and orthographic knowledge.* London: George Allen & Unwin.
Francis, H. (Ed.). (1985). *Learning to teach. Psychology in teacher education.* London: Falmer.
Gadamer, H.-G. (1960). *Warheit und Methode.* Tübingen: J. C. M. Mohr [English translation: Truth and method. (1975). London: Sheed and Ward.]].
Gagné, R. M. (1965). *Condition of learning.* New York: Holt, Rinehart & Winston.
Gagné, R. M. & Briggs, L. J. (1979). *Principles of instructional design.* New York: Holt, Rinehart, & Winston.
Gallagher, J. J. (1994). Teaching and learning: New models. *Annual Review of Psychology, 45*, 171–195.
Garcia, T. & Pintrich, P. R. (1994). Regulating motivation and cognition in the classroom: The role of self-schemas and self-regulatory strategies. In D.H. Schunk & B.J. Zimmerman (Eds.), *Self-regulation of learning and performance. Issues and educational applications* (pp. 127–153). Hillsdale, NJ.: Lawrence Erlbaum Associates Inc.
Gardner, H. (1987). *The minds new science. A history of cognitive revolution.* New York: Basic Books.

Genesereth, M. R. & Nilsson, N. J. (1987). *Logical foundations of artificial intelligence*. Los Altos, Calif.: Morgan Kaufmann.

Gibson, R. R. & Peterson, H. C. (Eds.). (1991). *Brain maturation and cognitive development. Comparative and cross-cultural perspectives*. New York: Aldine de Gruyter.

Giesecke, H. (1992). *Indføring i pædagogik* [Einführung in die Pädagogik]. København: Nytt Nordisk Forlag Arnold Busck.

Gilbert, J. (1994). The construction and reconstruction of the concept of the reflective practitioner in the discourses of teacher professional development. *International Journal of Science Education, 16*(5), 511–522.

Ginsburg, H. & Allardice, B. (1984). Childrens' difficulties with school mathematics. In B. Rogoff & J. Lave (Eds.), *Everyday cognition. Its development in social context*. Cambridge, Mass.: Harvard University Press.

Giroux, H. (1988). *Teachers as intellectuals*. Branby, Mass.: Bergin and Garvey Press.

Girmes-Stein, R. (1981). Grundlagen einer handlungsorientierenden Wissenschaft von der Erziehung. Zur Thematisierung des Theorie/Praxis-Verhältnisses bei Erich Weniger. *Zeitschrift für Pädagogik, 27*(1), 39–51.

Glaser, R. (1987). *Advances in instructional psychology*. Hillsdale, NJ.: Lawrence Erlbaum Associates Inc.

Glaser, R. (1990). The reemergence of learning theory within instructional research. *American Psychologist, 45*(1), 29–39.

Glaser, R. & Bassok, M. (1989). Learning theory and the study of instruction. *Annual Review of Psychology, 40*, 631–666.

Glasersfeld, E. v. (1987). *The construction of knowledge. Contributions to conceptual semantics*. Calif.: Intersystems Publications.

Glöckel, H. (1992). *Vom Unterricht* (2. Aufl.). Bad Heilbronn: Klinkhardt

Goldman, A. (1990). The relation between epistemology and psychology. In D. J. Cole, J. H. Fetzer, & T. L. Rankin (Eds.), *Philosophy, mind and cognitive inquiry* (pp. 305–344). Dordrecht: Kluwer.

Goldman, S. R. (1991). On the derivation of instructional applications from cognitive theories: Commenting on Chandler and Sweller. *Cognition and Instruction, 8*(4), 333–342.

Goldsmith, T., Johnson, P. & Acton, W. (1994). Assessing structural knowledge. *Journal of Educational Psychology, 83*, 88–96.

Gudjons, H., Teske, R. & Winkel, R. (Hrsg.). (1980). *Didaktische Theorien*. Braunschweig: Westermann.

Gudmundsdottir, S. & Shulman, L. (1987). Pedagogical content knowledge: Teachers' way of knowing. In Å. S. Strömnes & N. Søvik (Eds.), *Teachers thinking. Perspectives and research* (pp. 51–83). Trondheim: Tapir.

Gudmundsdottir, S. & Grankvist, R. (1992). Deutsche Didaktik aus der Sicht neuerer empirischer Unterrichts- und Curriculumforschung in den USA. *Bildung und Erziehung, 45*, 175–187.

Gundem, B. B. (1980). *Tradisjon—kritikk—syntese. En analyse av hovedtrekk ved samtidig tysk didaktikk—med en relatering til aktuelle spørsmål i nordisk sammenheng* (Rapport nr 7). Oslo: Pedagogisk forskningsinstitutt.

Gundem, B. B. (1989). *Engelskfaget i folkeskolen: Påvirkning og gjennomslag 1870-1970*. Oslo: Universitetsforlaget.

Gundem, B. B. (1991). *Didactics—aspects of impact, use and dialogue in Scandinavia*. Paper presented at the symposium "What is didactics?", Aarau, University of Zürich, Switzerland, Oct. 10–12, 1991.

Gundem, B. B. (1992a). Didaktik in Skandinavien. *Bildung und Erziehung, 45*(2), 189–200.

Gundem, B. B. (1992b). Notes on the development of Nordic didactics. *Journal of Curriculum Studies, 24*, 61–70.

Gundem, B. B. (1993). *Mot en ny skolevirkelighet?* Oslo: Ad Notam Gyldendal.
Gundem, B. B. (1995). Läroplansarbete som didaktisk verksamhet. In M. Uljens (Red.), *Didaktik-teori, reflektion, praktik.* Lund: Studentlitteratur (in press).
Gunstone, R. F. & Northfield, J. (1994). Metacognition and learning to teach. *International Journal of Science Education, 16*(5), 523–537.
Gurwitsch, A. (1964). *The field of consciousness.* Pittsburgh: Duquesne University Press.
Haag, R. H. (1988). *Filosofins väg* [Der Fortschritt in der Philosophie]. Göteborg: Daidalos.
Habermas, J. (1971). *Knowledge and human interests.* Boston: Beacon.
Habermas, J. (1987). *The theory of communicative action. Vol 2. Lifeworld and system: The critique of functionalist reason.* Cambridge: Polity Press.
Hameyer, U., Frey, K. & Haft, H. (Hrsg.). (1983). *Handbuch der Curriculumforschung.* Weinheim: Beltz.
Hamlyn, D. C. (1967). The logical and psychological aspects of learning. In R. S. Peters (Ed.), *The concept of education.* London: Routledge & Kegan Paul.
Hanson, N. R. (1958). *Patterns of discovery: An inquiry into the conceptual foundations of science.* London: Cambridge University Press.
Harbo, T. & Kroksmark, T. (1986). *Grundskolans didaktik.* Lund: Studentlitteratur.
Harva, U. (1965). *Systemaattinen kasvatustiede.* (Kolmas, muuttumaton painos, orig. 1960). Helsinki: Otava.
Haugeland, J. (1978). The nature and plausibility of cognitivism. *The Behavioral and Brain Sciences, 1,* 215–226.
Haugeland, J. (1985). *Artificial Intelligence: The very idea.* Cambridge, Mass.: MIT Press.
Hautamäki, A. (1988). *Kognitiotiede.* Helsinki: Gaudeamus.
Heimann, P. (1962). Didaktik als Theorie und Lehre. *Die Deutsche Schule, 54*(9), 407–427.
Heimann, P. (1976). Didaktische Grundbegriffe. In K. Reich & H. Thomas (Hrsg.), *Paul Heimann—Didaktik als Unterrichtswissenschaft* (pp. 103–141). Stuttgart: Klett.
Henz, H. (1991). *Bildungstheorie.* Frankfurt.
Herbart, J. F. (1993). *Konturer till föreläsningar i pedagogik* [1835]. Göteborg: Ordmånen.
Hergenhahn, B. R. & Olson, M. H. (1993). *An introduction to theories of learning.* Englewood Cliffs, NJ.: Prentice-Hall.
Heursen, G. (1994). Stichwort "Didaktik, allgemeine". In D. Lenzen (Hrsg.), *Pädagogische Grundbegriffe* (Band I, pp. 307–317). Reinbek bei Hamburg: Rowohlt.
Hewson, P. W. & Hewson, M. G. (1984). The role of conceptual conflict in conceptual change and the design of science instruction. *Instructional Science, 13,* 1–13.
Hieberg, J. & Lefevre, P. (1986). Conceptual and procedural knowledge in mathematics: An introductory analysis. In J. Hieberg (Ed.), *Conceptual and procedural knowledge: The case of mathematics* (pp. 1–27). Hillsdale, NJ.: Lawrence Erlbaum Associates Inc.
Hintikka, J. (1982). A dialogical model of teaching. *Synthese, 51,* 39–59.
Hirst, D. H. (1965). Liberal education and the nature of knowledge. In R. D. Archambault (Ed.), *Philosophical analysis and education* (pp. 113–138). London: Rouledge & Kegan Paul.
Hirst, P. (1971). What is teaching? *Journal of Curriculum Studies, 3*(1), 5–18.
Hollo, J. A. (1927). *Kasvatuksen teoria* [Theory of education]. Porvoo: Werner Söderström.
Hopmann, S. (1992). *Starting a dialogue. Roots and issues of the beginning conversation between European Didaktik and the American Curriculum Tradition.* Paper presented at the Annual Meeting of the American Educational Research Association, San Fransisco, April 1992.
Hopmann, S. (1994). *Comparative didactics.* Paper presented at the 22nd Congress of Nordic Association for Educational Research, March 10–13, 1994, Vasa, Finland.
Hopmann, S., Klafki, W., Krapp, A., & Riquarts, K. (Eds.). (1995). *Didaktik und/oder Curriculum (Beiheft 34 der Zeitschrift für Pädagogik).* Weinheim: Beltz.

Hopmann, S. & Künzli, R. (1992). Didaktik-Renaissance. *Bildung und Erziehung*, 45(2), 117–135.
Hopmann, S. & Riquarts, K. (1992). Didaktik—didaktikk—didactics. *Nordeuropa Forum, Berlin*, 2/1992, 21–24.
Hopmann, S. & Riquarts, K. (1995). Starting a dialogue: Issues in the beginning conversation between Didaktik and the curriculum traditions. *Journal of Curriculum Studies*, 27(1), 3–12.
Hull, C. (1943). *The principles of behavior*. New York: Appleton-Century-Crofts.
Hull, C. (1952). *A behavior system*. New Haven: Yale University Press.
Hume, D. (1986). *Om det mänskliga förståndet* [A treatise on human understanding, orig. 1738]. Göteborg: Daidalos.
Hunt, E. (1989). Cognitive science: Definition, status, and questions. *Annual Review of Psychology*, 40, 603–629.
Isberg, L. (1994). *Undervisningssituationen i ett ekologiskt perspektiv. Del 1: Bakgrund, undersökningsmodell och tidigare forskning* (Rapport 112). Uppsala: Uppsala universitet, Pedagogiska institutionen.
Itkonen, E. & Joki, A. J. (1969). "Taika". In E. Itkonen & A. J. Joki (Toim.), *Suomen kielen etymologinen sanakirja* (pp. 1196–1197). Helsinki: Suomalais-Ugrilainen Seura.
Jackendoff, R. (1989). *Consciousness and the computational mind*. Cambridge, Mass.: MIT Press.
James, W. (1958). *Talks to teachers on psychology: And to students on some life's ideals* [1899]. New York: Norton.
Jank, W. & Meyer, H. (1991). *Didaktische Modelle*. Frankfurt am Main: Cornelsen Verlag Scriptor.
Järvinen, A. (1989). Experiential learning and professional development. In S. Weil & I. McGill (Eds.), *Making sense of experiential learning. Diversity in theory and practice* (pp. 161–169). Milton Keynes: Open University.
Jarvis, P. (1987). Meaningful and meaningless experience: Toward an analysis of learning from life. *Adult Education Quarterly*, 37, 164–172.
Johnson-Laird, P. N. (1983). *Mental models: Towards a cognitive science of language, inference and consciousness*. Cambridge: Cambridge University Press.
Joyce, B. & Weil, M. (1980). *Models of teaching*. Englewood Cliffs, NJ.: Prentice-Hall.
Kagan, D. (1992). Professional growth among pre-service and beginning teachers. *Review of Educational Research*, 62, 129–162.
Kahl, R. (1971). *Selected writings of Hermann Von Helmholtz*. Middletown, Connecticut.
Kallós, D. (1989). Vilka frågor ställs om den svenska skolan och vilket intresse finns det för att få svar? In S. Franke-Wikberg (Red.), *Skolan och utvärderingen. Fem professorer tar ordet* (pp. 52–80). Stockholm: HLS Förlag.
Kansanen, P. (1987). The curriculum as a factor directing actual teaching. In P. Malinen & P. Kansanen (Eds.), *Research frames of the Finnish curriculum*. Helsinki: University of Helsinki, Department of Teacher Education.
Kansanen, P. (1989). *Didaktiikan tiedetausta. Kasvatuksen teoriaa didaktiikan näkökulmasta* (Tutkimuksia 70). Helsinki: Helsingin yliopiston opettajankoulutuslaitos.
Kansanen, P. (1991). Pedagogical thinking: *the* basic problem of teacher education. *European Journal of Education*, 26(3), 251–260.
Kansanen, P. (1992). *Kohti koulupedagogiikkaa. Lisää kasvatuksen teoriaa didaktiikan näkökulmasta* (Tutkimuksia 112). Helsinki: Helsingin yliopiston opettajankoulutuslaitos.
Kansanen, P. (1993a). Några allmänna reflexioner över didaktikens väsen. *Didaktisk Tidskrift*, 3/1993, 17–29.
Kansanen, P. (1993b). An outline for a model of teachers' pedagogical thinking. In P.

Kansanen (Ed.), *Discussions on some educational issues IV* (Research report 121, pp. 51–65). Helsinki: University of Helsinki, Department of Teacher Education.

Kansanen, P. (1993c). Onko pedagoginen ajattelu tutkimusta? In S. Ojanen (Toim.), *Tutkiva opettaja. Opetus 21. vuosisadan ammattina* (Oppimateriaaleja 21, pp. 40–51). Helsinki: Helsingin yliopisto. Lahden tutkimus- ja koulutuskeskus.

Kansanen, P. (1993d). *The Finnish didactics—finished or a new beginning?* Paper presented at the conference Didaktik and/or curriculum, October 5–8, 1993, IPN, University of Kiel, Germany.

Kansanen, P. (1995a). Tysk didaktik och amerikansk undervisningsforskning. *Didaktisk Tidskrift, 3/1995*, 26–48.

Kansanen, P. (1995b). Vad är skolpedagogik? In M. Uljens (Red.), *Didakuk-teori, reflektion, praktik*. Lund: Studentlitteratur (in press).

Kansanen, P. (1995c). The *Deutsche Didaktik. Journal of Curriculum Studies*, 27(4), 347–352.

Kansanen, P. & Uljens, M. (1990). Lärarutbildning i Finland—en konfrontation mellan tradition och reflektion. *Nordisk Pedagogik, 10*(3), 204–212.

Kansanen, P. & Uljens, M. (1995a). *Teacher education in Finland—current state and future perspectives*. Paper presented at ATEE (Association for Teacher Education in Europe) Winter university, January, 6–10, 1995, Falun, Sweden.

Kansanen, P. & Uljens, M. (1995b). Lehrerbildung und die zweite Welle der Dezentralisierung. Zur Analyse der heutigen Situation. In P. Kansanen (Ed.), *Diskussionen über einige pädagogische Fragen V* (Res. rep. 140, pp. 47–62). Helsinki: University of Helsinki, Department of Teacher Education.

Kansanen, P. & Uljens, M. (1995c). Eine systematische Übersicht über die finnische Didaktik. In S. Hopmann & K. Riquarts (Hrsg.), *Didaktik und/oder Curriculum. Grundprobleme einer international vergleichenden Didaktik* (Zeitschrift für Pädagogik, 33. Beiheft, pp. 299–307). Weinheim und Basel: Beltz Verlag.

Kansanen, P. & Uljens, M. (1996). What is behind the research on teacher education—The case of Finland. In: D. Kallós & I. Nilsson (Eds.), *Research on Teacher Education in Finland, Germany and Sweden* (pp. 47–65). Umeå: Umeå University. Monographs on Teacher Education and Research Vol. 1.

Kansanen, P. & Uusikylä, K. (1983). *Opetuksen tavoitteisuus ja yhteissuunnittelu*. Helsinki: Gaudeamus.

Karlsson, G. (1993). *Psychological qualitative research from a phenomenological perspective*. Stockholm: Almqvist Wiksell International.

Kaufman, A. (1966). Teaching as an intentional serial performance. *Studies in Philosophy and Education, 4*(Summer), 361–389.

Kieras, D. E. (1980). Knowledge representation in cognitive psychology. In L. Cobb & R. M. Thall (Eds.), *Mathematical frontiers of social policy and policy sciences* (pp. 31). AAAS Selected Symposia.

Kilpatrick, W. H. (1926). *Foundations of method*. New York: Macmillan.

Kivinen, J. (1992). *Problems in computational learning theory*. Helsinki: University of Helsinki, Department of Computer Science.

Klafki, W. (1958). Didaktische Analyse als Kern der Unterrichtsvorbereitung. *Die Deutsche Schule, 50*(10), 450–471.

Klafki, W. (1963). *Studien zur Bildungstheorie und Didaktik*. Weinheim: Beltz.

Klafki, W. (1964). *Das pädagogische Problem des Elementaren und die Theorie der kategorialen Bildung* (3./4. erw. Aufl.). Weinheim: Beltz.

Klafki, W. (1976). Erziehungswissenschaft als kritisch-konstruktive Theorie: Hermeneutik—Empirie—Ideologiekritik. In W. Klafki (Hrsg.), *Aspekte kritisch-konstruktiver Erziehungswissenschaft. Gesammelte Beiträge zur Theorie-Praxis-Diskussion*. Weinheim: Beltz.

Klafki, W. (1980). Die bildungstheoretische Didaktik im Rahmen kritisch-konstruktiver Erziehungswissenschaft. Oder: Zur Neufassung der didaktischen Analyse. In H. Gudjons, R. Teske, & R. Winkel (Hrsg.), *Didaktische Theorien* (pp. 11–27). Braunschweig: Westermann.

Klafki, W. (1984). Freizeitdidaktik und Schuldidaktik—zur Notwendigkeit einer Erweiterung des Didaktikbegriffs. In W. Nahrstedt, B. Hey, & H.-C. Florek (Hrsg.), *Freizeitdidaktik. Vom lehrerzentrierten Unterricht zum selbstorganiserten Lern-Environment. Teil I* (pp. 64–67). Pfeffer.

Klafki, W. (1985). *Neue Studien zur Bildungstheorie und Didaktik. Beiträge zur kritischkonstruktiven Didaktik.* Weinheim: Beltz.

Klafki, W. (1986). Die Bedeutung der Klassischen Bildungstheorien für ein zeitgemässe Konzept allgemeiner Bildung. *Zeitschrift für Pädogogik, 32*(4)455–476.

Klafki, W. (1991). Zur Unterrichtsplanung im Sinne kritisch-konstruktiver Didaktik [1980]. In B. Adl-Amini & R. Künzli (Hrsg.), *Didaktische Modelle und Unterrichtsplanung* (pp. 11–48). Weinheim: Juventa.

Klafki, W. (1993a). *Remarks about the problem of teaching and learning contents in school from the viewpoint of critical-constructive Didaktik as a concept founded on educational theory.* Paper presented at the Conference Didaktik and/or Curriculum, IPN, University of Kiel, October 5–8, 1993.

Klafki, W. (1994a). *Neue Studien zur Bildungstheorie und Didaktik. Zeitgemäße Allgemeinbildung und kritisch-konstruktive Didaktik* (4. Auflage). Weinheim: Beltz.

Klafki, W. (1994b). Zum Verhältnis der Allgemeinen Didaktik zu den Fach- und Bereichsdidaktiken. *Didaktisk Tidskrift, 1–2,* 33–53.

Klafki, W. (1995). Didactic analysis as the core of preparation of instruction (Didaktische Analyse als Kern der Unterrichtsvorbereitung). *Journal of Curriculum Studies, 27*(1), 13–30.

Knecht-von Martial, I. (1985). *Geschichte der Didaktik. Zur Geschichte des Begriffs und der didaktischen Paradigmen.* Frankfurt am Main: Fisher.

Knecht-von Martial, I. (1986). *Theorie allgemeindidaktischer Modelle.* Köln: Böhlau.

Kolb, D. (1984). *Experiential learning. Experience as the source of learning and development.* Englewood Cliffs: Prentice Hall.

Koort, P. (1974). *Edukation och planering.* Helsingfors: Gaudeamus.

Koskenniemi, M. (1946). *Kansakoulun opetusoppi.* (Toinen, täydennetty painos). Keuruu: Otava.

Koskenniemi, M. (1968). *Opetuksen teorian perusaineksia.* Helsinki: Otava.

Koskenniemi, M. & Hälinen, K. (1970). *Didaktiikka.* Keuruu: Otava.

Koskenniemi, M. (1971). *Elemente der Unterrichtstheorie.* München: Ehrenwirth.

Koskenniemi, M. (1974). *DPA Helsinki system for describing instructional processes. Manual* (Research Bulletin No 42). Helsinki: University of Helsinki, Institute of Education.

Koskenniemi, M. (1978). *Opetuksen teoriaa kohti.* Keuruu: Otava.

Kosslyn, S. M. (1987). The medium and the message in mental imagery: A theory. In A. M. Aitkenhead & J. M. Slack (Eds.), *Issues in cognitive modeling* (pp. 63–80). Hillsdale, NJ.: Lawrence Erlbaum Associates Inc.

Kroksmark, T. (1989). *Didaktiska strövtåg. Didaktiska idéer från Comenius till fenomenografisk didaktik.* Göteborg: Daidalos.

Kroksmark, T. (1993). *Didaskalos. Undervisningsmetodik vid vår tideräknings början med särskild inriktning mot Jesu undervisningsmetodik* (Rapport nr 3). Göteborg: Institutionen för metodik i lärarutbildningen.

Kroksmark, T. & Marton, F. (1988). Läran om undervisning. *Forskning om utbildning, 14,* 14–26.

Lahdes, E. (1969). *Peruskoulun opetusoppi.* Keuruu: Otava.

Lahdes, E. (1986). *Peruskoulun didaktiikka*. Keuruu: Otava.
Lahdes, E. (1988). Deskriptiivisen ja normatiivisen didaktiikan ongelma. In J. Kari (Toim.), *Tutkimuspohjaista koulutusta kohti. Professori Veikko Heinosen juhlakirja 7.5. 1988* (Julkaisusarja B, Teoriaa ja käytäntöä 21, pp. 157–172). Jyväskylä: Kasvatustieteiden tutkimuslaitos.
Laird, J. E., Newell, A. & Rosenbloom, P. (1987). SOAR: An architecture for general intelligence. *Artificial Intelligence, 33*, 1–64.
Leahey, T. H. (1987). *A history of psychology* (2nd ed.). Englewood Cliffs, NJ.: Prentice-Hall.
Lehtovaara, M. (1992). *Subjektiivinen maailmankuva kasvatustieteellisen tutkimuksen kohteena* (Ser. A, vol. 338) Tampere: Acta Universitatis Tamperensis.
Leinhardt, G. & Greeno, J. (1986). The cognitive skill of teaching. *Journal of Educational Psychology, 78*, 75–95.
Leino, J. (1985). Opetussuunnitelman toteutumisen esteet. In E. Kangasniemi (Toim.), *Opetussuunnitelma ja sen toimeenpano*. Jyväskylä: Jyväskylän yliopisto. Kasvatustieteiden laitoksen selosteita ja tiedotteita 268.
Leiser, D. & Gilliéron, C. (1990). *Cognitive science and genetic epistemology. A case study of understanding*. New York: Plenum.
Leontjev, A. N. (1977). *Toiminta, tietoisuus, persoonallisuus*. Helsinki: Kansankulttuuri.
Lilius, A. (1945). *Skolpedagogikens huvudfrågor* (3:e omarbetade uppl.). Helsingfors: Schildts.
Lippitz, W. (1984). Phänomenologie als Methode? Zur Geschichte und Aktualität des phänomenologischen Denkens in der Pädagogik. In W. Lippitz & M. Meyer-Drawe (Hrsg.), *Kind und Welt. Phänomenologische Studien zur Pädagogik* (pp. 101–130). Königstein: Anton Hein Meisenheim.
Locke, J. (1961/1690). *An essay concerning human understanding*. London: Dent.
Loser, F. & Terhart, E. (1994). Schule als Lebensraum—Schüler und Lehrer. In L. Roth (Hrsg.), *Pädagogik* (pp. 859–868). München: Ehrenwirth.
Lundgren, U. P. (1972). *Frame factors and the teaching process. A contribution to curriculum theory and theory of teaching*. Stockholm: Almqvist & Wiksell.
Lundgren, U. P. (1980). *Model analysis of pedagogical processes* (2nd ed.). (Studies in Education and Psychology 9). Stockholm: Stockholm Institute of Education, Department of Educational Research. Lund: Liber.
Lundgren, U. P. (1986). Den nygamla didaktiken i Sverige. *Norsk Pedagogisk Tidskrift, 70*, 202–208.
Lundgren, U. P. (1987). Didaktikens namn? *Forskning om utbildning, 14*, 27–38.
Lundgren, U. P. (Ed.). (1989). *Educational policy and control*. Oslo: Universitetsforlaget.
Lundh, L.-G. (1983). *Mind and meaning: Towards a theory of the human mind as a system of meaning structures*. Uppsala: University of Uppsala.
Macke, G. (1990). Disziplinenformierung als Differenzierung und Spezialisierung. Entwicklung der Erziehungswissenschaft unter dem Aspekt der Ausbildung und Differenzierung von Teildisziplinen. *Zeitschrift für Pädagogik, 36*(1), 51–72.
Manen, v., M. (1991). *The tact of teaching: The meaning of pedagogical thoughtfulness*. New York: SUNY Press.
Marc-Wogau, K. (1983). George Berkeley (1685–1753). In K. Marc-Wogau (Red.), *Filosofin genom tiderna. Del II* (pp. 216–220). Stockholm: Bonniers.
Marfo, R., Mulcahy, R., Peat, C., Andrews, J. & Cho, S. (1991). Teaching cognitive strategies in the classroom: A content-based instructional model. In R. F. Mulcahy, R. H. Short, & J. Andrews (Eds.), *Enhancing learning and thinking* (pp. 67–95). New York: Praeger.
Marková, I. (1982). *Paradigms, thought, and language*. New York: Wiley.

Marton, F. (1974). *Inlärning och studiefärdighet* (Res. rep. 121). Göteborg: University of Göteborg, Department of Education and Educational Research.

Marton, F. (1981). Phenomenography—describing conceptions of the world around us. *Instructional Science, 10*, 177–200.

Marton, F. (1982). *Towards a phenomenography of learning III. Experience and conceptualisation* (Res. rep. 1982:08). Göteborg: University of Göteborg, Department of Education and Educational Research.

Marton, F. (1986a). *Fackdidaktik. Volym I-III*. Lund: Studentlitteratur.

Marton, F. (1986b). Some reflections on the improvement of learning. In J. A. Bowden (Ed.), *Student learning: Research into practice. The Marysville Symposium* (pp. 205–224). The University of Melbourne: Center for the Study of Higher Education.

Marton, F. (1988). Phenomenography: Exploring different conceptions of reality. In D. Fetterman (Ed.), *Qualitative approaches to evaluation in education. The silent scientific revolution* (pp. 176–205). New York: Praeger.

Marton, F., Dall'Alba, G. & Beaty, E. (1993). Conceptions of learning. *International Journal of Educational Psychology, 46*, 4–11.

McClelland, J. L. & Rumelhart, D. E. & The PDP research group. (1986). *Parallel distributed processing: Explorations in the microstructure of cognition. Vol II: Psychological and biological models*. Cambridge, Mass.: MIT Press.

McDermott, D. & Doyle, J. (1980). Non-monotonic logic I. *Artificial Intelligence, 13*, 41–72.

McKeachie, W. R., Pintrich, P. R. & Lin, Y. G. (1985). Teaching learning strategies. *Educational Psychologist, 20*, 153–160.

McKeachie, W., Pintrich, P. R., Lin, Y.-G. & Smith, D. A. F. (1986). *Teaching and learning in the college classroom*. Michigan: University of Michigan, NCRIPTAL.

McShane, J. (1991). *Cognitive development. An information processing approach*. Oxford: Blackwell.

Mehan, H. (1979). *Learning lessons: social organization in the classroom*. Cambridge, Mass.: Harvard University Press.

Memmert, W. (1991). *Didaktik in Grafiken und Tabellen*. Bad Heilbrunn/OBB.: Verlag Julius Klinkhardt.

Menck, P. (1975). *Unterrichtsanalyse und didaktische Konstruktion*. Frankfurt am Main: Athenäum Fischer Taschenbuch Verlag.

Menck, P. (1987). Throwing two dice. The contents of a maths lesson. *Journal of Curriculum Studies, 18*, 219–225.

Menck, P. (1993). *Didactics as construction of content*. Paper presented at the symposium Didactic and/or Curriculum, October, 5–8. 1993 IPN, University of Kiel, Germany.

Menck, P. & Wierichs, G. (1991). Unterrichtsinhalt—erziehungswissenschaftlich analysiert. *Zeitschrift für Pädagogik, 37*(5), 787–805.

Mercer, N. (1993). Culture, context and the construction of knowledge in the classroom. In P. Light & G. Butterworth (Eds.), *Context and cognition. Ways of learning and knowing*. Hillsdale, NJ.: Lawrence Erlbaum Associates Inc.

Mercer, N. (1995). *The guided construction of knowledge. Talk amongst teachers and learners*. Clevedon: Multilinguamatters.

Mertaniemi, R. (1990). *Barns kontextberoende uppfattningar av inlärning* (Avh. pro gradu). Vasa: Åbo Akademi, Pedagogiska fakulteten.

Mertaniemi, R. & Uljens, M. (1994). Children's conceptions of the process of learning—dependence on content and context. In M. Uljens (Ed.), *Studier i inlärning, undervisning och utvärdering* (Publikation nr 9, pp. 19–34). Vasa: Åbo Akademi, Pedagogiska fakulteten.

Meyer, H. (1987). *Unterrichtsmethoden. I: Theorieband* (5 Aufl.). Frankfurt am Main: Cornelsen Scriptor.

REFERENCES 267

Meyer, H. (1991). Rezeptionsprobleme der Didaktik oder wie Lehrer lernen. In B. Adl-Amini & R. Künzli (Hrsg.), *Didaktische Modelle und Unterrichtsplanung* (pp. 88–118). Weinheim: Juventa.
Meyer-Drawe, K. (1984). *Leiblichkeit und Sozialität. Phänomenologische Beiträge zu einer pädagogischen Theorie der Inter-Subjektivität.* München: Fink.
Meyering, T. C. (1989). *Historical roots of cognitive science. The rise of a cognitive theory of perception from antiquity to the nineteenth century.* Dordrecht: Kluwer.
Mezirow, J. (1991). *Transformative dimensions of adult learning.* San Francisco: Jossey Bass.
Miller, G. A. (1956). The magical number seven, plus or minus two: Some limits on our capacity for processing information. *Psychological Review, 63*, 81–97.
Miller, G. A., Galanter, E., Pribram, K. (1960). *Plans and the structure of behavior.* New York: Holt, Rinehart & Winston.
Miller, G. A. (1987). Trends and debates in cognitive psychology. In A. M. Aitkenhead & J. M. Slack (Eds.), *Issues in cognitive modeling* (pp. 3–11). Hillsdale, NJ.: Lawrence Erlbaum Associates Inc.
Minsky, M. (1975). A framework for representing knowledge. In P. H. Winston (Ed.), *The psychology of computer vision.* New York: McGraw-Hill.
Myrskog, G. (1993). *Lärarstuderandes tankar om inlärning* (Rapport 6). Vasa: Abo Akademi, Pedagogiska fakulteten.
Neisser, U. (1976). *Cognition and reality.* San Francisco: Freeman.
Newell, A., Shaw, J. A. & Simon, H. A. (1958). Elements of a theory of human problem solving. *Psychological Review, 65*, 151–166.
Newell, A., & Simon, H. (1972). *Human problem solving.* Englewood Cliffs: Prentice-Hall.
Nisbet, J. (1992). *Issues. Curriculum reform assessment in question.* Paris: OECD.
Nohl, H. (1949). *Pädagogik aus dreißig Jahren.* Frankfurt am Main: Schulte-Bulmke.
Nordenbo, S.-E. (1993). *Danish didactics—an outline of history and research.* Paper presented at the symposium Didactics and/or Curriculum, IPN, October 5–10, University of Kiel.
Norman, D. (1980). What goes on in the mind of the learner? New Directions for Research, *Teaching and Learning, 2*, 37–49.
Norman, D. (1982). *Learning and memory.* New York: Freeman.
Norman, D. (1987). Twelve issues for cognitive science. *Cognitive Science, 4*, 1–33.
Novak, J. D. (1977). An alternative to Piagetian psychology for science and mathematics education. *Science Education, 61*, 393–395.
Nussbaum, J. & Novick, S. (1982). Alternative frameworks, conceptual conflict, and accommodation: Toward a principled teaching strategy. *Instructional Science, 11*, 183–200.
Osgood, C. E. (1956). Behavioral theory and the social sciences. *Behavioral Science, 1*, 67–187.
Ottelin, A. K. (1931). *Pedagogikens grunddrag.* Helsingfors: Söderström.
Paas, F. (1992). Training strategies for attaining transfer of problem solving skill in statistics: a cognitive load approach. *Journal of Educational Psychology, 86*, 122–133.
Palmer, S. E. (1978). Fundamental aspects of cognitive representation. In E. Rosch & B. B. Lloyd (Eds.), *Cognition and categorization.* Hillsdale, NJ.: Lawrence Erlbaum Associates Inc.
Passmore, J. (1980). *The philosophy of teaching.* Cambridge, Mass.: Harvard University Press.
Perkins, D. N. & Salomon, G. (1989). Are cognitive skills context-bound? *Educational Researcher, 18*(1), 16–25.
Peterson, D. L., Marx, R. W., & Clark, C. M. (1978). Teacher planning, teacher behaviour and student achievement. *American Educational Research Journal, 15*, 417–432.
Phillips, D. C. (1987). *Philosophy, science and social inquiry. Contemporary methodological*

controversies in social science and related applied fields of research. Oxford: Pergamon Press.
Piaget, J. (1953). *The childs construction of the world* [1929]. London: Palladium.
Piatelli-Palmarani, M. (Ed.). (1980). *Language and learning: The debate between Jean Piaget and Noam Chomsky*. Cambridge, Mass.: Harvard University Press.
Pintrich, P. R. & DeGroot, E. V. (1990). Motivational and self-regulated learning components of classroom academic performance. *Journal of Educational Psychology, 82*, 33–40.
Pintrich, P. R., Marx, R. W., & Boyle, R. A. (1993). Beyond cold conceptual change: The role of motivational beliefs and classroom contextual factors in the process of conceptual change. *Review of Educational Research, 63*(2), 167–199.
Plato (1956). *Protagoras and Meno*. London: Penguin.
Popper, K. (1972). *Objective knowledge*. Oxford: Clarendon.
Popper, K. (1976). *Unended quest*. La Salle, IL.: Open Court.
Posner, G., Strike, K., Hewson, P. & Gertzog, W. (1982). Accommodation of a scientific conception: Toward a theory of conceptual change. *Science Education, 66*, 211–227.
Pramling, I. (1990). *Learning to learn: A study of Swedish preschool children*. New York: Springer.
Pratt, D. D. (1992). Conceptions of teaching. *Adult Education Quarterly, 42*(4), 203–220.
Prawat, R. (1992). Teachers' beliefs about teaching and learning: A constructivist perspective. *American Journal of Education, 100*, 354–395.
Prosser, M., Trigwell, K. & Taylor, P. (1994). A phenomenographic study of academics' conceptions of science learning and teaching. *Learning and Instruction, 4*(3), 217–231.
Putnam, H. (1960). Minds and machines. In S. Hook (Ed.), *Dimensions of mind* (pp. 138–164). New York: Collier.
Putnam, H. (1988). *Representation and reality*. Cambridge, Mass.: MIT Press.
Pylyshyn, Z. W. (1984). *Computation and cognition: Toward a foundation of cognitive science*. Cambridge, Mass.: MIT Press.
Rauhala, L. (1978). *Ihmistutkimuksesta eksistentiaalisen fenomenologian valossa*. Helsinki: Helsingin yliopisto, Soveltavan psykologian.laitoksen julkaisuja 3.
Rauhala, L. (1990). *Humanistinen psykologia*. Helsinki: Yliopistopaino.
Reichenbach, H. (1938). *Experience and prediction*. Chicago: Chicago University Press.
Reid, D. K. & Stone, C. A. (1991). Why is cognitive instruction effective? Underlying learning mechanisms. *Remedial and Special Education, 12*, 8–19.
Reif, F. & Larkin, J. (1991). Cognition in scientific and everyday domains: Comparison and learning implications. *Journal of Research in Science Teaching, 28*, 733–760.
Rein, W. (1912). *Pädagogik im Grundriss* (Fünfte Aufl.). Leipzig: K. D. Köschesche Verlagshandlung.
Ricoeur, P. (1989). Phenomenology and hermeneutics. In P. Ricoeur (Ed.), *Hermeneutics and the human sciences* (pp. 101–128). Cambridge: Cambridge University Press.
Rogers, C. (1969). *Freedom to learn*. Columbus, O.: Merrill.
Rorty, R. (1979). *Philosophy and the mirror of nature*. Princeton: Princeton University Press.
Royer, J. M., Cisero, C. A., & Carlo, M. S. (1993). Techniques and procedures for assessing cognitive skills. *Review of Educational Research, 63*(2), 201–243.
Rumelhart, D. E. (1981). *Understanding understanding*. La Jolla: University of California, San Diego. Center for human information processing.
Rumelhart, D. E. & Norman, D. A. (1987). Representation of knowledge. In A. M. Aitkenhead & J. M. Slack (Eds.), *Issues in cognitive modeling* (pp. 15–62). Hillsdale, NJ.: Lawrence Erlbaum Association Inc.
Rumelhart, D. E. & Ortony, A. (1976). The representation of knowledge in memory. In R. C. Anderson, R. J. Spiro, & W. E. Montague (Eds.), *Schooling and the acquisition of knowledge*. Hillsdale, NJ.: Lawrence Erlbaum Association Inc.

Ryle, G. (1990). *The concept of mind* [1949]. London: Penguin.
Sacerdoti, E. D. (1977). *A structure for plans and behaviour.* New York: Elsevier North-Holland.
Sajama, S. & Kamppinen, M. (1987). *A historical introduction to phenomenology.* London: Croom Helm.
Säljö, R. (1991). Learning and mediation: Fitting reality into a table. *Learning and Instruction, 1,* 261–272.
Säljö, R. (1995). Begreppsbildning som pedagogisk drog. *Utbildning och Demokrati* 4(1), 5–22.
Salomaa, J. E. (1947). *Koulukasvatusoppi.* Helsinki: Söderström.
Sampson, E. E. (1981). Cognitive psychology as ideology. *American Psychologist, 36*(7), 730–743.
Sandberg, J. & Barnard, Y. (1991). Interview on AI and education: Allain Collins and Stellan Ohlsson. *AICOM, 4*(4), 132–144.
Schank, R. C. & Abelson, R. P. (1977). *Script, plans, goals, and understanding: An inquiry into human knowledge structures.* Hillsdale, NJ.: Lawrence Erlbaum Association Inc.
Scheffler, I. (1960). *The language of education.* Springfield, IL.: Charles C. Thomas.
Schleiermacher, F. (1957). Pädagogische Schriften. In E. Weniger (Hrsg., Unter mitwurkung von T. Schulze), Band 1: *Die Vorlesungen aus dem Jahre 1826.* Düsseldorf/München: Verlag Helmut Küppers vormals Georg Bondi.
Schnotz, W. (1993). *Understanding logical pictures* (Research Report 1). Jena: University of Jena, Institute of Psychology, Department of Educational Psychology.
Scholz, G. & Bielefeldt, H. (1978). *Kompendium Didaktik-Schuldidaktik.* München: Ehrenwirth.
Schröder, H. (1992). *Grundwortschatz Erziehungswissenschaft. Ein Wörterbuch der Fachbegriffe.* München: Ehrenwirth.
Schulz, W. (1980). *Unterrichtsplanung.* München: Urban und Schwarzenberg.
Schulz, W. (1991). Ein Hamburger Modell der Unterrichtsvorbereitung—Seine Funktion in der Alltagspraxis. In B. Adl-Amini & R. Künzli (Hrsg.), *Didaktische Modelle und Unterrichtsplanung* (pp. 49–87). Weinheim: Juventa.
Schulze, T. (1978). *Methoden und Medien der Erziehung.* München: Juventa.
Schulze, T. (1993). Aussichten für eine Theorie der Unterrichtsmethode. In B. Adl-Amini, T. Schulze & E. Terhart (Hrsg.), *Unterrichtsmethode in Theorie und Forschung* (pp. 135–166). Weinheim: Beltz.
Schön, D. A. (1983). *The reflective practitioner.* London: Temple Smith.
Seegers, G. & Boekerts, M. (1993). Task motivation and mathematics achievement in actual task situations. *Learning and Instruction, 3*(3), 133–150.
Selz, O. (1924). *Zur Psychologie des Produktiven Denken und des Irrtums.* Bonn: Cohen.
Shannon, C. E. & Weaver, W. (1949). *The mathematical theory of communication.* Urbana: University of Illinois Press.
Shavelson, R. J. (1973). What is *the* basic teaching skill? *Teacher Education, 24,* 144–151.
Shavelson, R. J. (1987). Teachers' judgements. In M. Dunkin (Ed.), *The international encyclopedia of teaching and teacher education* (pp. 486–490). New York: Pergamon.
Shiffrin, R. M. & Schneider, W. (1977). Controlled and automatic human information processing, II: Perceptual learning, automatic attending, and a general theory. *Psychological Review, 84,* 127–190.
Shuell, T. J. (1986). Cognitive conceptions of learning. *Review of Educational Research, 56*(4), 411–436.
Shulman, L. (1987). Knowledge and Teaching: Knowledge growth in teaching. *Educational Researcher, 15,* 4–14.

REFERENCES

Siegler, R. S. (1990). How content knowledge, strategies and individual differences interact to produce strategy choices. In W. Schneider & F. E. Weinert (Eds.), *Interactions among aptitudes, strategies and knowledge in cognitive performance*. New York: Springer.

Siegler, R. S. & Richards, D. D. (1982). The development of intelligence. In R. J. Sternberg (Ed.), *Handbook of human intelligence* (pp. 897-971). Cambridge, Mass.: Cambridge University Press.

Silver, E. A. (1987). Foundations of cognitive theory and research for mathematics problem solving instruction. In A. Schoenfeld (Ed.), *Cognitive science and mathematics education* (pp. 33-60). Hillsdale, NJ.: Lawrence Erlbaum Associates Inc.

Simola, H. (1995). *Paljon vartijat. Suomalainen kansanopettaja valtiollisessa kouludiskurssissa 1860-luvulta 1990-luvulle* (Rep. no 137). Helsinki: Helsingin yliopiston opettajankoulutuslaitos.

Simon, N. (1979). Information processing models of cognition. *Annual Review of Psychology, 30,* 363-396.

Singley, M. K. & Anderson, J. R. (1989). *The transfer of cognitive skill*. Cambridge, Mass.: Harvard University Press.

Sjöberg, J. (1994). Pedagogikens huvudfåror och didaktikens sidoströmmar—en teoretisk betraktelse över relationen mellan två discipliner och dess konsekvenser för vuxenpedagogikens territorium. In J. Sjöberg (Red.), *Pedagogik och relevans* (Diskussion och dokumentation 1/1994, ss. 85-103). Vasa: Åbo Akademi, Osterbottens högskola, Pedagogiska institutionen.

Skinner, B. F. (1938). *The behavior of organisms*. Englewood Cliffs, NJ.: Prentice-Hall.

Skinner, B. F. (1954). The science of learning and the art of teaching. *Harvard Educational Review, 24,* 86-97.

Skinner, B. F. (1957). *Verbal behavior*. Englewood Cliffs, NJ.: Prentice-Hall.

Smith, B. O. (1956). The anatomy of teaching. *Journal of Teacher Education, 7,* 339-346.

Smith, B. O. (1987). Definitions of teaching. In M. J. Dunkin (Ed.), *The international encyclopedia of teaching and teacher education* (pp. 11-15). Oxford: Pergamon.

Soininen, M. (1901). *Opetusoppi* I. Helsinki: Otava.

Soininen, M. (1906). *Opetusoppi* II. Helsinki: Otava.

Steindorf, G. (1972). *Einführung in die Schulpädagogik*. Bad Heilbrunn/Obb.: Klinkhardt.

Stenbäck, L. (1855). *Om paedagogien och dess närvarande utveckling*. Helsingfors: Frenckell.

Sterelny, K. (1991). *The representational theory of mind. An introduction*. Cambridge, Mass.: Basil Blackwell.

Sternberg, R. J. (1987). The triadic theory of human intelligence. In J. T. E. Richardson, M. W. Eysenck & D. W. Piper (Eds.), *Student learning. Research in education and cognitive psychology*. Milton Keynes: Open University Press.

Stormbom, J. (1986). *Pedagogik och didaktik. Den herbartianska grunden*. Stockholm: CWK Gleerup.

Strike, K. A. & Posner, G. J. (1992). A revisionist theory of conceptual change. In R. Duschl & R. Hamilton (Eds.), *Philosophy of science, cognitive psychology and educational theory and practice*. Albany, NY.: SUNY Press.

Sundqvist, R. (1995). *Didaktiskt tänkande hos lärarstuderande* (Rapport nr. 10). Vasa: Åbo Akademi, Pedagogiska fakulteten.

Suortti, J. (1981). Opetussuunnitelma ongelmana. Teoreettista analyysia opetussuunnitelman ehdoista. *Kasvatus, 12*(4), 262-266.

Suppes, P., Pavel, M. & Falmagne, J.-C. (1994). Representations and models in psychology. *Annual Review of Psychology, 45,* 517-544.

Swartz, R. (1982). Alternative learning strategies as a part of the educational process. *Science Education, 66*(2), 269-279.

Sweller, J. (1994). Cognitive load theory, learning difficulty and instructional design. *Learning and Instruction, 4*(4), 313–329.
Taba, H. (1966). *Teaching strategies and cognitive functioning in elementary school children.* San Francisco: San Francisco State College.
Terhart, E. (1983). *Unterrichtsmethode als Problem.* Weinheim: Beltz.
Terhart, E. (1989). *Lehr-Lern-Methoden. Eine Einführung in Probleme der methodischen Organisation von Lehren und Lernens.* Weinheim: Juventa.
Terhart, E. (1991). Pädagogisches Wissen. Überlegungen zu einer Vielfalt, Funktion und Sprachlichen Form am Beispiel des Lehrerwissens. In J. E. Oelkers & H. E. Tenorth (Hrsg.), *Pädagogisches Wissen.* (Zeitschrift für Pädagogik, 27. Beiheft, pp. 129–141). Weinheim: Beltz.
Terhart, E. (1994). *Lehrerprofessionalität.* Vortrag im Rahmen der Herbsttagung der Kommision "Bildungsorganisation, Bildungsplanung, Bildungsrecht" der DGfE zum Thema "Zukunftsfelder von Schulforschung" Universität Dortmund, 9–10. Sept. 1994.
Terhart, E. & Wenzel, H. (1993). Unterrichtsmethode in der Forschung: Defizite und Perspektiven. In B. Adl-Amini, T. Schulze, & E. Terhart (Hrsg.), *Unterrichtsmethode in Theorie und Forschung. Bilanz und Perspektiven* (pp. 12–56). Weinheim: Beltz.
Tolman, E. (1920). Instinct and purpose. *Psychological Review, 27*(Sept.), 217–233.
Tolman, E. (1948). Cognitive maps in rats and men. *Psychological Review, 55*(4), 189–209.
Tulving, E. (1972). Episodic and semantic memory. In E. Tulving & W. Donaldson (Eds.), *Learning strategies* (pp. 383–408). New York: Academic Press.
Tulving, E. (1983). *Elements of episodic memory.* Oxford: Oxford Psychology Series 2.
Turing, A. M. (1950). Computing machinery and intelligence. *Mind, 59,* 433–460.
Uljens, M. (1989). *Fenomenografi—forskning om uppfattningar.* Lund: Studentlitteratur.
Uljens, M. (1992a). *Phenomenological features of phenomenography* (Report no 1992:03). Göteborg: University of Göteborg, Department of Education and Educational Research.
Uljens, M. (1992b). *What is learning a change of?* (Report no 1992:01). Göteborg: University of Göteborg, Department of Education and Educational Research.
Uljens, M. (1993a). *Den pedagogiska flugan—en analysmodell för didaktiskt handlande* (Publikation nr. 2). Vasa: Åbo Akademi, Pedagogiska fakulteten.
Uljens, M. (1993b). Skoldidaktik—mot en förståelse av det pedagogiska handlandet i skolan. In S-E. Hansén & Å. Holmström (Red.), *Undran inför undervisningen. Essäer i didaktiska ämnen* (Skrifter 51, pp. 81–105). Vasa: Svensk-Österbottniska Samfundet.
Uljens, M. (1993c). The essence and existence of phenomenography. *Nordisk Pedagogik, 13*(3), 134–147.
Uljens, M. (1994a). Att bedöma lärarkandidaters undervisningsförmåga—en översikt och utvecklingsförslag [1989]. In M. Uljens (Red.), *Studier i inlärning, undervisning och utvärdering* (Publikation nr 9, pp. 87–125). Vasa: Åbo Akademi, Pedagogiska fakulteten.
Uljens, M. (1994b). *A study on the foundations of cognitivism.* Vasa: Via Mathesis Press.
Uljens, M. (1994c). Skoldidaktik—en didaktisk modell. *Didaktisk Tidskrift, 4*(3), 31–51.
Uljens, M. (1995a). Grunddrag till en skoldidaktisk teori. In M. Uljens (Red.). *Didaktikteori reflektion, praktik.* Lund: Studentlitteratur (i tryck).
Uljens, M. (1995b). Nationalsocialismen och bildningsteoretisk pedagogik. *Utbildning och Demokrati 4*(1), 116–121.
Uljens, M. (1995c). *The structure of consciousness and teachers' didactic intentionality.* Vasa: Unpublished manuscript.
Uljens, M. (1995d). *School didactics and reflective pedagogical practice.* Paper presented at the conference Didaktik and/or Curriculum—A Continuing International Dialogue, August 9–13, 1995, University of Oslo.
Uljens, M. (1995e). A model of school didactics and its role in academic teacher education. In S. Hopmann & K. Riquarts (Eds.), *Didaktik and/or Curriculum* (pp. 301–332,

Report 147). Kiel: Institut für die Pädagogik der Naturwissenschaften an der Universität Kiel.
Uljens, M. (1996). Skoldidaktik som pedagogiskt forskningsfält. *Didactica Minima. 10*(2), 58–66.
Uljens, M. (in press). *Didaktik-teori reflektion, praktik.* Lund: Studentlitteratur.
Uljens, M. & Myrskog, G. (1994). Context-related differences in conceptions of learning. In M. Uljens (Red.), *Studier i inlärning, undervisning och utvärdering* (Publikation nr 9, pp. 35–70). Vasa: Åbo Akademi, Pedagogiska fakulteten.
Uusikylä, K. & Kansanen, P. (1988). *Opetussuunnitelman toteutuminen. Oppilaiden tyytyväisyys oppiaineisiin, opetusmuotoihin ja kouluelämään peruskoulun ala-asteella* (Tutkimuksia 66). Helsinki: Helsingin yliopiston opettajankoulutuslaitos.
von Wright, G. H. (1971). *Explanation and understanding.* London: Routledge & Kegan Paul.
von Wright, G. H. (1985). Determinismi ja ihmistutkimus. In G. H. von Wright, *Filosofisia tutkielmia* (pp. 49–77). Helsinki: Kirjayhtymä.
von Wright, J. (1992). Reflections on reflection. *Learning and Instruction, 2*, 59–68.
Vosniadou, S. (1994). Capturing and modeling the process of conceptual change. *Learning and Instruction, 4*(1), 45–69.
Vosniadou, S. & Brewer, W. F. (1987). Theories of knowledge restructuring in development. *Review of Educational Research, 57*(1), 51–67.
Wallin, E. (1988a). Didaktik—fågel eller fisk? *Nordisk Pedagogik, 8*, 17–23.
Wallin, E. (1988b). Notes on didactics as a field of research. *Scandinavian Journal of Educational Research, 32*, 1–7.
Ward, M. & Sweller, J. (1990). Structuring effective worked examples. *Cognition and Instruction, 7*, 1–39.
Watson, J. B. (1929). *Behaviorismen och dess metoder.* Stockholm: Natur och Kultur.
Weinstein, C. (1991). The classroom as a social context for learning. *Annual Review of Psychology, 42*, 493.
Weinstein, C. E. & Mayer, R. M. (1986). The teaching of learning strategies. In M. C. Wittrock (Ed.), *Handbook of Research on Teaching* (3rd ed.). New York: Macmillan.
Wenestam, C-G. (1993). A critique of research on cognition and cognitive processes. *British Journal of Educational Psychology, 63*, 34–45.
Weniger, E. (1930). Die Theorie der Bildungsinhalt. In H. Nohl & L. Pallat (Hrsg.), *Handbuch der Pädagogik. Band III* (pp. 1–55). Weinheim: Beltz.
Weniger, E. (1952). *Didaktik als Bildungslehre. Teil 1. Die Theorie der Bildungsinhalte und des Lehrplans.* Weinheim: Beltz.
Weniger, E. (1963). *Didaktik als Bildunglehre. Teil 2. Didaktische Voraussetzungen der Methode in der Schule.* (2. Aufl.). Weinheim: Beltz.
Weniger, E. (1990). Theorie und Praxis in der Erziehung [1929]. In E. Weniger (Hrsg. B. Schonig) *Ausgewählte Schriften. Band 6: Ausgewählte Schriften zur geisteswissenschaftlichen Pädagogik* (pp. 29–44). Weinheim: Beltz.
Westbury, I., Hopmann, S., Künzli, R. & Riquarts, K. (in press). *Didaktik as Reflective Teaching.* Chicago.
White, R. T. (1992). Implications of recent research on learning for curriculum and assessment. *Journal of Curriculum Studies, 24*(2), 153–164.
Willman, O. (1903). *Didaktik als Bildungslehre nach ihren Beziehungen zur Sozialforschung und zur Geschichte der Bildung. Band I & II.* (3 aufl.). Braunschweig: Friedrich Bieweg und Sohn.
Winne, P. H. (1987). Students' cognitive processing. In M. J. Dunkin (Ed.), *The international encyclopedia of teaching and teacher education* (pp. 496–501). Oxford: Pergamon Press.

Winne, P. H. & Marx, R. W. (1977). Reconceptualizing research on teaching. *Journal of Educational Psychology, 69,* 668–678.

Winograd, T. (1980). What does it mean to understand language? *Cognitive Science, 4,* 209–241.

Winograd, T. C. & Flores, F. (1986). *Understanding computers and cognition. A new foundation for design.* Norwood, NJ.: Ablex.

Wistedt, I. (1994). Reflection, communication and learning mathematics. *Learning and Instruction, 4*(2), 123–138.

Wittgenstein, L. (1953). *Philosophical investigations.* Oxford: Basil Blackwell.

Wittrock, M. C. (1974). Learning as a generative process. *Educational Psychologist, 11,* 87–95.

Wittrock, M. C. (1986). *Handbook of research on Teaching* (3rd ed.). New York: Macmillan.

Yrjönsuuri, Y. (1994). *Opetuksen ymmärtäminen.* Helsinki: Yliopistopaino.

Yrjönsuuri, R. & Yrjönsuuri, Y. (1994). *Opiskelun merkitys.* Helsinki: Yliopistopaino.

Zeichner, K. (1983). Alternative paradigms of teacher education. *Journal of Teacher Education, 34*(3), 3–9.

Zimmerman, B. J. (1990). Self-regulated learning and academic achievement: An overview. *Educational Psychologist, 25,* 3–17.

Author Index

Abelson, R.P. 168, 173, 188
Acton, W. 214
Adl-Amini, B. 57, 71–72, 88, 94
Aebli, H. 49, 73
Aitkenhead, A.M. 148
Allardice, B. 77
Anderson, J.R. 157–159, 188–189
Andersson, H. 25, 47
Andrews, J. 224
Anthony, M. 151
Apel, H.-J. 90
Arfwedson, G. 57, 83, 85–87
Arfwedson, G.B 47, 57, 87
Ashman, A. F. 163, 223–224
Atkinson, R. 187, 222
Ausubel, D.P. 156–157, 198

Baddeley, A.D. 187
Bannister, D. 5, 127
Barnard, Y. 152
Bartlett, F.C. 144
Bassok, M. 152
Beaty, E. 77
Bechtel, W. 133, 151
Beckman, H.-K. 90
Bempechat, I. 77
Bengtsson, J. 250
Benner, D. 17, 90, 96
Bennett, N. 59, 247
Berkeley, G. 178
Bereiter, C. 37, 59, 117, 152–153, 163–164, 209
Bergqvist, K. 42
Bielefeldt, H. 93
Biggs, N. 151
Bjørndal, H. 58
Blankertz, H. 44, 996, 106, 111, 113, 122
Bloom, B.S. 201
Bock, I. 25
Boekerts, M. 233
Bourdieu, P. 111, 210
Boyle, R. A. 161, 208
Bransford, J.D. 163
Bredo, E. 175

Brewer, W.F. 160–164, 204, 208
Brezinka, W. 55, 113
Briggs, L.J. 16, 155, 218
Broadbent, D.E. 144, 169, 187
Brown, A.L. 155, 207, 228
Brown, J.S. 16, 158–159, 184
Brown, R. 222
Bruhn, K. 93
Bruner, J. 156, 198
Bråten, I. 224
Bunge, M. 189

Calderhead, J. 247
Campione, J.C. 222
Carey, S. 28–29, 160–163, 188
Carlo, M.S. 233–234
Carré, C. 59, 247
Carter, K. 247
Champagne, D.B. 206
Chandler, P. 184, 232
Chi, M.T.H. 163
Cho, S. 224
Chomsky, N. 143, 164, 188
Churchland, P. 145, 189, 190
Cicero, C.A. 233–234
Clandinin, D.J. 68, 246
Clark, C.M. 62, 69, 75
Cleve, Z.J. 90
Cole, D.J. 148
Collins, A. 16
Comenius, J.A. 45
Connelly, F.M. 246
Conway, R.N.F. 163, 223–224
Corno, L. 222
Cube, F.v. 45
Cummins, R. 141

Dahllöf, U. 61
Dale, E.L. 25
Dall'Alba, G. 77
Danner, H. 8
DeGroot, E.V. 233
Dennett, D.C. 190
Descartes, R. 178
Desforges, C. 127

Dewey, J. 15
Dilthey, W. 8, 57
Diedeich, J. 3, 15, 20, 84, 88
Doyle, J. 168
Doyle, W. 46, 78, 200, 247
Duguid, P. 16
Dunne, E. 59, 247
Dweck, C.S. 77

Eckblad, G. 225
Egglestone, J. 64
Einsiedler, W. 90
Eisner, E. 15
Engelsen, B.U. 47, 68
Engeström, Y. 25, 239, 250
Englund, T. 47
Eraut, M. 247
Eysenck, M.W. 140, 146–147, 159, 165, 183, 185, 187

Falmagne, J.-C. 141
Fend, H. 87
Fenstermacher, G.E. 16, 39, 57, 240, 244
Ferrara, R.A. 222
Fichte, J. G. 48
Flavell, J. 155, 228
Flores, F. 173
Fodor, J. 145, 148, 150, 152, 188–191, 207
Francis, H. 3, 77
Frege, G. 143
Frey, K. 48

Gadamer, H.-G. 9
Gagné, R. M. 16, 110, 155, 198, 218
Galanter, E. 185, 222
Gallagher, J.J. 198, 223
Garcia, T. 219–223
Gardner, H. 141, 148–150, 183
Gelman, R. 29
Genesereth, M.R. 143
Gertzog, W. 162, 204
Gibson, R.R. 29
Giesecke, H. 248
Gilbert, J. 247

AUTHOR INDEX

Gilliéron, C. 145
Ginsburg, H. 77
Giroux, H. 253
Girmes-Stein, R. 252
Glaser, R. 54, 152–154, 163–164, 173–174, 185, 205, 209, 221, 223
Glasersfeld, E.v. 164
Glöckel, H. 89
Goldman, A. 133
Goldman, S.R. 184, 234
Goldsmith, T. 214
Grankvist, R. 46
Greeno, J. 78
Gudjons, H. 45
Gudmundsdottir, S. 46, 59
Gundem, B.B. 46–47, 57, 61, 67, 106, 246
Gunstone, R.F. 155, 206, 228
Gurwitsch, A. 227

Haag, R.H. 178
Habermas, J. 25, 112, 210
Haft, H. 48
Hälinen, K. 46, 79, 83, 93
Hameyer, U. 48
Hamlyn, D.C. 177–178, 217
Hanesian, M. 157
Hanson, N.R. 210
Harbo, T. 120
Harva, U. 55
Haste, H. 156
Hastings, J.T. 233
Haugeland, J. 141, 147
Hautamäki, A. 141
Heimann, P. 11, 23, 69, 93–95, 106–107, 110–111
Helmholz, H.v. 180–181
Henz, H. 99, 121
Herbart, J.F. 17, 48, 50, 57, 73, 121
Hergenhahn, B.R. 158, 207
Heursen, G. 44
Hewson, P.W. 162, 204–205
Hewson, M.G. 205
Hieberg, J. 219
Hitch, G. 187
Hintikka, J. 81
Hirst, D.H. 217
Hirst, P. 38
Hollo, J.A. 5, 10, 23, 53, 77

Hopmann, S. 46, 48, 57, 95–96
Hull, C. 142–143
Humboldt, W.v. 121
Hume, D. 178–179
Hunt, E. 146, 148, 182

Isberg, L. 57
Itkonen, E. 14

Jackendoff, R. 192
James, W. 53
Jank, W. 57, 93–94, 107, 120, 252
Järvinen, A. 247
Jarvis, P. 117–118
Johnson-Laird, P.N. 173
Johnson, P. 214
Joki, A.J. 14
Joyce, B. 198–199, 208

Kagan, D. 247
Kahl, R. 180
Kall—s, D. 82
Kamppinen, M. 176
Kansanen, P. 21, 39, 44, 46–48, 59, 62, 71, 79, 88, 90, 995, 113–114, 242–245
Kant, I. 144, 179–180
Karlsson, G. 8
Kaufman, A. 59
Keane, M.T. 140, 146–147, 159, 165, 183, 185, 187
Kieras, D.E. 214, 216
Kilpatrick, W.H. 15
Kivinen, J. 151
Klafki, W. 45–47, 57, 59, 61, 70, 89, 93, 95–96, 98, 100–105, 108–109, 120–122
Klopfer, C.E. 206
Knecht-vonMartial, I. 44, 48, 57, 94
Kolb, D. 59, 117–118, 250
Koort, P. 25
Koskenniemi, M. 23, 39, 46, 54, 59, 72, 76, 79, 83, 93, 114, 118, 251
Kosslyn, S.M. 186
Krapp, A. 46
Kroksmark, T. 44, 46, 120

Künzli, R. 46, 57

Lahdes, E. 46, 93, 118–120
Laird, J.E. 159
Larkin, J. 210
Leahey, T.H. 142–143
Lefevre, P. 219
Lehtovaara, M. 79, 120
Leinhardt, G. 78
Leino, J. 61
Leiser, D. 145
Leontjev, A.N. 29
Lieberg, S. 58
Lilius, A. 90
Lin, Y.G. 219, 221
Lippitz, W. 70, 84
Locke, J. 170, 177, 178, 179–180
Loser, F. 26
Lundgren, U.P. 26, 47, 82, 86
Lundh, L.-G. 144

Madaus. G.F. 233
Macke, G. 993
Manen, M.v. 10, 79
Makarenko 49
Marc-Wogau, K. 178
Marfo, R. 224
Marková, I. 178
Marton, F. 41, 46, 58, 77, 175, 227, 228, 234
Marx, R.W. 59, 699, 161, 208
Mayer, R.M. 218–219
McDermott, D. 168
McKeachie, W.R. 219, 221, 223
McClelland, J.C. 187
McShane, J. 147, 169, 172, 186, 187
Mehan, H. 78
Memmert, W. 45
Menck, P. 26, 57, 71, 73–74, 87–88
Mercer, N. 42, 83
Mertaniemi, R. 26, 77, 140
Meyer, H. 57, 71, 93–94, 107. 120, 252
Meyer-Drawe, K. 70
Meyering, T.C. 179–181
Mezirow, J. 253
Miller, G.A. 170, 185, 203, 222, 232

AUTHOR INDEX

Minsky, M. 168, 173, 188
Montessori, M. 50
Mulcahy, R. 224
Myrskog, G. 26, 140, 247

Neisser, U. 144, 148, 169, 174, 206
Newell, A. 149, 159, 168, 173, 185, 188
Nilsson, N.J. 143
Nisbet, J. 241
Nohl, H. 96, 100–101, 253
Nordenbo, S.-E. 47
Norman, D. 59, 146, 152–153, 157–158, 171–173, 186, 200, 202
Northfield, J. 155, 228
Novak, J.D. 157, 160
Novick, S. 205
Nussbaum, J. 205

Ohlsson, S. 153
Olson, M.H. 158, 207
Ortony, A. 168
Osgood, C.E. 143
Ottelin, A.K. 79
Paas, F. 232
Palinscar, A.S. 207
Palmer, S.E. 171
Passmore, J. 15
Pavel, M. 141
Peat, C. 224
Perkins, D.N. 163
Pestalozzi, J.H. 48, 73, 121
Peterson, H.C. 29
Peterson, D.L. 69
Phillips, D.C. 214–217
Piaget, J. 144, 188
Piatelli-Palmarani, M. 164
Pintrich, P.R. 161, 208, 219–223, 233
Plato 164
Popper, K. 137, 215–216
Posner, G. 161–162, 204–205
Pramling, I. 228
Pratt, D.D. 3
Prawat, R. 3
Pressley, M. 222
Pribram, K. 185, 222
Prosser, M. 3
Putnam, H. 10, 182
Pylyshyn, Z.W. 146, 148, 150, 190
Ratke, W. 44
Rauhala, L. 120

Rees, E. 163
Reichenbach, H. 134
Reid, D.K. 224
Reif, F. 210
Rein, W. 5, 53, 73
Richards, D.D. 162, 169
Ricoeur, P.
Riquarts, K. 446, 57
Rogers, C. 8
Rosenbloom, P. 159
Rorty, R. 210, 213, 251
Royer, J.M. 233–234
Rumelhart, D.E. 157, 163, 168, 171–173, 186
Russell, B. 143
Ryle, G. 15

Sacerdoti, E.D. 168
Sajama, S. 17
Säljö, R. 25, 225
Salomaa, J.E. 90
Salomon, G. 16
Samavapungavan, A. 208
Sampson, E.E. 127
Sandberg, J. 152
Scardamalia, M. 37, 5
Schank, R.C. 168, 173, 188
Scheffler, I. 15
Schleiermacher, F.D.E. 8–9, 12, 18, 48, 57, 121
Schneider, W. 233
Schnotz, W. 74
Scholz, G. 93
Schön, D. A. 250
Schröder, H. 17, 45, 51, 58–59, 88, 90, 93, 99, 120–121
Schulz, W. 11, 45, 106–107
Schulze, T. 26, 71, 73
Seegers, G. 233
Selz, O. 144
Shannon, C.E. 144, 169
Shavelson, R.J. 78, 199
Shaw, J.A. 149
Shiffrin, R.M. 233
Shiffrin, M. 187, 222
Shuell, T.J. 30, 153–154, 157, 162, 164
Shulman, L. 48, 59
Siegler, R.S. 162, 169, 224
Silver, E.A. 186, 197
Simola, H. 70, 8
Simon, H.A. 149, 168, 173, 185, 18
Simon, N. 152
Singley, M.K. 157

Sjöberg, J. 93
Skinner, B.F. 58, 142
Slack, J.M. 148
Smith, B.O. 14–15, 240
Smith, D.A.F. 221
Snow, R.E. 222
Soininen, M. 93
Soltis, L. 16, 399, 57, 240, 244
Steindorf, G. 90
Steiner, R. 49
Stenbäck, L. 24, 59
Sterelny, K. 169
Sternberg, R.J. 155, 157
Stone, C.A. 224
Stormbom, J. 46
Strike, K.A. 161–162, 20
Sundqvist, R. 247
Suortti, J. 75
Suppes, P. 141
Swartz, R. 209
Sweller, J. 162, 184, 232

Taba, H. 134, 198
Taylor, P. 3
Terhart, E. 26–27, 36, 71–73, 83, 120
Teske, R. 45
Tolman, E. 141–143
Trigwell, K. 3
Tulving, E. 187, 230
Turing, A.M. 144

Uljens, M.
    8, 22, 26, 61, 84, 119, 122, 131–133, 135, 140, 178, 185, 189, 220, 224, 227, 230, 234, 245, 248
Uusikylä, K. 62, 79, 242

VanLehn, K. 159, 184
Vosniadou, S. 160–164, 204

Wallin, E. 47
Ward, M. 232
Watson, J.B. 142
Weaver, W. 144, 169
Weinstein, C. 78, 218–219
Weil, M. 198–199, 208
Wenestam, C-G. 214
Weniger, E. 72–73, 75, 96, 100–101, 120–121, 252
Wenzel, H. 120
Westbury, I. 46
White, R.T. 213

Wiener, N. 169
Wierichs, G. 71
Willman, O. 71, 100–101, 231
Winkel, R. 45
Winne, P.H. 59, 140, 185, 199–202, 219–222, 231
Winograd, T. 149, 173
Wistedt, I. 40
Wittgenstein, L. 143
Wittrock, M.C. 57, 157, 218, 234
Wright, G.H.v. 60, 76
Wright, J.v. 226
Yinger, R.J. 62, 75
Yrjönsuuri, Y. 37, 40, 57
Yrjönsuuri, R. 37, 57

Zeichner, K. 253
Zimmerman, B.J. 165

Subject Index

Accommodation 157, 160f, 203, 209
Associative rules 178, 181
Awareness 60, 131, 225
 of impression 30
 ontological problem of 132
 epistemological problem of 130

Bildung 18, 51, 99–102
Brainstates 171

Cognitive
 load 232
 map 143
 mechanism 181
 processes 140, 154f
 science 142, 145
Computationalism 147
Cognitivism 136, 140ff
 and learning 151
Conceptual conflicts 204
Contents 26, 65, 129, 242
 and methods 137
 and psychology 70
 and studying 37
 as Bildungsinhalt 129
 choice of 70
 types of 71
Context 65
 construction of 83
 of teaching 83–85
 historical 10, 97
 school as 85
 social 78
Competence
 and learning 34, 38
 modeling 207
 reaching of 37f
Classroom processes 66, 78, 83, 201, 240
Culture 41f
 as framing teaching 25, 65
 continuity of 25
 local 65, 85
 of school 42, 83
Cultural-historical theory 29, 139
Curriculum
 as context 85

community level 62
 levels of 61, 68, 96, 246
 national 62, 79
 school based 245

Design of study 5–7, 136
Descriptivity 51, 53, 55, 112, 115
Didactics 23
 a model of 65, 93
 a reflective theory 114
 and learning theory 52ff
 and values 55, 114–115
 and reflection 249
 and related disciplines 23
 as a thought model 10, 248
 as doctrine 21–22, 48
 Berlin model of 106ff
 comparative 46
 concept of 44, 87, 92
 context of 103
 critical-constructive 103
 critical-communicative 45
 didactics of 97
 erudition centered 95ff
 German 56
 general 87
 history of 44
 human science 96
 ideology of 104
 narrower and wider 102f
 Nordic 47
 normative 21–22, 47, 49, 104, 254
 object of 23
 hilosophical reflection of 112
 School 64–65, 87, 91–92, 115
 scools of 45
 triangle of 15, 84, 137
 universality of 9
Didaktik 44–49, 57, 94
 renaissance 46
Didaktische Analyse 98
Dualism 132
 epistemological 193
 interactionist 189

mind-physical instance 190
 substance 132
 property 189, 194

Empiricism 178f
Erfahrung 30, 76, 250
Erlebnis 30, 250
Erziehung 18, 51, 99–102
Ethics 66
 deontological 243f
 teleological 243f
Evaluation 63–65, 81, 111, 212
 levels and types of 81–82
Epistemology 131
 and learning 133
Epoché 8
Equilibration 205
Existential dimensions 79
Experience 29
 didactic 75–76, 250
 learning 75
 learning from 29ff
 lived 99
 of performance 76
 phenomenal 172

Frame factors 86
Functionalism 189f

Goals 68
 collective 113
Goal-model 204
Goal-state 233
Grading 26

Heneutics 7–9

Identity theory 191
Information 168ff, 181, 192
 and teaching 231
 familiarity of 207
 meaning of 205
 processing 150
 relevant 206
 reresentation of 173
Instruction 49
Instructional psychology 53

SUBJECT INDEX

Intention 17, 24, 60, 65, 76, 240
and method 71, 129
as planning 67f
as purposiveness 39, 242
pedagogical 59
student's 40
Interaction 25, 66, 78, 201
dynamics of 65, 76
existential dimension of 74
teacher and learner 65, 75
Internalization 214

Learning
and experience 29

and mind–brain problem 133, 134
and mind-world problem 133, 135
and instruction 4, 128
and pedagogical decisions 127ff
and personality 35
and philosophy of mind 133
as discovery 32f
as inventing 31
as reaching of teachable competence 38
bringing about 38
cognitivist theory of 156ff, 239f
experience of 77
from teaching 200
intentions of 36ff, 40, 246
knowledge of 127
teachers' understanding of 127
theory of 4, 137, 151ff
paradox 31–32, 164, 174
parameters 232
practice 26
preconditions of 29
process and result of 27–28, 133–137
process 182, 225
strategies 181, 218
understanding of 3, 5
unintentional 37
Learning strategies
awareness of 225

content dependence 163, 223
learning of 222–224
teaching 220

Maturation 29
Media of teaching 73, 242
and contents 129, 137
and learning 124
Memory 173, 184, 187
theories of 187
and teaching 130
Metacognition 154–155, 227
Methods 26, 71, 73, 129, 197ff, 242
Mind–Brain problem 131, 133, 194
Mind–World problem 131, 136, 167, 192
Mind's eye 177
Misinformation 206

Neuropsychology 229
Normativity 21–22, 49, 55, 104, 112–113, 115

Object theories 94
Object of experience 176
Ontology
as problem 132
and learning 135

Pedagogical
activity 61, 63
contract 41–42
criterion 101
decisions 127–129, 137
implications 136–137, 197ff
intentionality 59
practice 54, 77
practice and theory 5–9
programmes 49
reality 19, 55, 97
reflection 60, 117, 248–249
relevance 134–135
Perception 170, 177
causal theory of 79f, 193
forms of 179
directed by cognition 212
object of 176f
Phenomenology 7ff, 131–132, 150

Phenomenography 139, 175, 227–228
Philosophy of Mind 133. 137
Planning 63, 65, 67
Prescriptivity 21, 53, 126
Problem solving 184ff

Reality 172
noumenal 180
pedagogical 19, 55, 97
representation of 171f
Realism
epistemic 10
hypothetical 180
Reflection 14, 20, 60, 65, 243, 247
critical 253
epistemic 252
didactic 114, 127f, 248
object of 76
on experience 29f
on one's model 204
pedgogical 60, 76, 247, 250
scientific 55, 118
self 30, 251
Reflective didactics 114, 249
Representation 149, 177
and teaching 73, 248
level of 183, 186
type of 186
Rescources 85
Restructuring 157ff
weak 160
radical 161

Schema 144, 162, 173ff, 181, 183, 200
School didactics 64–65, 87, 91–92, 115
and Berlin didactics 107ff
and critical-constructive didactics 102–109
and curriculum theory 106
and educational policy 116
and erudition-centered didactics 102ff
and lerning theory 125, 250
as a subfield 66, 87, 92
as a thought model 105, 248

as a research model 67, 105
as theory and practice 115, 248
as reflective theory 114, 249
autonomy of 67
historicity of 97
ideological loading of 109, 112f
goal neutrality 110, 114–115
knowledge perspective 115–116
School pedagogics 89
Self-reflection 251
Social contract 41–42, 80
Student
  as teacher 77
  interests of 64, 246
  personal integrity 79
Subject matter 26, 70
Studying 37, 39
  activity 34, 36, 39, 80
  and learning 36
  and teaching 39, 80
  as trying to learn 37
  control of 206
  experienced by teacher 76

intentions 40

Teaching 13–18, 24
  a definition 23
  affecting learning indirectly 39
  and didactic theory 117, 247ff
  and information 231
  and knowledge of learning 127
  and learning 4, 35, 80, 203
  and memory 230
  and studying 39, 80
  as an art 53
  as based on learning 22, 53
  as educative instruction 50–51
  as intentional 15, 39, 240
  as moral craft 22
  as necessary element 36
  as success 15, 240
  awareness of 41, 53
  beliefs of 3–4, 69
  develoment of 248–252
  experienced by student 75ff

intentional 39
  methods of 197ff
  of learning strategies 220
  personality 25
  principles of 54, 126, 128
  productive 33
  reproductive 33
  resonsibility 78, 109
  student's 76
  theory of 4, 55
Teacher
  as learner 77
  cultural role of 25
  education 19, 77, 97, 127, 248
Theory and practice 19, 117, 248–252
TSL process 13, 15, 43–44, 65
  as a cultural phenomenon 25

Values 16, 21, 104, 127
  and didactics 52
  and psychological teory 127
  behind school didactics 112f, 115